The Floral Hand of God

Secret Healing Codes of Flowers Revealed

Dr. Brent W. Davis

Nature Force
Publishing

Nature Force Publishing
550 Rosedale Avenue
Nashville, TN 37211

Printed in the United States of America

Permission from Prof. William Tiller to quote extensively from his texts, and his preparation of original material that is included in this book, is gratefully acknowledged. Thanks also to biologist William Brown for his preparation of original material that is included herein, and to Pier Rubesa for his exquisite scientific measurements of the frequency characteristics of uncut flower essence samples sent to him by the author. I am enormously indebted to my editor, Catherine Dees, for her insights and suggestions. I am grateful for the keen eye of George Makris who scanned the manuscript for corrections, and for the final editorial review by Pamela Ann Davis.

ISBN 978-0-9960043-4-3

Library of Congress Control Number: 2014913507

1. Body, Mind & Spirit: Inspiration & Personal Growth
2. Self-Help: Personal Growth
3. Medical: Alternative Medicine
4. Health & Fitness: Alternative Therapies
5. Psychology/Emotions

The Floral Hand of God is a trilogy in one book:

• **Part 1** describes peak experiences in Dr. Brent Davis' continuing search in the realm of flowers for "the Beloved"… that power of attraction that enables us to more easily fulfill our fondest dreams and wishes – to draw to our self the experience of greater love, understanding, and appreciation in our life.

• **Part 2** presents landmark scientific discoveries relating to the mode of action of flower essences prepared in a powerful new way. It penetrates the mysteries of the spiritual mind, examining leading edge theories in quantum biology and physics to explain how specially selected flower frequencies may install into our brain/being spiritual impulses from the "Heavens" to improve our life… at a rate faster than the speed of light.

• **Part 3** concludes with a self-help rapid reference. It describes the manner in which selected flower frequencies can infuse us with codes of light that allow us to receive more love (and hence more energy), and transmute what has held us back in life. It describes a new method to remove core causes of stress at the deepest level – the level of the subconscious mind silently replaying negative messages that wear us down. It will teach you how to accelerate personal transformation by applying the life-force of Dr. Davis' newly discovered UNCUT flower essences… the powerful next generation of frequency healing.

You will learn how to "overwrite" and eliminate your particular brand of negative self-talk that all humans carry in the unconscious mind, and how to replace it with healing and uplifting "Source information" found in rare flowers from around the world.

Transformational flower frequencies described in this book are to be used as an adjunct to all practices that support the evolution of consciousness, and are never intended to be used as a substitute for self-reliance and responsibility on the path to greater awakening.

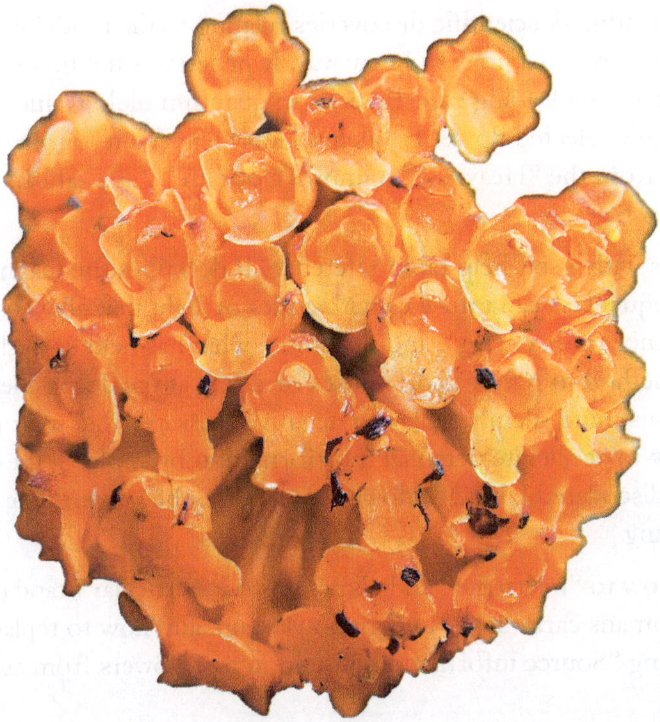

One Thousand Voices

Table of Contents

PART 2 (continued)

Toward A Science of Flower Frequencies:
Changing The Address of Our Quantum Mind

PART 3

How to Use Specific Flower Frequencies
For Personal Transformation & Evolution

APPENDICES

Preface

Into the Light

This is a book about how we can increase happiness and contentment in life. At the same time it is about how the subconscious mind can sabotage our happiness and keep us in a perpetual state of self-limitation, despair and even chronic illness. And though it deals with thought transformation, it is not a book about psychology. It is, instead, about the existence of potent healing frequencies given off by certain flowers – subtle but targeted vibrational essences that, when consumed in drinking water and/or sprayed around our body, can "overwrite" and remove those sabotaging thoughts and limiting beliefs and lead to a cascade of healing within the body/emotional complex. This is no small thing to promise, I realize.

My purpose for writing *The Floral Hand of God* is simply to tell you how I came to discover these transformational flower frequencies and how they work. I believe that is what I am supposed to do with this knowledge. As you will see, this will not be an ordinary story of scientific study and discovery.

Many people have asked me, "How on earth did you think of this? How did you know?"

The simple answer has been, I did not.

I can say with conviction born of experience that no single human being could have devised and implemented the mind/spirit transformation system that has been unveiling before me. During its evolution it has required the alignment and integration of so many pieces and components of life experience in order to become manifest – along with the input of key information at precisely the right time – that it is inconceivable I could have come to this alone.

A compelling activity for me has been the practice of continuously asking, "What if it were possible?" and to offer to my willing and open-minded patients a new way to transform their unconscious mind...a true partnership with Nature...a fast-track process of movement into the light.

This Book Is Dedicated To *You*

Introduction

I have loved flowers and herbs since I was a child. Though when I was young I had no conscious idea of plants as healers. They were simply my cherished and most constant companions. In retrospect I see that in their natural environment they served as a sort of enlightened ancestral community, providing balance in my life as I grappled with the challenges of growing up.

My early years were privileged with respect to material setting. I lived in a spacious Tudor house in a West Los Angeles suburb at the foot of the Santa Monica Mountains. Like so many children born in the last half of the twentieth century, some of my family members seemed too frequently to be embroiled in inner conflict as they tried to make sense of their life in a highly materialistic culture. I remember often lying on my back in the grass near the house, staring overhead into the clouds, or being tucked away high in one of the lofty pine trees in our back yard, only to have my reverie broken by strident screaming – the cacophony of another family quarrel. I was confused by the intensity of dissatisfaction that manifested because I could seldom find reason for it.

When there was discord, my antidote was to escape. And how fortunate I was that a large, uninhabited canyon, complete with creek and luscious plant growth was just across the street. I took many other opportunities as well to explore that "wilderness" close by whenever possible. I spent many hours and days there alone each year between the ages of seven and fourteen.

Accompanied by a walking stick and a small knife strapped to my belt, I furtively crept on the property line between two houses at the canyon's edge and made my way through thickets of towering bamboo until I reached a clearing. I paused to look over the expanse of chaparral on the edge of the serene canyon across from Will Roger's State Park. It was a steep descent to the bottom, punctuated by many stops to observe, smell and sit among the varied plants, enjoying a sort of kinship with them. Only years later did I learn Native American and other uses of the herbs I encountered.

When I reached the bottom of the canyon, several trails were available. If I needed solitude or healing I generally went to a marvelous area where the creek passed through stone canyon walls. Above the water there were flat rocks to lie on heated by the sun, and at the creek's edge a few remarkable "chairs" had been carved out of the rock over time by the flowing stream. I sat comfortably in the earth for hours sometimes, isolated from the sounds of civilization, entranced by the voices of the water, the fragrance of herbs, and the whispering breeze. Eventually my thoughts evaporated into blissful nothingness. I had the opportunity as a child of experiencing oneness with life that is much harder to find as an adult. Something very precious was transmitted to me in that place. Looking back, it seems I was instructed in an ancient point of view by intelligences in Nature, and a course in life was charted for me much different than what my family envisioned. You see, I was being groomed to become an upstanding and socially acceptable medical doctor.

There were a few problems with the plan, however. Foremost was the fact that my undergraduate education at UCLA took place when anti-establishment student unrest of the sixties and early seventies had not been entirely forgotten. Several dedicated instructors had the opportunity at that time to speak with unusual candor about the causes of societal ills. They hoped to cultivate in their students the ability to find real motives behind outward appearances; not to be swayed by glossy advertising, carefully managed information fed to the media, corporate propaganda, or science conducted for financial gain rather than being motivated by a search for truth.

I actually spent one whole trimester in a sociology class reviewing case studies of white-collar crime. We examined the lives of people who were socially elite, who maintained a fascade of integrity due to their affiliations with charities, service organizations, and churches, and who, at the same time were involved in unethical or criminal conduct to advance their selfish interests.

That class provided important object lessons to help me avoid some of life's potential pitfalls, but at the same time it was disheartening and disempowering. It made me question a great deal of what I thought was true, or what was being represented as truth. Such a questioning process leads, at least temporarily, to indecisiveness – a characteristic incompatible with the confident ego structure required to succeed in medical school.

While I was pre-med, I had a second major in anthropology. Many of those classes examined social structures and institutions from a cross-cultural perspective. We were diligently taught to avoid "ethnocentrism," which can be defined as the propensity of dominant cultures to ascribe value to their ways and to denigrate or dismiss the views of less materially developed societies. So when I began to encounter descriptions of ancient healing practices that seemed unscientific, I did not regard them in that way. In fact, as a result of my childhood experiences in the canyon, I felt drawn to native medicine and to the herbal kingdom that had provided so much energy to uphold and nurture me.

I spent whatever spare time I had in the last two years of college reading about ancient medical systems and herbal usage. I particularly enjoyed studying ethnology reports of the nineteenth and early twentieth centuries in which Native Americans and other "informants" were interviewed by anthropologists regarding their traditional healing uses of plants.

After a time, I began to feel I could tell when "informants" were intentionally supplying bogus information to the academics studying them. Sometimes I howled to myself in laughter, because when the anthropologists were condescending and arrogant, they were setting themselves up for a ride. They recorded so seriously what they were told, unaware they were being duped. When interviewers wrote with respect or occasionally with reverence and awe when they felt they had found a truly wise native person, the herbal character and indications described to them seemed to be authentic.

One course in physical anthropology was devoted to the study of the modern scientific method of investigation. Great pains were taken to show that the definition of the experimental framework or frame of reference in a scientific study is critical to its outcome and merit. If there are too many variables in an experimental frame of reference, it makes it logistically difficult or impossible to scientifically determine the relative importance of each variable (let alone combinations of variables). So generally just a few variables are selected to determine how they relate to the experimental question. Though the variables chosen for study are at the discretion of the investigators, they are normally directed by precedents and normative views of institutional science. And, of course, they are very much influenced by the sources that fund the study. I concluded that when only a few variables are studied out of the many in real life that are acting concurrently, then it is possible that we no longer have an accurate representation of reality. I began to wonder how often that phenomenon took place in mainstream medical research.

A pivotal event in my life occurred in my sophomore year at UCLA. It was a work-related injury.

I worked through college as a house painter whenever I could find the time. I was on a second story balcony cleaning a banister before painting it when it broke. I was thrown off balance and fell two stories down to a concrete slab with all my body weight landing on one foot. As with two previous serious injuries, I must have had angels hovering around me, because ostensibly I didn't have anything wrong. My foot and ankle were X-rayed in the emergency room and I was told "no fractures...you're fine to go home."

Unfortunately the docs in the emergency room were unaware of the critically important physiology that chiropractors and some osteopaths appreciate. I had received a serious sheering injury at the sacroiliac joint (in the pelvis), translating all the way up and into my skull via a connection of tough fibrous tissue called the dura. A strong twisting injury occurred deep within the skull as well. This type of injury commonly causes chronic energy loss, and, because of damage to structures within the skull, can wreak havoc with nervous system and hormonal balance. Apparently I needed to work against a tremendous obstacle, because after this injury, I was plunged into chronic illness that took me many years to reverse. I experienced about every symptom and malady that is associated with chronic fatigue. It is easy to see one of the motivating factors that caused me to undertake training in therapies aimed at resolving chronic illness.

For a long time I operated on will power alone. I made a valiant effort to cope, but the injuries were a crowning blow on top of the emotional abuse with which I grew up. I could not participate in normal socialization. The great passion I have for life was trapped inside. I felt so vulnerable that I shut away my heart, and, sadly, retreated into my head. Time after time when I reached points of hopelessness, I would be guided to a new herb, chiropractic technique, holistic practice, or homeopathic remedy that would rekindle faith that I could be healed. For a long time the only love affair I had was an impersonal one with the herbal kingdom – and that kept my heart from breaking.

The journey of my recovery is what prepared me to unveil the healing power of "chosen" flowers. Though my chronic illnesses left, my love of the heart and soul of herbs has only grown stronger.

A remarkable event took place in my Junior year of college which I still find amazing to this day. The second quarter seemed to be charmed. I didn't work very much and got good marks. I relaxed the most of any other time in college. Almost every day in the late morning I went to a comfortable place on the lawn at the side of Royce Hall (University of California at Los Angeles–UCLA) and lay on my back as I used to when I was a child. On several occasions, as I looked up into the canopy of the tree above me, I saw moving pictures of my future life. I saw myself traveling to many regions worldwide doing herbal research and finding new plant healers. Many of those images have come to pass, actually occurring in real life.

I saw images of myself in a high mountain valley with enormous rock walls on its sides. I was surrounded by gigantic forms and angelic forces of Nature communicating with me, upholding me, beseeching me to hear their offerings of assistance, and impelling me to bring their floral healing frequencies into the world. In 2002 I felt directed to travel to the high Andes, and was guided so that I encountered the valley and the forces of Nature I had seen so many years before. In that remote fifteen thousand foot setting, as I looked around myself, awestruck in the presence of God, I was breathless literally and figuratively. The flower frequencies that I extracted in that region are incomprehensively powerful in their ability to transform one's life.

When I experienced those future visions in college, I was amazed and at the same time troubled by them. I wondered if what I was seeing was manifesting out of personal instability and illusions.

Now, many years later, I see that was not the case. I no longer question God's invisible hand that has directed my life, for it has led me on an intriguing voyage and one in which I see a purpose that can greatly benefit humanity.

Part 1

The Discovery Adventures

1

Measuring Our Invisible Mind Activity

Before we can observe changes in a phenomenon, first we obviously have to witness that the phenomenon exists. In order for us to recognize changes in our subconscious mind programming, which is invisible to our rational, conscious mind, we first have to have a way to measure subconscious mind activity. A whole new field of body/mind healing emerged in the 1980's which provided a way to measure something that previously had always been invisible – namely our thoughts and beliefs, i.e., the commands being generated by our unconscious mind.

As a young member of the ICAK–International College of Applied Kinesiology (the body that teaches proper use of holistic diagnostic muscle testing), I remember attending an annual conference in Dearborne, Michigan in the late nineteen eighties. The importance of that meeting was only clear in retrospect. There a paper was presented that challenged conventional wisdom with respect to the merit of using affirmations, and as practitioners, the potential benefits of recommending affirmations to our patients.

In this era, holistic practitioners were busy helping patients identify their limiting beliefs, and then constructing affirmations for the patient to state with conviction. This was to act as a counter-measure to self-sabotaging beliefs with the intention of nullifying them.

The doctor presenting the paper discussed the confounding nature of a discovery he had made clinically. In the course of interviewing his patient during an office visit, the patient happened to mention that on his own he had created an affirmation to help himself break out of a mind pattern. His affirmation was something along the line of, "I am confident I will be financially successful this year." The patient had been repeating this several times per day.

With the proper use of muscle testing and self-referential statements, it is possible to measure response in an individual to what he himself says. When the doctor asked his patient to repeat the "I am confident…" phrase and then performed a muscle test on a muscle that was strong prior to the statement, after the statement, the muscle collapsed in weakness. This is, in a sense, like a lie detector test. If the initially strong muscle had remained strong after stating the affirmation, it would indicate subconscious mind coherence (agreement) with the positive affirmation – in other words, that the statement was true for the individual, and he actually did believe he would be financially successful. If the statement weakened a previously strong muscle, it would indicate a conflict, i.e., non-coherence, and the unconscious mind would be telling us that with this statement, it is not true for the patient.

Even though the patient was repeating this positive affirmation many times per day, it did not cause him at the unconscious level to believe it was true. In fact, quite the opposite. It was actually weakening him every time he said it because there was a clash between his conscious intention and his firmly established unconscious mind belief. This was a profound finding.

For the rest of that conference many of the docs attending were discussing it. Eventually the phenomenon was named "reversal" – the mind's ability to distort conscious belief (and/or positive intention) 180 degrees out of phase, producing a negative mind/body outcome. This discovery prompted many ICAK members to explore the phenomenon of "reversal" and to learn how to eliminate it. The first ICAK member to bring this concept widely to the attention of the general public was Roger Callahan, Ph.D. (psychologist) who wrote the NY Times best selling book, "The Five Minute Phobia Cure."

What began as a collaboration between chiropractic physician and ICAK founder, George Goodheart, D.C., other chiropractors, psychologists, and a holistic psychiatrist, eventually gave rise to a whole new field now known as "energy psychology." The greatest number of health professionals employing energy "psychology" in practice are not psychologists at all; they are chiropractors with training in applied kinesiology.

However, under the influence of psychologist, Fred Gallo Ph.D., who trained with Dr. Goodheart, an organization was formed in 1999 called ACEP–The Association For Comprehensive Energy Psychology. Its membership of about 700 consists of psychologists, other mental health professionals and various holistic practitioners. They host conferences and publish newsletters which showcase dozens of reflex and other techniques to eliminate destructive beliefs and improve mental health.

Identifying the phenomenon of "reversal" was just the beginning. What followed was a period of experimentation with various practitioner-mediated techniques to induce coherence.

The question I posed to myself was: Could there be a way to consistently induce coherence – not dependent on the presence of a particular practitioner – that could create the desired positive shifts in the unconscious mind (healthfully aligning the subconscious/conscious mind complex)? And if there were such a process, exactly how would it work?

As we shall see in following chapters, I found the answer in the almost surreal realm of flower frequencies.

2

Message on the Mountain

I jokingly refer to the period between the years 1987 to 1999 as my "lost years". They really weren't lost. Actually they were very productive. What I lost was a normal orientation toward most things conventional and mainstream. A great deal happened in this period which prepared me for the discovery of the most effective way to extract the totality of healing frequencies from flowers while they are living, uncut, and pulsing with life.

With my newfound ability to clinically test my patients for "reversal", and a phenomenon closely related to it called "switching", I found a high percentage of my patients were affected by conflicts between their conscious desires and sabotaging unconscious mind patterns they were unwittingly expressing. To remedy this problem for my patients I used the first therapeutic methods developed from chiropractic disciplines such as applied kinesiology and bio-energetic synchronization technique (B.E.S.T.) as well as PSYCH–K (developed by Rob Williams).

While having the patient visualize and hence activate stored memories of trauma, the practitioner, by using his hands to hold reflex areas (or by stimulating acupuncture points or spinal areas), could essentially erase the trauma of memories stored in the brain and re-pattern and normalize the nervous system. In many cases this produced remarkable alleviation of stress symptoms and physical complaints.

Even though I was delighted to see the wonderful results that could be obtained using these methods, at a level beyond thinking I had an awareness that a way existed to re-pattern human beings at the primordial level of soul and Spirit which would likely influence the subtle crystalline matrix of our DNA. I was vaguely aware that this method would use vast field energies of Nature and would be so enormously encompassing that it would be incomprehensible to the mind.

If you think about it, that's not really a lot to go on! That awareness provided no road map to discover this magical process that I felt must exist. I could only imagine that the "mysterium" I was seeking would be revealed by reverting to what I had learned as a child – sitting in stillness in Nature.

As often as I could I would make "pilgrimages" to wilderness areas – places that I felt would be specially touched by the Divine. I would often have an inner prompting to take such a trip, and then I would ask for inner guidance at to where the trip needed to be. Due to the fact that I was constantly researching wild plants for my herbal company, Phytotherapy Research Labs.[1]

I always had the camping and other necessary gear ready to go when the prompting "hit". I had only to notify my patients that I would be gone for a while.

I had a special fondness for the Native American wild plant called Oshá (Ligusticum porteri). It is a potent immunomodulator, used often to recover from flu, and to clear excess mucous and lung congestion. It was always a challenge to find supply sources for the herb that were harvesting the root in an eco-conscious manner, taking care not to excessively deplete wild populations.

I strongly intuited that I would have a wonderful experience if I were to "meet" the plant in person. Since I felt that the herb was threatened due to declining populations, it seemed that I had the ideal opportunity to take the time I needed in Nature and at the same time study Oshá in its optimal wild habitats.

With advanced research, I knew more or less where the plant was growing in Colorado, New Mexico, and Northern Mexico. I decided to fly from Los Angeles (where I had my practice) into Albuquerque, New Mexico, rent a car, and drive up to Taos to meet a field botanist I had contacted previously for pointers as to where I should go on my expedition.

In the usual manner, the airplane pilot came on to the PA system to announce to passengers that we should especially look out the window at such and such "area of interest" (landmarks that are always on the OTHER side of the plane). Of course I couldn't see what he was referring to, but I did gather that we were just entering air space over New Mexico. For some reason it felt like I should pull out my detailed map of Northern New Mexico to look at the topography over which we were flying.

I located Taos on the map, and my eyes wandered upwards into southern Colorado, noticing things like Culebra Peak (at about 14,000 feet elevation), and further to the West, Mesa Verde National Park. Then my eyes drifted downwards (south) towards the central part of northern New Mexico and suddenly stopped over an area called Chama. I had never heard of this area, but there seemed to be something very special about it. I saw a tiny blue spot on the top of Chama mountain. It must have been a small lake, noted at just over 11,000 feet on the map. Perhaps that was it, the place I needed to go?

Soon we started our decent into Albuquerque, landed smoothly, and without delay I obtained my rental car and took off north to get to Taos in the late afternoon in time to meet the botanist at the appointed forestry station. I had good directions so I found it easily. With map in hand I entered inside and mentioned that I had an appointment. The receptionist signaled to Wayne who came over and greeted me hospitably. We exchanged a bit of small talk. He told me about his familiarity with Oshá, and showed

[1] In 2012 Phytotherapy Research Labs, Inc. changed its brand name to Forest Center Herbs (ForestCenterHerbs.com is the forthcoming new website.)

me on area maps where he had seen it growing. He explained it was quite spotty and didn't know of any areas where it grew abundantly. He felt my finding it would be hit and miss.

I finally had the opportunity to ask him about the area that struck me while I was in the plane. I pointed to the small lake on Chama Mountain and asked him if he happened to know that piece of land (about 70 miles away). He smiled and shook his head. "Well, that's quite a coincidence," he said " I just saw Frank across the street about 45 minutes ago. His dad owns that piece of land with the lake on it. It's quite something, about 4,000 acres. He's care-taking it now, harvesting fallen timber to make special beams for custom homes. He doesn't live here, so let me call him to see if I can catch him while he's still in town."

Well, Frank Simms was still in town, and within a few minutes I had the opportunity to meet with him to ask for permission to explore his dad's ranch. Wayne warned me not to be too hopeful because he said the Simms were very private about that piece of land, using it only for family retreats and the like.

Frank listened to me explaining my interest in natural medicine, the fact that I had a holistic practice, and that I had an herb company known for its care of ecologically harvested plants. I told him that I had spotted his piece of land at the time I was just about flying over it, and my excitement must have grown to such a pitch that it broke through his reservations! He gave me permission to enter through the gates at the lower end of the property (at about 8,000 feet elevation). He explained the lay of the land a bit and that he would be near the cabin quite a ways up the mountainside. He asked me to check in with him after the first day I was on the land. I happily agreed.

I was so focused on getting to Chama that I had failed to take account of the fact that my rented Toyota Corolla would be swallowed up by the rutted terrain that Frank described I would encounter – only passable to 4-wheel drive vehicles! "Let's see," I thought to myself, "how am I going to pull this one off. Well, there must be jeep rentals here in town. I'll just leave the Corolla here and take off in a Jeep for a few days." Seemed pretty plausible at the moment.

What I didn't realize was that although there are many 4-wheel drive rental companies in Taos, they NEVER rent vehicles to drive out of the region (especially 70 miles away). "I am sorry sir, I understand your predicament, but it's company policy, and we just can't rent you a Jeep to drive that far away." By the time I got to the third or fourth 4-wheel drive rental company, I suspect that my eyes were bulging out with the fury and the fervor of a hell-and-damnation preacher! I think I dazed the poor lone gal at the rental desk of the last place. Having no one to turn to, and in what may have been a mesmerized state, she agreed to rent to me.

She explained, "Now you understand, sir, this is very irregular and probably dangerous. Our vehicles have no tops or doors on them because they are just for day use here locally. And you're going to drive off across the state? I really can't recommend this, sir." I just kept nodding my head at the appropriate points, let her speak her piece, got the keys and got out of there as quickly as possible!

I was delighted to have my beautiful new metallic blue Jeep with no top and NO doors! The no doors part turned out to be fantastic. I shall never forget the ride from Taos to Chama. I started out at dusk, heading west across high plains with my stocking hat pulled over my ears and parka zipped tight. No doors and no top. I was hurling through space (about 38 degrees F) with an unimpaired 270 degree view of the land and the starry sky. It was a crystal clear night for which New Mexico is famous. In the absence of moon, the firmament was thick with sparkling stars highlighted against the black sky. In the altered state of this peak experience, I felt a benediction from the planets, the stars, and beyond into galaxies.

When I reached the area near the Simms' ranch, my reverie was broken because it was so challenging to figure out where I was. I never could find the entrance gate at night so I just had to settle for camping on a spot I presumed to be near to the ranch. After packing up my tent the next morning and eating a bit, I headed off. Turns out that I was about a mile away from the entrance gate to Frank's property. I navigated ruts and boulders in the dirt road, crossing through several gates. As I left the access road behind and got out into the open, I saw beauty so spectacular that I could not fathom it.

I was looking out into a large valley with a stream crossing at the bottom of it. Stretching up Chama Mountain at 3000 feet in elevation were red rock cliffs lower down with patches of trees and beautiful meadows as one progressed upwards. The colors seemed surreal as if one had dialed up the vibrancy level beyond the attributes of this earth. I got out of the Jeep and walked to an observation point to get a sense of where to go. I was enthralled, searching for words within myself to describe what I was seeing and feeling. Enchantment. Yes, that was the feeling (remembering the word that aptly appears on New Mexico's license plates, "the land of enchantment").

I plotted a course through the valley below and up the mountainside. The first place I stopped was on the other side of the river at a meadow facing red rock cliffs. I waded through a large patch of wild Arnica cordifolia and sat down in lavish grass with the blue and purple heads of several types of wild Gentian peaking out at me. I was made to be still. What was I sensing? Choruses of voices echoed from the rock cliffs.

So… I realized… I was in the company of native Elders. I had traveled to many magnificent parts of the U.S. in search of herbs while on a path of inner discovery from the eastern woodland forests to the Great Lakes to the Cascade and Rocky Mountains to the western deserts of California and Arizona, yet I had never been gripped by such a commanding presence.

There were many voices seemingly echoing messages that had been given but rarely ever heard. At first, I could only understand the general theme of what was being communicated. Then after a while, it was as if one voice spoke a narrative to me, addressing me personally relating to my quest. What I was told astonished me.

Part of what the Elder spoke to me was as follows:

> "My son, we have seen you in your travels, searching for the love that flows from the heart of Nature and imbues herbs with their healing power. You have worked hard to find this love that once flowed abundantly, but in this country at this time you will not find what you particularly seek. It has been killed off. The destruction of Earth in the pursuit of wealth and the repeated betrayal and killing of the ancestors have ruptured the heart of my brothers, and broken their critical link with the natural realm that has flowed for eons.
>
> "Your exploiters of Nature in this country do not understand. We are co-creators with the great Mother. When we are broken, the Earth is broken. When we neglect her, we neglect ourselves. And though she wishes always to nurture and provide for us, beyond a point she can no longer. In your lifetime, what you seek from Nature here will be reborn in these lands. But for now, it is gone. To find what you seek now you must travel abroad. Go to the Southern Continent [South America] where native peoples still hold the sacred link with the earth. There you will still find the deepest healing."

I could not easily integrate the power of this message. I briefly broke down emotionally and sat immobilized in the most beautiful place I had ever seen. Of course I had to continue, but it cast a powerful influence into my life.

My visit to Chama Mountain was nevertheless splendid. At about 10,500 feet I found an old logging site where trees had rotted forming a rich humus. In that area of at least 60 acres grew what was probably the largest, densest, and healthiest stand of Oshá in existence anywhere. I dug a little of the herb's roots but mostly spent the day walking through its unusually scented blossoms, singing an internal song of joy with the plant.

My return trip to Los Angeles was unremarkable. I resumed my practice through the end of the summer and into the fall of 1987. Just before the new year, I received an intriguing invitation and one that would forever change my life.

3

The Invitation

On an ordinary day in West Los Angeles I made a routine trip to the mailbox and found something quite out-of-the-ordinary. With all the bills and promotional flyers in the heap of mail I scooped up, one piece stood out especially. It was a little bit different size than one normally sees, and it just seemed to be, well… foreign looking. I placed it carefully on my desk to take a look at it after I had finished working on my afternoon patients.

That evening I returned to my desk to examine the piece of mystery mail. It came from Peru, but I didn't know anyone in Peru. I noticed that it was addressed "Dr. Brent Davis" so I figured it came from someone who obtained health professional mailing lists from licensing boards. No matter. What was on the outside of the folded brochure was fascinating to me: "II Congreso Internacional de Medicina Tradicional." It was an announcement of the upcoming II International Congress on Traditional Medicine that would be taking place in Lima, Peru, June 1988 – half a year away. My instinctual response was, "Wow, this would be neat to attend. I wonder how though?"

Then my mind started popping up very rational reasons why that trip would be impractical. First was the fact that I had a solo practice, and it seemed it would be very difficult to leave for a long period of time. I had been wanting to go to Peru ever since my year-long anthropology studies at UCLA on various aspects of ancient Peruvian culture. At the time I was taking these classes, little did I know that any benefit would ever come from them. Turns out that they were some of the most useful classes of my whole education.

Due to that long-standing desire to travel in Peru, I couldn't imagine taking a short trip. There was so much to see! "Six weeks" – that is the length of time I would need in Peru that initially popped into my mind. End of January? "No, that's impractical." End of February? "The cost of leaving practice for six weeks is untenable." End of March? "I don't know even one person in Peru, and I have no idea where to start my herbal studies in such a botanically rich country." Middle of April? "Why do I keep thinking about this trip so much?" Beginning May: "I'm going. Everything will just have to fall into place. I'll meet whom I need to at the congress." Decision made. Soon thereafter I sent out notice to my patients of the period my office would be closed.

Actually, one of the reasons that I thought so much about the trip to Peru was that personally I was experiencing emotional pain and loneliness as a result of the internal prompting which, six months before, caused me to move away from an intentional community where I had lived most of my adult life. I felt as though I had just lost all support of the adopted "family" that I had grown to depend on and who meant the world to me emotionally. It occurred to me that I might encounter a mystical transformational force in Peru that could help me heal and enable an opening to a more joyful existence. I was feeling dissatisfied with life in general, and I did not want that frame of mind to continue, yet I did not know what to do to shift it. I had a deep yearning for change.

It is much easier to travel in Peru now than it was in June of 1988. The airport and admission processing of tourists are both vastly improved. Significantly, the political climate is less volatile. Research in advance of my trip revealed that the Maoist guerilla group, El Sendero Luminoso (The Shining Path), was very serious about terrorism, and as a result, certain regions of Peru that were a stronghold for them were too unsafe for travel. That turned out to be a relevant point after I arrived.

I noticed that the congress was being held in a former "grande dame" of hotels, The Crillon. The hotel, like most of Lima, had lost its former glory but was still described as comfortable.

During my taxi ride from the airport to the hotel, it was clear that the once opulent colonial city of Lima was now definitely third world. I was so excited to be in Peru, and yet as I coursed through the streets, I felt a pervasive sadness that did not seem to arise just from the obvious poverty and from seeing mountains of trash everywhere. I was soon to discover the cause of what I was feeling.

I arrived a day before the congress started, checked into my room, quickly unpacked, and changed into some non-descript clothing so as not to stand out too much as a "gringo." I had a strong sense that I needed to get out of the hotel and sit among the local people. I had the perfect opportunity just a block away in the beautiful Plaza San Martin, which consisted of lovely neo-classical buildings built in the 1920s. On the edge of the central square, now dilapidated, there were some stone steps facing a busy pedestrian area – a perfect place for people watching.

Within just a few moments after sitting down, an oppressive heaviness enveloped me, and I was confused because I was so excited to be in Peru. Then as I watched the body language and the faces of the passers-by, mostly dark-skinned indigenous natives, I soon understood what I was sensing.

I did with the local people what I learned to do with plants when I "meet" them for the first time. I opened a blank space in my mind and asked for the meaning of what I was observing to appear there internally and communicate with me. It became clear that I was sensing the collective unconscious of the many people walking by me. Mostly they were poor and seemed to be hopeless and hapless. But there was something more.

Then it struck me: I was feeling the pain behind the masks people had put on. A narrative voice seemed to speak.

> "You are witnessing the effects of colonial exploitation, even as it masquerades as the progress of industrialization. The listless eyes, the heavy feet, the ever

so slightly stooped posture, are all signs of something deeper – a broken heart. The people you see in front of you are here in this metropolis out of desperation, for they have lost their land and their great purpose as caretakers of the Earth. They work for money only, subsisting in artificial jobs, and not as they once did when they were in contact with Gaia as they plowed her fields and tended her forests. Though that life was very difficult and austere in its own ways, they still felt joy from the harmony of Nature."

"While you are here do not inhabit the cities. Find the wild areas where the old methods of living are still being followed."

I understood that is what I would have to do.

The next morning in the hotel's large conference area, the congress organizer, neurosurgeon Dr. Fernando Cabieses, gave the inaugural address. I was amazed by the attendance – throngs of 4 ½ to 5 ½ feet tall native people packed into the central room and overflowing into numerous side room wings. I mention height because as a 6 foot, very Caucasian-looking fellow, I stood out like a large reflector! What made my presence more glaring was the fact that there were virtually no other "reflectors" (tall white guys) in attendance! I asked myself, "Where is the U.S. contingent?" The lovely color brochures produced in English must have been sent out to a lot of people. "What happened?" I wondered.

I had corresponded with Dr. Cabieses before the congress, and as a result he had set aside time at the end of the first day for me to interview him for an article I intended to write. I brought a video camera as well to document our meeting, and unwittingly that bit of technology attracted the attention of the people I didn't know but needed to meet. Wow! Bunches of attendees gathered around to watch the "Hollywood" production.

The first question I asked Dr. Cabieses was, "Why is there virtually no one here from the U.S.?" Shaking his head he replied, "We don't know. We sent out 10,000 invitations to the U.S. Besides you and Dr. Norman Farnsworth (a well known pharmacognosist from the University of Chicago) there are only a couple of other Americans here so far, and there will be an overall attendance at this Congress of about 4,000 people. The only thing we can think of is that virtually all of the U.S. mailbags were lost. Somehow a couple of invitations got through." I didn't show it but felt stunned. Once again serendipity had acted. Why was I one of only a few who received the congress announcement? "Maybe there's going to be some real significance to this trip," I thought to myself.

As Dr. Cabieses was replying to my questions I kept feeling a set of eyes fixed upon me from within the gathered crowd. As time went by, the "owner" of the eyes moved into plain sight, and I noticed he had an oriental but somewhat Peruvian appearance. He was a Peruvian of Japanese decent named Jorge, and he was the key that opened the door for me to the wonders of Peru on this trip and for many years to come. He turned out to be a spiritual brother, worthy of great love and admiration, and became a life-long friend.

When I finished the interview with Dr. Cabieses and was packing up my video gear, several people formed a queue to ask me various questions. There at the end of the line was Jorge, patiently waiting for everyone to finish. When Jorge and I finally had the opportunity to speak, I was flooded with feelings of warmth, congeniality, and familiarity. It felt like I had known him forever. Many of the apprehensions I had about how my trip would unfold seemed to dissolve, and quite soon I understood why.

It turns out that Jorge had a background that was so especially aligned with my interests that he understood exactly what I was supposed to accomplish on this trip. Moreover, he intuited immediately that I needed emotional repair in addition to whatever physical objectives might arise. I was overjoyed that without having to say a word about my emotional vulnerability, he knew what I required for healing. He exercised with me great kindness and patience.

In a very Catholic country, Jorge had moved beyond the confines of Catholicism. He had explored eclectic philosophies and various religions. He developed a great respect for and eventually adopted many of the tenets of the teachings of Dr. Rudolf Steiner, a German Christian mystic of the early twentieth century, who founded the Anthroposophical Society. Steiner deeply understood the living realms of Nature, having been influenced by the teachings of the German mystic, Goethe. (Steiner was, as well, familiar with the teachings of the Theosophical Society that incorporated wisdom of the adepts of India.) As I had just recently finished quite a review of Anthroposophical literature (especially its early contributions to holistic medicine), Jorge and I shared a common language – a humanistic view of life and an appreciation of Nature as a direct expression of the Divine.

There was a unique "frequency" about Jorge that I had never encountered before. He exhibited definite male characteristics but was not like a normal "guy." What was it that was so unusual about him? Then I found out. His specialized training and true devotion was in apiculture. He was one of the foremost authorities in South America on the cultivation of bees and on the start-up requirements for small-scale rural industry resulting in the commercial production of honey. In that capacity he worked for NGOs who provided funding to develop rural income for the economically disenfranchised.

Now you might not understand this, but it was very clear to me. Jorge was a "human bee." If you have ever sat without fear in the company of the true honeybee, Apis mellifica, there is an extraordinary single-minded lovingness and gentleness about these creatures. They are here for one purpose: to ensure the continuity of plant life –and our life– on earth. There is a sense of blessing about these little beings and something I have never found in any other life form. Though they will sting, they would really prefer not to, and if they do, they lose their own life.

There was virtually no rural region in Peru that Jorge had not traversed on foot, and he left a wake of friends behind him wherever he went. I found later that he seemed to know everyone in his country that had to do with natural products and ecosystems management. Everywhere I might need to go, he had only to call for someone to assist me. Who, I wondered, had directed Jorge to meet me? It seemed beyond coincidence.

Jorge mentioned that there were people I would appreciate meeting. Soon we were making a "bee line" directly toward two young holistic physicians, Irma Luz and Oscar. They too possessed very eclectic philosophical and spiritual views. With dispatch they introduced me to herbal authorities presenting papers at the congress (some of whom were their teachers). They seemed to be aware, as was Jorge, that I had some sort of mission to accomplish, and they were a great help in that respect.

By the end of the second day, it was all arranged. When the congress was over I would meet with a small advanced study group of holistic Peruvian medical doctors who had spent about the last ten years of clinical practice identifying what they felt were the most important herbs in Peru by testing how they worked on their patients. I made plans to visit socially with Jorge and his family, Irma Luz and Oscar after the meeting was over.

One of the presenters at the congress brought samples of the highest quality Cat's Claw (Uncaria tomentosa) herb, which does not come from the bark of the vine (what is now sold commercially). What I obtained was the root and inner wood of the trunk of the vine (and only a small percentage of bark) in dried powdered form.

I knew from my training in classical homeopathy how to conduct what is called a "proving" – a way to use one's senses and observational skills to discover the energetic action of an unknown substance under investigation.

Alone at night in my hotel room, with a still mind, I "met" the herb for the first time. I placed a small spoonful of powdered Cat's Claw in my mouth and slowly chewed it. It had a very characteristic and totally distinctive taste due to high content of what are called oxindole alkaloids. Physically I experienced the powerful sensation of increased secretory activity in my digestive system, a strong antispasmodic effect in the intestines, and an opening of my lymphatic circulation. But what I experienced psychically was far more profound. I felt encompassed by a balm of safety, as if the greatest of my trials were shifted and lifted off of me. It was incomprehensible yet wonderful. I had received a huge blessing. I knew I had to find and study this plant in the wild, but where?

When the congress was over, I met with the docs in the study group over two days. I discovered that between them, they had thousands of case studies which represented the greatest practical resource imaginable. With their input I was able to construct a prioritized numbered list of the most valuable Peruvian herbs and the optimal habitats where they grew. I was incredulous at what I had just been given. I realized that the herbal products industry would soon kick into high gear in the U.S., and what I now possessed had enormous value in the commercial marketplace. I had always viewed herbs as a resource to protect rather than to exploit, so I had an inner directive to identify the herbs that would most likely be commercially exploited. I then needed to understand how to safeguard their habitats while, if possible, allowing a sustainable supply of them.[1]

There was a unanimous consensus that Cat's Claw was by far the most important of all Peruvian herbs. The doctors provided volumes of information to me about its various applications. They told me "insider" information about what makes the plant the most bioactive – how it should be harvested and more. They explained the altitude at which it optimally grows and that the best herb came from particular areas in the province of Junin. Problem: the Maoist guerilla group, Sendero Luminoso, had heavily infiltrated that region. Any trucks carrying Cat's Claw in that area were held up at gunpoint at makeshift road blockades that would spontaneously appear overnight. If you didn't pay a bribe, the truck and the herb didn't pass. They quickly convinced me that if I ventured there I would probably not return. They mentioned that the herb grew in safer regions in the north, Iquitos, all the way to the south ending in the precinct of Madre de Dios.

At the congress I just happened to meet and note a contact phone number of a representative from a tribe a few miles outside of Iquitos. With Jorge's assistance we contacted the phone number I had taken, communicated with the tribe, and arranged for me to be picked up by boat and transported to near the tribal reserve on a tributary river outside of Iquitos. Little did I know what I was getting into.

Never, I repeat, never ask an aboriginal person the distance or the time required to reach a particular landmark. That question doesn't seem to compute. They operate outside our normal time/space continuum.

[1] At the end of the nineteen eighties one of my grateful patients gifted me with substantial funds to allow me to fulfill one of my dreams – to start a non-profit 501(c)3 organization I called The Foundation for Herbal Healing & Conservation (FHHC). The FHHC had one amazing and ambitious project that was nearly successful. It ran for six years and was a landmark study of the potentially valuable food and medicine crops on a large site in a remote Peruvian tropical forest/jungle ("Bosque Gamitana" in the Madre de Dios precinct. See the "Jungle Photos" in Doc's Photo Journal on page 324).

The intention of this project was to demonstrate that by simply harvesting the wild nut, fruit, and medicinal plant resources from this tract of land a substantial income would result with NO cutting of tropical forest wood or other depleting practices and a significant ability to hire workers locally. Over 7000 hectares of publicly held land in Peru was scheduled to be passed to the FHHC once a comprehensive forestry management study was completed by an FHHC-employed forestry professor at the Lima, Peru University of La Molina. The forestry inventory study was completed over a period of one year with all necessary documentation for the land to pass to FHHC's care.

Once the FHHC paperwork was placed in the regional magistrate's office in this remote precinct, a logging company was tipped off about the study. They stole the documents, placed their name on the documents, and when the study was approved, they obtained the rights to use this land for logging first, which they did, and then for "ecotourism" once the destruction of logging was finished. This was a heart breaking experience.

I was hoping the guide sent to retrieve me from where I was dropped at the river's edge did not intend to deceive me. However, I was becoming exasperated hearing several times from him that the tribal land that was our destination was "just up the way–close." Two hours later it was still "just up the way–close." Keep in mind that I was only partly through my long period of debility mentioned in the book's introduction. I still had chronic fatigue and weighed in at a measly 140 pounds (I am now a healthy 175.) It was 100 percent humidity, about 92 degrees Fahrenheit, I was carrying a backpack, and it felt like my guide was trying to catch a Kenyan distance runner! I was truly spent by the time we reached the village that was our destination.

Fortunately I remembered reading an ethnology account of a jungle fruit the Jivaro indians used as a tonic. They rubbed the juice of the fruit over their bodies to revive themselves. I asked my hosts if they could please find some of this fruit and bring it to me. They thought it an odd request, but about half an hour later they delivered me a broken little plastic bucket of the freshly picked fruit. I crushed it up and rubbed it all over my legs, my arms and my face. Then I turned orange. They were amused.

But the stuff worked! It actually allowed me to get through the rest of the day.

My guide thoughtfully found an area relatively close to the village where I was able to observe a large stand of old growth Cat's Claw, a giant vine that can reach more than a hundred feet into the forest canopy. (See the "Jungle Photos" in Doc's Photo Journal beginning on p. 324. My herbalist guide thoughtfully showed me how to sample the enormously healing juice that flows from the freshly cut Uña de Gato vines). I asked to be alone for a while, mentioning that I would return to the village when I was through.

Cat's Claw vines can run along the ground for many feet, eventually turning straight upward, growing into the treetops. I found an old vine about 7 inches in diameter and sat on the forest floor close to where it exited the earth, holding it. Notwithstanding the drone of many insects, the stillness of the jungle was astounding. My body swayed almost imperceptibly, joining the pulsing life-energy of this spot. I cleared my being to receive an impression from the plant.

I was able to somehow merge into the "body" of the huge Cat's Claw vine and perceive its character. The hundreds of water-filled tubules that form the diameter of the vine together act as an enormous antenna, an energy transfer conduit that receives input from the Earth's grid and from the heavens. It is powerfully linked to the whole of life.[2]

Beyond that impression was an encompassing awareness in the moment and an emotional response to a precious act of love.

The super-consciousness of this Cat's Claw "being" enveloped me in a "shawl of surcease." My psychic pain coming from identifying with apparently insurmountable

[2] See Jungle 1 photos in Doc's Photo Journal.

obstacles in my life vanished. I was held in the embrace of the Great Mother and the Great Father. I was completely safe and whole. I received blessings from the farthest reaches of Creation. It was not only this one vine that renewed me. It was the whole community of them over a range of hundreds of miles, for they are all linked in an unwavering dedication.

My life was never the same after this incident. My perceptive abilities increased and helped me to better assist my patients. I became more tuned to the "supersensory world" in which Rudolf Steiner lived and from which he drew his insights. In retrospect I realize this was THE critical step that set up the possibility for me to work effectively with the invisible but powerful energy of flowers.

When specially chosen flowers are prepared by a method I would discover years later, without cutting them or bending them into water, they often deliver an even more profound healing than just mentioned. (The traditional method of preparing a flower essence is to cut the flower and place it in a bowl of pure water for extraction of the energy. This ruptures bio-coherence in the collected frequencies. As I will later describe in detail, I found a method that extracts all energy from the entire surface area of a whole flower while it is alive and uncut, in its normal spatial alignment with the earth. This enormously enhances the coherence and power of the flower's healing frequencies.)

A core strength was restored to my nervous system and marked the beginning of my return to health which still would take many more years. Had it not been for the inspiration Cat's Claw provided me (and for the healing which I derived from consuming this herb intermittently over the next couple of years), I never would have had the initiative and the energy to move from Los Angeles to start a new life in a remote forest in the third least developed county in the state of Tennessee.

And had I not moved, I would have missed my transformational and mind-bending adventures with the incredible Eli – a young man you are about to meet…

4

Being Broken...
(and unusually tamed)

Almost everyone has a stored mental image of a wild horse being broken. It is likely a memory from a big screen dramatization or from some re-run of an old television series such as Bonanza, Rawhide or Maverick.

Most often the cowboy protagonist asserts his dominance over the rearing and rebellious animal, taming him after a bucking and grueling battle of endurance. Only seldom did we ever see the Redford-esque "horse-whisperer" approach[1] whereby kindness, perceptiveness, and patience are the trainer's tools to transform traumatized or unruly beasts into dutiful creatures. I was fortunate to be "tamed" by the latter method.

In 1993, my life began to unfold in an extraordinary way, when the willful, independent, and impulsive "steed" in me was transported from Los Angeles to the third least populated and most impoverished of the 96 counties in Tennessee. It was a case of first world entitlement running headlong into third world forbearance where the self-centered first world imperative of "do it now in this way" was constantly transcended into "the job will be done in keeping with the balance of the community."

Beginning around 1989 I had felt a strong inner prompting to leave Los Angeles – to purchase forest land where I could start an organic herb farm and build my own energy independent, off-the-grid home. At the time it seemed to be a dream so large as to be implausible, yet it just kept getting stronger.

I began searching for land in the Southeastern states of W. Virginia, North Carolina, Tennessee, and Kentucky. I wanted a place where I could experience the four seasons (without digging out of snow), and I required hardwood forests for the many wild herbs that grow there natively. Not having any family or friends in those states made my search very challenging. In communities where realtors came up with potential land prospects, I hired local folks to independently assess the land parcels. On a couple of occasions I flew back to look at places myself, but to no avail. After three years and a lot of hope, I gave up the search. Within two weeks of that surrender a remarkable thing happened.

It was 1992, and a new patient named Barbara showed up in my West Los Angeles

[1] In the 1998 Movie titled "Horse Whisperer," Robert Redford played the part of Tom Booker, a sort of mystical healer of horses.

office. Before the exam, as I usually do, I took a few minutes to chat and get to know her. Barbara and I shared similar views and had a good rapport. Turns out she was an administrator at Self Realization Fellowship, a spiritual community founded by Paramahansa Yogananda in 1920, dedicated to disseminating worldwide his teachings on India's ancient practices and philosophy of Yoga and its tradition of meditation.

For some reason, at the end of our conversation I mentioned my futile efforts to find land in the Southeast. I left the room for a moment to wash my hands before the exam. When I returned, we went through her history, and then she hopped up on the adjusting table (lying face up) for me to begin muscle-testing assessment. As I was about to give her instructions for the procedure, she looked directly into my eyes and said, "I know just where you need to be." I stuttered, "Um… what?" She smiled, "Oh, I mean, I know where your land is." What Barbara said still did not compute in my head. She continued, "I have owned a piece of property for several years in the central part of rural Tennessee. It is right on the edge of a wonderful Mennonite [similar to Amish] community, and they're great neighbors. I think it is just what you are looking for."

I purchased airline tickets and within 10 days Barbara and I were on a plane to Nashville for her to introduce me into her community and to find out if there was land for sale. I rented a truck, and we drove west about one and a half hours from the airport to Perry County – physically beautiful terrain that seemed to be largely uninhabited. I had no idea of the rare treat I was about to experience and that I would essentially be entering a time warp taking me back 200 years.

When we were just a few blocks away from the start of the community, situated off an unpaved country road, there was a palpable stillness. It profoundly affected me, just having come out of the hyperactive energy of Los Angeles. No sooner than Barbara mentioned we might not see another motor vehicle at all in this area, an open-air, long, horse-drawn buggy appeared on the rise in the lane ahead. Mom and Dad were on the bench seat in the front with two youngsters wedged between them, and on the flat bed behind them eight other children were packed together, well behaved and apparently content.

I slowly drove over the rise in the road, and for a moment, I was breathless. To the right I saw an idyllic scene that could have been a painting of an eighteenth century French countryside. Two weather-tanned women were cultivating a field set against a backdrop of verdant forest. They were both barefoot, wearing dove grey and blue full-length dresses. White head scarves concealed their hair. One woman was riding the plow-horse bareback. The other followed behind guiding the plow with attention focused on the cultivator blade to keep it within one to two inches of the young seedlings.

We passed several other farms and fields with intriguing images as well. I looked, astonished, as a log on a saw buck was being cut by two men pulling and pushing back and forth furiously with a six foot long hand saw. Almost silently and in a harmonious rhythm, they appeared to be moving through the log at nearly the speed of a chainsaw (that incredibly useful time-and-labor-saving device that is an ecological abomination).

I soon found out that this Mennonite community was nearly the end of a "dying breed." For they held fast to the longstanding traditional Mennonite (and Amish) practice of not using modern tools that require gas or electricity. Tools and appliances (including washing machines!) were all run by hand or by ingenious horse-powered drive trains. Transportation was by foot, horse, buggy and wagon. "Wow," I thought to myself, "this is gonna be intriguing!" I had encountered a third world "country" right in the U.S.

Due to the amazing character of this community, "outsiders" were always looking to buy surrounding land, as it might come available, so they could experience a more simple life. No land was for sale at the time I arrived.

Barbara had arranged for me to stay in the home of the Mennonite community patriarch, John Shirk, whom I eventually got to know very well. It would take a whole book to describe this extraordinary, honorable, complex and "simple" man. Let's just say that he did not beget ordinary children.

I came to know six of his eleven children, five of whom were living on his farm when I first arrived. His youngest child, a son named Eli, had recently married Lydia (all names were biblical), and intended to purchase a portion of a neighbor's farm to start his own family. Therein was my entré. Eli knew that I would need lots of help (actually vast amounts) to build the dream I envisioned and had described to him. He was confident he could be a good foreman for all the work that would be required, and that would provide him with the cash he needed without having to leave the community to earn income.

The question was, where would my land come from?

Eli had a composed and yet dynamic presence. He had a huge amount of cellular energy or "chi." His body type was strong with a very similar appearance to the famous painting called, "The Pugilist." The subject in that artwork had markedly downward sloping shoulders, which, when combined with strong arms, trunk, and legs gives a wrestler or a boxer a great mechanical advantage. That kind of fellow can simply get the job done!

"Outsiders" in the surrounding towns knew how unique Eli was. They often solicited help from him that required numerous talents and abilities – from tracking a wounded deer at midnight that no one else could find, to repairing odd structural building damage that contractors wouldn't touch, to figuring out prospective gravity flow water systems that posed seemingly insurmountable obstacles. With no formal education, Eli was nevertheless a genius.

With all of Eli's talents, I discovered eventually that there was something precious which he needed but could not obtain on his own, and that he felt my arrival was a sign from God that I would be able to facilitate his heartfelt desire.

Eli was hence motivated to find me a place in the community, but the question was how, since there was apparently no land available for sale.

As fate would have it, before the Mennonite community had formed in the nineteen eighties, Memphis resident, Jack Wilcox, had bought a 160-acre forest parcel (with 7 acres of open fields in the center) that sat in the midst of what eventually became several of the Mennonite community farms. A couple of times a year Jack would drive his trailer onto this land to rest for a few days or to hunt when it was the season. He left caretaking of the land to Eli, who in exchange was given permission to graze his animals there.

Eli had the idea to call Jack to see if he might be convinced to "cut loose" his property and allow me to purchase it. I stood by when Eli made the call to Jack. The upshot of the conversation was that Jack had intended to retire on the property in question but that a serious financial demand had just arisen, and he was faced with the possibility of having to sell it. Eli explained that I would be an asset to the community.

It didn't take long for Jack to agree to sell me his property, carrying the papers on it for a fair percentage interest with payoff in 5 years! The first of many "miracles" had just occurred. (My ability to deal with the huge challenges of the land transformation that would become my farm and forest retreat, concurrent with the building of a residence there and the construction of my herb company's manufacturing facility in town three miles away was profoundly aided by the steadfastness, support, and selfless nature of my former wife, Lynn. The angels smile down on her.)

After I completed the move to Tennessee in 1993 (and started married life in a temporary apartment near to Lynn's hospital work), I discovered the nature of the "magical key" I possessed that had enabled me to obtain the earlier support of Eli in obtaining the land that I was seeking.

It took close to six months before I found out that Eli's new bride, Lydia, was barren. A Mennonite man could hardly suffer a worse fate than having no children. All the natural healing resources that Eli sought out had failed to reverse his wife's infertility, and from our first meetings he had adopted enormous confidence that somehow I would be able to find the remedies and administer the care that would reverse his wife's condition.

Lydia's case was the most challenging of that type I had seen, for she was born with a very weak constitution. Fortunately, she had an unsinkable spirit, and I witnessed by the method of her relating that she had great love and adoration for her mate whom she knew transfused her with energy to buoy up her strength.

Eli gave me something beyond material compensation. He helped deliver to me my dreams. And I was able to give back to him. It took me a year and a half of careful treatment to reverse Lydia's infertility. I provided for her advanced structural chiropractic work, major nutritional therapies, and most of all "divinely guided" homeopathic prescribing. Eli is now the father of 10 healthy and extraordinary children.

He lives in a community about 200 miles from my farm.

The next miracles that would occur required my personal growth, and there was a lot needed in that department! Those changes could not all occur during the short "tenure" of Eli (and the presence of the Mennonite community) – only three years – but a great deal was accomplished in that time. Due to Eli's extraordinary character and the tempering physical demands of what we were faced with almost daily, I experienced substantial transformation rather joyfully and without too much personal drama.

The common undesirable character traits I had when I arrived (L.A. city dweller-dysfunctional family sufferer-no dad-overbearing mother-stuff) were able to shift more readily when reflected against attributes I found in my new setting: in essence a mirror by which to measure humility, humor, and allowance.

The following three topics summarize key elements that were a defining part of my experience in this special place in rural Tennessee. They describe essential parts of a personal shift that later allowed me to find and develop transformational and evolutionary flower frequencies.

I. Certainty of fulfillment of what is right

This principle is the exact opposite of the neurotic fears, worries, and doubts that commonly arise as a result of today's dysfunctional families and single parent households, absent the support and solidarity of two balanced parents and true spiritual community.

While I could not embrace the narrow Christian doctrinal approach of the Mennonite faith (especially their views on the "sinfulness" of the sensual world) and adopt it as my own, I developed inestimable respect for the constancy of my neighbors' daily practice of valuable religious teachings that very much influence their children's development.

In the common vernacular, they "walk their talk." Every day I spent with my unusual "third world" neighbors pointed out to me the value of a healthy family and large extended families. Though in the "outside" world it is not sustainable and environmentally tenable to have a family with a "herd" of children (and stay-at-home moms harnessed to so many dependents have little personal time for reflection, career, or recreation), very beneficial character traits can develop in a functional multi-sibling (and multi-parenting) environment. It is how children have been successfully reared for most of history until recently.

When I think of "certainty of fulfillment of what is right" I immediately see two images from my memory.

Image A is of sitting in the simple, welcoming living room-dining-room-kitchen of my next-door Mennonite neighbors at mealtime. The wholeness of the moment is calming, happy and without artifice.

Image B is substantially different – occurring in a period when I still lived in Los Angeles. This image is unfortunately representative of a great many families and single-parent households in materially advanced societies. It is a snapshot of the kitchen–living room/den area in my friend's house as I was visiting in the early afternoon a couple of days before New Year's.

Image B:

I am standing for a few minutes in a doorway that lets me see and speak with Susan (in the kitchen) and her children in the living room. I greet the children, Ryan and Rachel, letting them know I will be playing with them after taking a moment to say "hi" to their mom.

I notice that Ryan (three years old), surrounded by a huge array of new acquisitions, is in the midst of being momentarily delighted and then disinterested in one toy at a time. I am witnessing conspicuous consumption in its infancy. Taking no note of the fact that I am in conversation with his mother, he loudly talks over what I am saying to her–again and again.

Rachel (nine years old), enveloped in an over-stuffed chair, is operating the joy stick of her new video game. She is completely disconnected from everything and everyone around her. She too insists loudly that I need to pay attention to HER.

It is natural that children, delighted with their toys, should be excited around Christmastime. However, something seems truly out-of-balance. It is the fact that the children are demanding attention and are repeatedly interrupting the adults' conversation, speaking over whatever was being said. I was wondering what would happen with those ego structures so well developed at an early age.

They had not experienced nor had been taught by their parents the essential lessons of simple courtesy and patience. Furthermore, they had not received the profound support of true community. As a result, it did not allow me the privilege of the proper timing so that I could be happily present with them.

That was disappointing for everyone.

Image A:

At twelve o'clock sharp (the appointed time for lunch each working day) the father, his adult sons and two adult male neighbors, having washed their hands after hard field labor, stand around the kitchen table, looking for cues from the women in the kitchen preparing lunch that they should sit down. Two adult sisters who are helping their mother with meal preparation move their heads together and laugh, the mother tips her head quizzically as she looks at them with a warm, slight smile. Various "encampments" of children and women who are part of the extended family sit in different places around the small room. Two toys are visible: a four-inch disc that had been band-sawed and sanded smooth and a home-made rag doll. Boys, perhaps six and eight years of age, quietly rolled the disc back and forth on the hardwood floor. A four-year old girl silently clutches the doll as she watches her older sisters who were taking care of a little girl just about ready to start walking. Anyone speaking could easily be heard because there was considerable stillness in the room, even with so many people.

When the women from the kitchen quietly signaled, the men sat down, and all the children gathered together quickly to sit on a long bench alongside the table. Everyone bowed in silence as the man at the head of the table said a simple grace. No politics were discussed, no serious topics, just a recounting of some of the wonder of the morning's experiences that had been perceived through keen eyes.

Quite often there were belly laughs. There was often recounting of anecdotes similar to the priceless stories told in the book, and later in the television series, "All Creatures Great and Small." Serious topics were discussed away from the table, privately, or in council or other special meetings.

Wait a minute, you say! Something's wrong with that picture. Sounds worse than TV series of the 50's and 60's where apparently dutiful housewives were presumably seething inside, unfulfilled, unappreciated, living quiet lives of desperation, abused in a male chauvinistic society!

No, actually, not at all. This family was genuinely happy. They had truly embraced good religious codes of conduct, and like others in the community, had accepted their roles and responsibilities, pledging to live life honorably and with good humor.

Now, in retrospect, after having studied Eckhart Tolle's *A New Earth*, I realize that what was most striking about this setting was the complete absence of ego.[2] Real and honest humor and levity flourish in the absence of ego, and that is the single-most reason I so enjoyed this household.

After several months of living with my Mennonite neighbors (as I was constructing my nearby house) I witnessed many of the features that give them "certainty of fulfillment of what is right." A few of the most important are:

- They do not carry debt and are relieved of the consequences of that enormous burden.
- While maintaining true love and support of their children, they do not support the development of ego structure in them and therefore are reasonably sure that they will be upright and not cause harm. (This approach to child rearing in no way diminished the childrens' levels of confidence and performance.)
- There is a prohibition against the use of attorneys. All community conflicts

[2] Tolle did something with his book in a grand way that no one before him has ever accomplished. He laid out chapter and verse, with every detail, the subtleties of how the ego operates so that it can destroy life in service of itself… AND get away with it! Then, unbelievably, he got people all over the world to actually read and study what he wrote. Millions of them! How did he do it? Maybe it wasn't just him.

are resolved within by asking for God's spiritual authority to preside over their council meetings of elders that issue final decisions. If outsiders threaten community members with legal intervention, they generally walk away from the matter even if it results in financial loss. Within the community, the concept of someone else's legal liability for them or their children is utter nonsense. They train their children by example to be highly observant, and this is generally sufficient to avoid problems. If the occasional accident occurs, everyone comes together to share the burden and to provide support for the injured, including community coverage of hospital bills if that is required.

In short, my Mennonite neighbors created a social structure that allows them to practice something that lies in a mandate seemingly reaching in scope beyond the Ten Commandments (though they might not agree on that). I found a good description of the code they live by (with two noted exceptions) in a rare Tibetan text whose title translates as *The Seven Point Thought Transformation*. This is part of the practice of Lo Jong – turning the mind from non-virtue to virtue.

The Tibetans seemed to have had something psychologically clever up their long orange sleeves, because instead of giving ten "commandments" (which our desire body could easily interpret as rigid and demanding and hence disregard), they instead invite us to "Be aware of actions and their results, and abandon the ten non-virtuous acts" which are:

– Three unskillful actions of body:

Killing any sentient being [With their penchant for hunting and animal husbandry, Mennonites miss on this one.]

Taking that which is not given

Engaging in sexual misconduct

– Four unskillful actions of speech:

Lying

Slandering - creating division between people

Speaking harshly by scolding, swearing, or being sarcastic

Foolishly chattering - engaging in senseless conversation

– Three unwholesome actions of the mind:

Greed

Hatred - ill will toward others

Holding on to such wrong views as:

a) disbelief in the law of cause and effect, and

b) disbelief in the ability of attainment of the awakened state.
[Mennonites would surely interpret (b) differently than Tibetans!]

As we are globally immersed in the evolution of consciousness and in personal individuation, I realize why it is necessary for the dissolution of entrenched attitudes and dogmatic practices of conventional religions and social structures. Earlier in my life I could not have imagined that around the world, as we shall see, a set of frequencies lies hidden in special flowers that if "unlocked" can precisely assist such a transformation.

II – Pace Yourself

Before I could move my existing organically-grown herb company from Los Angeles to rural Tennessee, a whole lot of things had to take place and in a particular order. I would have to give one month's notice on the building I had leased in Van Nuys, CA; have the building I was newly constructing ready with an inventory already stocked there; move the whole company and all remaining inventory; and have worked out how I would keep the company there going while I was developing the raw land and building a house at the same time. (My former wife, Lynn, in a true spirit of support had already gone ahead, as she was able to obtain a physical therapy job in a nearby rural hospital.)

Boy, was I was a young man with a mission! But there was a huge catch. Natively, by nature, I am a contemplative. I am not normally the hyperactive, super-business-kind-of-guy. When I have the choice, I associate with such fellows because their skill set is very useful when stuff has to get done. But there weren't any of them around, so I had to assume the role by default. It was the largest test of my life, and it put my nervous system completely on edge. All the poise one might hope for leaves when one feels the pressure of needing to move at "mach 3 hair-on-fire."

So you might imagine the true puzzlement of my new Mennonite farm development foreman, Eli, when I would fly by nervously overlooking work on the farm that was being done. When Eli and his first assistant, Aaron, were doing wonderful things like laying out the fields and beginning cultivation, I would join in where I could.

Eli watched me work hard for several weeks, never saying a word. One day I joined in the massive job of trenching one half mile of land to lay in a pipeline bringing spring water from a higher altitude to where we were installing a water turbine that produces electricity from the head of pressure the water produces. (It is worth noting that in initial stages of land development, motorized equipment was used by "my" Mennonites to perform enormous jobs.)

There were areas where the trenching machine could not be used, and we had to dig by hand. Eli and Aaron seemed to rather effortlessly move a lot of dirt. And they worked at such an even pace! Try as I might to follow in their footsteps, my work just wasn't the same as theirs. I am sure of that because I noticed from time to time that Eli would cock his head slightly, with a slim expression of puzzlement, while looking at me intently as if he were mentally calculating what would be the actual output from my "unhandy" (a Mennonite expression) efforts.

I would shovel as long as I could, then quite exhausted I would have to stop for a while to catch my breath. His numerous assessments of me took only a moment, and would generally end with a fleeting glimpse of a smile. Finally, when I was very red in the face and probably badly dehydrated, Eli figured he'd have to say something. He looked at me while he continued to dig with the hallmark slight cocking of his head, as if he were about to say something.

Then I saw him stop digging altogether and in a fluid set of movements, back out of the trench, place the shovel in front of him, raise up his right foot to rest on the shovel while relaxing his upper body as he loosely held the shovel handle, straighten his left knee slightly, and look me in the eyes kindly with a father-like gaze. Eli had the most impeccable timing. He knew how to "get to me." When he noticed that I was aware he would be saying something of note, he did.

"Brent!" he said in a stout and modulated voice, "If you… don't …learn… to pace… yourself, you are goin' to plum tucker yourself out."

I was speechless and nothing more was said. After about three seconds of Eli's kindly projection of energy toward me, he got back in the trench and continued digging.

How could so few words have such a huge effect on someone's life? Well, of course, it wasn't just the words. It was the totality of Eli's remarkable being and his intention and choice of timing.

That one event caused me to look deeply at life to see what would lead a person to operate out of balance. The list is a long one, and in many cases, a sad one: poor self esteem, sense of isolation from life, hopelessness, lack of trust, hypersensitive reactivity to the threat of emotional or physical abuse, feeling unsafe, worthlessness, and not the least of these, shame, which is often the origin of hurt and on top of that, rage.

How much we express those common characteristics all comes back to the inheritance we bring with us at the beginning of life and to the circumstances that arise in our childhood that enable us to identify our weaknesses, and early on, with proper mentoring from balanced parents and right community, transmute those weaknesses into strengths.

Only rarely does that idyllic childhood occur, and so, in general what we see are wounded personalities with large areas of development missing. Life experience will eventually fill in the missing development, but often at the cost of heartbreak, ruptured relationships, unplanned and unwanted children, and more.

The three years that I worked alongside Eli and Aaron, I suspect, will always be among the most memorable in my life. Even though there was much work to be done (fortunately I did not have a health care practice at the time), there was a great deal of time for me to sit in the stillness of the magnificent forest I had been gifted. Much like my childhood canyon experiences mentioned at the outset of this book, now, in a different setting, the "tree people" were informing me of what I would soon need to do.

As I reflect on this period, it seems that I was unconsciously being "encoded" with a set of "awareness frequencies" correlating with the developmental personality deficits that are most common in the world, and that, if removed, make life much more enjoyable.

In retrospect, apparently those "awareness frequencies" acted as attractor fields, pulling and shaping the malleable fabric of our quantum universe so that I might have the opportunity of encountering flowers containing frequencies to nullify the unhealthy unconscious beliefs we all carry in our subconscious mind.

This huge (outlandish?) concept will be explored much more in coming chapters.

III - Don't Panic

This topic is naturally aligned with the one above, "Pace Yourself." It is the brief recounting of my experiences with another wonderful young man named Shane, who was also a gift in my life.

He helped me with the insane vision I had of completely finishing the inside of my house without the assistance of professional carpenters: milling from raw lumber with a planer all of the cherry wood trim around the hardwood floors and windows (well over 800 feet of it!); building out a rather exotic walk-in closet with all cedar drawers and clothing storage spaces; in one trial producing finished Corian counter tops for the kitchen (the stuff is expensive and you don't want to be "experimenting" on it), and producing laminated kitchen cabinets with red oak trim doors (a nightmare of router work).

Crazy? Yes, because the totality of my preparedness for this undertaking (which required very skilled labor) was a one semester wood shop class I took at Santa Monica City College before I left L.A. for Tennessee. What did I produce for my final grade in that class? Six little pieces of walnut, nicely milled, cut, and glued together in a hexagon to form a picture frame!

To this day that frame still houses one of my favorite things: a collector plate of a Native American scene titled *Great Spirit,* depicting a brave in full regalia sitting atop his bowed-head steed with his arms raised in praise to heavenly Creator.

I was really proud of that frame… but it was six little pieces of wood!

Whenever I have had a deep dream of something that felt like I needed to accomplish, people somehow show up for it to happen. In this case, from the slim pickings of 900 people in the nearest town, I was fortunate to find Shane.

Shane was a country boy, born and raised all American. An adorable fellow that surely had a way with women, he was most certainly not a Mennonite. But there was a very important characteristic that he shared with the Mennonites: integrity. He was a kind and decent young man. He had a wicked sense of humor and perfect timing in his delivery. His stand-up joke routines could have played in any comedy club. And for the job we had to tackle, he was truly "handy."

Shane had a wonderful relationship with his father who taught him a great deal. He idolized him. It sounded to me like his father was skilled at parenting and had passed on wonderful traits to his son. I was fortunate, in a second-hand way, to be able to absorb some of that mentoring by simply working with Shane.

The development of my herb company was taking longer than expected due to a lot of farm delays. I felt that at some point soon I would need to return to practice, and so, you guessed it, I was a nervous wreck. It was hard to stay nervous though when Shane was always providing outstanding comedy routines. We got the work done and done well, but we were pretty slow. Constant laughter kind of slows things down! (Wonderfully, that constant laughter became part of the fabric of my house.) I suspect that it was the same outstanding mentoring from a great father that fostered in Shane, like Eli, a wonderful depth of character and insight. He just didn't get flustered.

We labored arduously for two weeks to learn how to fabricate and eventually succeed in producing a finished Corian counter top. The glue and the resin smell horrible and are very toxic. I was really reluctant to install the counter top in my kitchen because of the outgassing of the building material.

There is one way to rapidly get rid of that, and it is by applying heat. The noxious vapors evaporate to a large extent quite rapidly. But how do you heat up 10-foot long sections of a Corian counter top? The sun is not hot enough to do it quickly. The solution? My herb drying shed which had just been finished alongside my herb company. Though we dry herbs at 105 degrees, it could be raised to about 120. That would work we thought.

We dragged the thing from my farm on a flatbed trailer and set it up on saw horses in the drying shed. I cranked up the heat and let it run for two days, smelling the exhaust vents to make sure the gasses were leaving. Yup, it worked. We were ready to open the doors of the shed for the "extraction."

The doors flew open and there, lo and behold…was… this pathetic, drooping excuse of a counter top. The heat had deformed the once straight and true beauty we set in there just two days ago!

"Oh, my God!" I started out. I think I banged my hand on the side of the shed. There were lots of expletives. All in all, I was pretty LOCO. Shane, much like Eli, was quite implacable as he quietly examined the situation. He stood rather patiently waiting for my own "venting" to pass.

With perfect timing, he interjected just the right words before I was going to go at it all over again: "Brent! … Don't… panic."

The solution was to rapidly move the drooping and flexible countertop to the even mounting surface in the kitchen and weight it down for it to flatten. I still appreciate that great countertop to this day.

Later I realized the real, deeper reasons why people panic. Perhaps their mother was deeply distressed when they were undergoing development in-utero (in my case true). Perhaps they had a frightening and uneasy delivery (a powerful premise of rebirthing). Perhaps they witnessed their mother being abandoned by the father (in my case true), and on and on the examples run. (Perhaps as a result of those occurrences they suffer a common neurological deficit that is virtually unrecognized – a condition called "retained primitive reflexes" – that can be the root cause of a life-long exaggerated core stress response.)[3] The theme is the same. Our personal and social problems often derive at the root from trauma or lack of balance in the formative years and from the misfortune of not having wise mentors to help correct family deficiencies.

From 1993 to 1996, in the midst of the hardest physical work of my life, I nevertheless had the most meaningful "vacation" a person could ever experience. I was given the opportunity time and time again to observe and contemplate how tranquility and non-reactivity, essentially the absence of trauma, created a rich life experience, even in the materially poor surroundings of my "Mennonite village."

I had to adapt to a tremendous shock when, in 1996, I learned that 25 neighboring families, essentially the whole community of Mennonites (excepting a handful of people that fortunately included my immediate adjoining neighbors) intended to pick up and relocate very quickly.

For reasons of doctrinal interpretation having to do with fundamental issues about how to live a "simple life," the traditional Mennonite adherents in the community where I lived had been in conflict with the neighboring and slightly larger Mennonite community three miles away. The larger community was gradually adopting modern implements including gas powered chain saws, electric motors, a few telephones, and more. Rather than quarrel with them, the smaller community agreed it was easier to leave and to start a newly inspired community 200 miles away in southern Kentucky.

It was the second time in my life that I felt like I was losing my family, and it took me several years to adapt to this loss. From 1997 through 1999 I had to "dig deep" to better understand the meaning of impermanence. Further, I was challenged by the fact that having grown more in touch with who I really was as a person created an awareness relating to my wife, and that revealed our resonance as a couple had attenuated to nearly nothing.

She was retreating into late hours at work, spending weekends at church and with friends, and reverting more and more to her Catholic underpinnings which gave her the familiarity and security she knew during her youth.

[3] An enormously healing flower essence formula to remove this horrible condition is explained in Part 3 (p. 238)

Probably it was in 1999 that I suspected my marriage would have to be terminated, and I kept expecting that my wife would realize that as well and address the issue with me. That did not happen, so in 2002 I initiated a conversation that I knew was inevitable and would be painful.

In essence, I suggested divorce as the only answer to our situation. My wife's Catholic ideology took hold, and she was very resistant to the idea. At this point in time I was much more in touch with my body, and I realized I was literally dying. There was no turning back for me. Our divorce was final in the summer of 2003.

Since that time a deep theme has emerged for me concerning what it is that produces "aliveness" and meaningful connection between men and women. My fascination with that enormously important topic continues to this day, and is integrally a part of the flower essence transformation process I have been witnessing personally and with many patients and consumers internationally.

What has now become a simple three-tiered model for more joyful living evolved from 2003 to 2007. That model was developed for me by the guiding intelligences that seem to lead me to particular flowers that have specific transformational frequencies.

Retrospective analysis shows that the characteristics of the flowers I found and continue to find and the order in which they are discovered are not at all arbitrary. The model is this:

1. Repair our body field energies and stored subconscious brain memories that have been damaged by the experience of emotional and physical trauma and/or abuse;
2. Re-awaken our process of receiving that is generally turned off when one suffers trauma;
3. Understand and embrace what I call the "Law of Alignment," which is changing and further enhancing our spiritual resonance so that we can align with the frequencies that will activate the positive Law of Attraction. This is the beginning of the cycle of empowering the higher parts of our self. **We then become ready for manifestation of the right sort.**

With a smile I often tell people, "Somebody that's really smart up there already has this whole thing figured out. For me now it's just a matter of finding the flowers that are the chosen ones!"

Several of the coming chapters deal with my adventures as I search the world for the frequencies of especially transformational flowers.

5

The Dream

I was living at my farm in 1999 when, one lovely spring morning, I awoke in an astonished state, remembering every detail of a revelation I had experienced the previous night. I say "revelation" because that was the only thing I could think to call it. The first part of my dream had centered around an historical figure well known in the field of natural medicine, Dr. Edward Bach, yet I had not thought of him at all for many years. His writings had impressed me when I was a pre-med student.

At that time I had the good fortune of discovering Dr. Bach's classic booklet, *Heal Thyself.* It was enormously inspiring to me because it discussed the true origins of disease. Dr. Bach articulately described the fact that modern medicine had lost sight of the true causes of disease, concentrating solely on the materialistic nature of illness rather than more essential psycho-spiritual causative factors – the roots of illness – which mature for a long time before manifesting. He wrote that when disease is attacked as if it were solely material, it removes attention from the primary cause – "the result of conflict between Soul and Mind" – causing illness to become more entrenched. He observed that when our personalities are in harmony with our soul we will experience happiness, peace and health, and when we stray from that path, we will suffer conflict that will compromise wellness.

Dr. Bach described a conceptual framework wherein something as gentle and subtle as flower extracts could reach deep into the human psyche and transform the origins of disease arising from unhealthy thinking, attitudes and beliefs. After reading Dr. Bach's work while in college and during post-graduate studies, I felt I would have to learn how to make flower essences according to his directions, and I hoped to discover the uses of flowers by intuition as he had. I had no idea what a long process it would be.

On several occasions I had prepared flowers according to Bach's extraction method. Oddly, I'd always felt uncomfortable every time I did. I would take time locating the perfect flowers and, following Dr. Bach's precedent, set up a small crystal bowl of pure spring water beside them. Then I would attempt to communicate my healing intentions to the flowers. I was unsettled though because I felt I could not create sufficient harmony within myself to override the shock I would be causing the flowers by following the traditional method of essence preparation: cutting them before placing them in the crystal bowl for extraction. I knew the shock would be a part of the subtle spiritual "medicine", and that seemed untenable.

And yet Dr. Bach wrote about the importance of gentleness and alignment with Universal Coherence:

"There are two great errors: first, to fail to honor the dictates of our Soul, and second, to act against Unity.

If we have in our nature sufficient love of all things, then we can do no harm; because that love would stay our hand at any action, our mind at any thought which might hurt another. (*Heal Thyself*, Chpt. 3)

The real victories of life come through love and gentleness, no force whatever must be used. (*Heal Thyself*, Chpt. 5)"

Toward the beginning of my practice I purchased a complete commercial set of Dr. Bach's flower essences to begin evaluating on my patients. By using applied kinesiology muscle testing and other methods, I screened many patients to ascertain their need of Bach's remedies, and I seldom found them to be indicated.[1]

I was discouraged because I believed so much in Bach's work, yet I could not obtain significant results on my patients using his flower essences. I resolved that one day all the necessary factors would align so that flower essences would heal my patients. I didn't know then that I would have to wait so many years for that "one day" to arrive – but arrive it did.

My dream revelation that spring morning was astonishing in that it showed me vivid details of how to create a device and a process that would produce flower essences while the flowers remained UNCUT and pulsing with life. The energy of the entire flower could be collected as a result of using the apparatus I saw, and that would not be possible any other way. Here was the harmless extraction method that I had hoped might be developed "one day." Had I triggered the dream by my subconscious holding of that thought? I don't know.

I could hardly contain my enthusiasm, and yet I spoke to no one about my unusual experience. I knew that somehow I had been given a marvelous gift and had been charged with bringing it into physical reality. I carefully gathered the components necessary to create the apparatus that would produce my first living extract from uncut flowers. It took a couple of weeks before I was ready.

I was filled with anticipation and hope the first time I set out on my land to give my flower essence extraction process its trial run. I wondered if it would work. But there was another feeling, a greater presence surrounding me that was not my own.

After my grandfather, with whom I was very close, passed away years before, I would occasionally feel his presence watching over me. But I knew this "energy" I felt now was not his, although it was benevolent and fatherly as well. I wondered who or what it was, but I continued to go about my work nevertheless.

I walked slowly along the forest margin as it met open fields. I felt suspended in a

[1] "Old-Timer" colleagues in the International College of Applied Kinesiology told me they observed the same thing I did, and that Dr. Bach's remedies seemed to have worked better in the 1970's and before.

timeless state, being prompted to assess the energy of numerous flowers, wondering if somehow I would "know" which one to extract. I finally selected a flower among the profusion of wild flowers and then began an awkward extraction procedure that now, years later, has become efficient and streamlined.

When the extraction vessel was in place, I was ready to harmlessly collect the full spectrum of energy from the UNCUT living flower, its entire surface area covered with pure water. I was able to step back from the apparatus to move my energy out of the field of the flower, leaving it undisturbed and in its normal spatial relationship to the earth. As soon as all was calm, every millimeter of the entire flower surface was being extracted at once.

When I saw that the process was working, I felt both the exuberance and excitement of a child – and the greatest sense of accomplishment I had ever known.

The steady presence that I had felt earlier now became a pronounced voice. I knew without doubt whose it was. "Well done, lad, well done!" said the voice of Dr. Edward Bach. "I was hoping you would carry out this special living flower extraction. For this, I have waited a long time."

I had the awareness that Dr. Bach was communicating to me that this discovery would enable a new level of spiritual healing and that is was deeply needed in this cycle. I felt inspired, imagining that from a higher state of perception his spirit would be helping me find flowers to protect against the tremendous challenges of this era.

Although I felt amazed to experience this level of communication, I also felt a deep sense of ease and gratitude. After a twenty-year commitment to Dr. Bach's principles of flower use without being able to utilize them effectively in my own practice, I was finally able to create a new process that now, after years of use, I see produces tremendous results for my patients and those of colleagues.

From time to time, when I am making a new flower essence by the UNCUT Flower method, I feel the presence of Dr. Edward Bach smiling down on me.

6

A Forest "Gift"

With my background in energy healing techniques ranging from classical homeopathy to hands-on methods such as the wonderful chiropractic technique called Bio-Energetic Synchronization Technique (BEST), I have often observed the dynamics of exchange between the energy donor (doctor, healer) and the recipient (patient, client). I have happily been a recipient of frequency healing many times myself.

It is a complex phenomenon because there are so many variables. With hands-on techniques such as BEST or Reiki (and for that matter conventional chiropractic adjusting), the "energy" of the practitioner is of utmost importance. He cannot give a highly coherent and deeply healing session if he is unstable. The potential derived benefits are operator dependent. Therapeutic substances such as homeopathic and herbal extracts similarly are technology and operator dependent, and the therapeutic "energy" in them varies tremendously with respect to how they are made.

Conscientious holistic practitioners are aware that their state of internal balance is important for the success of their practice and for the benefit of their patients and clients. Yet no matter how we might try, even if we intend to be in a very clear space, we leave some "energy signature" on those we treat. We do our best, and we trust that it is an uplifting one.

> *Most practitioners would probably agree that if it were possible to dispense "pure divine energy" (free of other signatures) in drops from a dropper bottle so that a patient could access it wherever they went throughout the day, it would be a momentous advent in healing and a great step forward to aid the evolution of consciousness.*

Just after my extraction method discovery, I was under the impression that I had been given a gift that allowed just that. Now, after many years of seeing people respond to the uncut flower essences prepared by the method I described in the previous chapter, I have seen evidence that that is true.

It would be useful to take an aside here to discuss briefly the many ways different individuals are making flower essences and to compare the energy outcome from those methods to the outcome using the apparatus I was shown in the dream state. I hope, then, that you will be able to understand why I was overjoyed to begin exploring "my" (the FlorAlive) one hundred sixty acre forest from a new perspective, searching for special flowers that had been "touched by the divine," so that I could collect their energies and see how it could benefit my patients.

Oral tradition from India and Egypt points to the use of flower essences in ancient times. It was a practice then (and still is now) to collect dew drops from flowers to be diluted and made into flower essences. Among all conventional flower essence manufacturing methods, this is probably the purest. The flower is left alone, intact and alive, it is in its normal spatial relationship with the earth (if it is not touched during collection), and the small amount that is collected has very coherent energies *restricted to the area on the flower surface where the dew was resting.*

Fast forward a few millennia to the nineteen twenties in England, and we encounter the great healer who popularized flower essences, Dr. Edward Bach. He made his flower essences by cutting wild flowers and rapidly placing them in a bowl of pure water exposed to sunlight for a few hours. Then he strained, decanted, and preserved the water with brandy, later to dilute it for the final dosing remedy. (Dr. Bach's method is the standard method now used by most flower essence companies worldwide.)

By being cut, the energy of the flower is ruptured and the all-important energy coherence (bio-coherence discussed in chapter 7 and in Part 2) is broken, so this is the least desirable method to use. What is amazing, however, is that the essences Dr. Bach personally made (which apparently lasted into the 1970's) were very therapeutic, despite cutting of thc flowcr. When I studied Dr.Bach's work, I wondered how this could be. I speculated that he was an unusually evolved spiritual being, that his own energy was highly coherent, and that it acted as an "energy bridge" to attenuate the shock of cutting the living flower, so the essences turned out to be very healing in spite of the methodology. Flowers that are cut and made into essences nowadays still do have healing benefits though less than originally. It is just a matter of degree.

The last stop in our brief historical flower essence review is the nineteen eighties and nineties. Around the world, in that era, several individuals must have perceived at nearly the same time that it would be better to prepare flower essences without cutting the flowers. As a result, several different methods of preparation were employed:

(1) Collecting dew drops as mentioned above. A very good method, but it only captures for direct energy transfer the area of the flower on which the dew is sitting and misses the powerful information that can only be collected as a complete array.

(2) Dripping water over the surface area of different parts of the flower and catching the water as it cascades off the flower surface. This is very operator dependent (contains the energy signature of the person making the extract) and does not allow a complete energy transfer from the surface of the petals to the water drops moving over them. As the flower is moved about it disrupts the bio-coherence of the flower.

(3) Bending the living flower over so that parts of it are immersed in a water bath. Despite good intentions, when the stem of a flower is bent, it causes energetic (electric) cell signaling changes in various flower parts, and this low level shock can disturb pure energy transfer. It also contains the personal signature of the person preparing the essence. Most important, I have found that some flowers must not be disturbed in their spatial relationship to the earth and to the heavens. When they are extracted in their normal growth position they transfer the most coherent healing frequencies. I am familiar with individuals in companies using the bending-flower approach, and they are devoted to their craft and produce fine products.

(4) "Angel-assisted" flower essences. By this process a container of pure water is placed or held beside the living flower and the human "mediator" calls in the assistance of higher beings to transfer energy from the flower to the water-filled container. This method is obviously highly variable, and essences prepared in this way contain the signature of the individual mediating the process as well as "angelic energy." Some of these preparations are magnificently healing. Others seem to fall short of the intention.

On a clear April morning in 2000 I awoke on a Friday with a real inspiration to walk over half the perimeter of the FlorAlive forest to see what wild flowers were blooming. I saw a few areas that still had Bloodroot's telltale grey-green leaves that look like folded up "wings". Its beautiful creamy white flowers were nearly all past. Several species of Bethroot were blooming in profusion. While traversing the forest I kept seeing a small bright white flower that looked like a star. At first it seemed insignificant. Then when I entered a particularly beautiful moist hollow, that little "star" simply stopped me! It was so energized, and it seemed to call out for my attention.

I had to kneel down so I could inspect it more closely. I knew that it was a species of chickweed (Stellaria), but I didn't know which one, so I dubbed it "star spirit flower." When the flower had just freshly bloomed, at the tip of the stamen was a vibrant but tiny orange-colored ball forming the anther. I didn't want to get up because there was something so "magnetic" and charming about the flower.

It was a long walk back to my farmhouse, but I decided that I must return to assemble my extraction equipment so I could make an essence with it. I got my gear and my photographic equipment, jumped on my four-wheeler, and was back to the magical hollow in no time at all.

Since my dream revelation, I had used my extraction equipment enough that it was no longer novel but was nevertheless very special. And now, many years later, it still is.

The deepest meditation in my life occurs when I am sitting in the presence of a flower I intend to extract. All thoughts vanish. Nothing else in the world exists but the flower. I look into the face of the flower as I will embrace the eyes of my beloved when she finally appears.

A feeling of fullness and love occurs that is transcendent. The flower "communicates" a sense of adoration, that it exists only to benefit all of life, that it will use all the energies it has concentrated into its complex geometry, fragrance, and unique colors to mediate the deepest healing allowable.[1]

Until I am finished, I do not entirely leave that timeless state, but the changing shadows remind me of earthly time and that I must make the extract or lose the opportunity on that day.

I next take close-up photos of the flower and capture some of the beauty I have been witnessing. Then I take all the time necessary to set up the extraction process that is unique to each flower. When the rooted and uncut living flower is extracting, still and in its natural orientation between heaven and earth, I move away from its field and leave it alone in its peaceful environment to transfer its phenomenal transformational power to the water, which covers every millimeter of its entire surface. In this instance I left it late morning and returned to collect the extract after lunch a couple of hours later.

I normally remove the water extract with a glass pipette and rubber suction bulb. The bulb was missing so I had to very carefully draw up the liquid into the pipette without letting it touch my mouth. As I was on the last "draw" I must have lost focus because I got a mouthful of the extract. Since I would have to throw that out, I decided to enjoy it – to take a bath so to speak! With the full dropper I ceremoniously drizzled the essence on the top of my head (acupuncture point Bai Hui (GV20), and it dripped down all sides of my body to the ground. Then I squirted gulps into my mouth a few times, and it was gone. I was happy with that bit of hydration. I gathered my gear and rode back to the house to take a rest. It must have been about 2 pm.

After flower essence work I normally rest very deeply, but on this day I could not. I was fidgeting on the bed for about an hour, and then I had to get up because I was so agitated. I went into my home office to see if I could catch up on mail, but I didn't get very far – for the strangest reason. My office was messy. There were papers that needed to be sorted and stuff that had just been sitting around for way too long. In the past, however, that had never stopped me from working and completely ignoring the mess! But something was different. I HAD to tidy things up.

[1] See "San Juan Mountains" photos in Doc's Photo Journal beginning on p.329.

My energy kept accelerating until I was in a full fledged paper sorting frenzy, punctuated by the emptying of trash, vacuuming, dusting and re-arranging. When I finally came to my senses it was about 2 am the next morning. I couldn't figure out what had come over me initially but appreciated the increased sense of organization in my office. I got only a few hours of sleep and continued my obsessive cleaning and organizing all of Saturday through Sunday afternoon.

When I finally sat down on Sunday and reviewed the weekend, I realized that something bizarre had just occurred. I began asking myself what could account for my unusual behavior. Then I remembered that I showered myself with Star Spirit Flower. Could that have been responsible, I wondered? Did this marvelous little flower boot out the hidden procrastinator lurking inside me? I prepared a bottle of its extract to begin testing on my patients the following Tuesday morning.

There is a consistent "serendipity" that occurs when I have a new flower essence to test. Invariably, among the first few patients I see someone really needs the newly prepared and uncharacterized essence. How on earth could that happen? But it does!

It did not take me long to test my suspicions about the properties of Star Spirit Flower. The next week when I was in my clinic, one of my patients, Mari, described that she had a vague malaise, that she was "stuck" and couldn't make herself tackle the work she needed to get done. She explained that she experienced that problem quite often.

Using Holographic Scanning,[2] an energy screening technique I developed (and teach in an instructional video) for the purpose of testing the affinity of a therapeutic substance on a patient, I found that Mari's body resonated positively with the frequencies in Star Spirit Flower. That was the first indication that she would probably benefit from taking it. Then I began the next evaluation stage consisting of measuring the effect of self-referential statements by applied kinesiology muscle testing (which I explained in chapter 1). To recap, here is how it works:

The procedure begins by identifying a strong test muscle (normally in the patient's arm). The individual being evaluated repeats aloud test phrases that, due to mind/body reflex connections, effect changes in muscle strength. In this particular case, I wanted to see what was going on in my patient's subconscious mind with respect to procrastination, the resistance to doing what must be done. So I created the test phrase for Star Spirit, "I am free from the effects of procrastination." Upon making that statement, if Mari's previously facilitated (strong) arm muscle were to weaken, it would indicate that the conscious statement was colliding with the opposite and stronger subconscious belief. The arising conflict would cause muscle weakness, meaning that at the subconscious level – the level that truly directs our life – Mari was NOT free from the effects of procrastination. In other words, she was prone to procrastination. In fact, that is what we found.

[2] See Appendix 9 p.315.

After I administered test drops of Star Spirit Flower on Mari's tongue so that she was exposed to the powerful frequencies in the extract, when she repeated the test phrase, she no longer weakened. That meant that the new frequencies of Star Spirit apparently dislodged from brain memory Mari's unconscious pattern of procrastination. I provided a dropper bottle of the Star Spirit essence for Mari to use, and when I checked her in my office a couple of weeks later she was breezing through her tasks and felt she never really looked back.

Mari was a new patient at that time. She is still a patient of mine today, and she has received many of my other flower essences since this first one. But she still remembers the powerful evolutionary effect Star Spirit had on her life. We did not know at the time the more profound transformational force residing within that precious flower.

After a couple of years of using Star Spirit, another of its properties was revealed and gave rise to a new and rather chilling test phrase:

"My mistakes are unforgiveable."

Can you imagine? How amazing that a flower could contain frequencies that appear to "overwrite" and remove from our mind such an incredibly damaging belief, memory, trans-generational inheritance, or karmic pattern (whatever is valid for you). This belief – unforgiveable mistakes – was probably resident in Mari originally (it is not now), and quite possibly that is the deeper reason why Star Spirit helped her so much.

If a person somehow believed at a core level that "their mistakes were unforgiveable", would it not impair functioning in many areas of their life? It could certainly give rise to what superficially would appear to be simple procrastination.[3]

Over the next two years I discovered several more great flowers from the FlorAlive forest, and I adopted the habit of "bathing" myself in each one of them.

When I am in the forest alone I naturally tend to abandon mental content (a la recommendation of Eckhart Tolle), and, exiting that state sometimes leads to interesting musings.

One of my favorite themes just after the turn of the millennium was (but is no longer) speaking to the trees: "So God, why do I have to be the personal testing ground for all these new flower frequencies? Why do I have to look at all my stuff? It's not always fun having the stuff…ing knocked out of me!! Come on, just give me the flowers to clear out my life once and for all, and I promise I'll pass it on!" Well, of course, God wouldn't be God if he/she/the One didn't see the larger picture. When I eventually "got" that notion firmly established a few years ago, life became much more of a delight.

Now to prepare me for where I had to go beyond where I was around the turn of

[3] From the standpoint of stress management, few things could be a greater persistent stressor than a belief that one's mistakes are unforgiveable.

the millennium (so that I could find more powerfully evolutionary frequencies) required another installment of wondrous discovery, blessings, and serendipity. That came in the form of meeting Bruce Lipton, Ph.D. and his psychologist collaborator, Rob Williams, (as outstanding but not as funny as Robin Williams, actor) when they taught a seminar in Nashville, summer of 2002.

7

New Forms of Thought Transformation

(& How Flowers Can Initiate It)

I had seen notices in 2002 about a PSYCH-K workshop and Dr. Lipton's lecture for three months prior to it taking place, and though it looked interesting, I decided I did not have the time then to give up a weekend. Little did I know!

At 5:30 a.m. the morning of the workshop, I awoke startled, as if someone pulled me upright from my recumbent position in bed. I had an awareness, a knowing… I had to go to the workshop! I left the guest bedroom (where I had been sleeping solo the last couple of years) to tell my wife (still asleep in the master bedroom) about the impelling force that was urging me to go. In short order I was on the road, making the fast, wide-open 80 mile drive from my farm to Nashville.

The workshop began around 9:00 a.m. and was attended by 15 people quite evenly split between men and women. Including myself, there were only two docs. There was a nurse, several reiki and massage therapy practitioners, and the rest were natural-healing-savvy "civilians" simply interested in the subject of thought transformation.

Before describing the basic premise and technique of PSYCH-K (which helps one understand the domain in which flower frequencies act), a brief mention of thought and mind transformation as it has been practiced around the world historically would be a nice way to set the stage.

In Eastern spiritual traditions, the mind of the average person who has not practiced disciplines of internal alignment and transformation is called a "monkey mind." If you imagine the animated facial expressions and grimaces of a little chimpanzee – his arms waving as he jumps up and down, vocally protesting things undesirable or threatening – that is what the unexamined mind is like in most people.

Stored painful memories, traumas, failings of one sort or another (what Eckhart Tolle aptly named the "pain body") all combine to form the distracting chatter of the unconscious/subconscious mind.

When we suffer from a restless mind it makes it difficult to encounter life's opportunities because we are reverberating in the past or projecting into the future.

In the East, the cure for the chattering mind was various forms of meditation and for a significant number of young men (especially in Tibet), the opportunity of receiving monastic training. Under the guidance of master teachers, by way of disciplines that would be incomprehensibly difficult by today's standards, the illusions in the candidate's mind (the source of chatter) were unveiled, analyzed, and transformed. Life was a commitment to enlightenment.

In less structured spiritual traditions of aboriginal peoples, rites of passage were enacted that required a focused mind and especially absence of fear to emerge successfully. Often the "spirits" within Nature and of animals were adopted as guides to help reveal to us on our journey what is real.

The spiritual traditions of native people of the Americas varied tremendously from the Nagual master teachers of the Mesoamerican Toltecs to the shamans of the Andes, who rely on hallucinogenic cactus, and those of the jungles who employ hallucinogens in a mixture called Ayahuasca to pierce through stored memories and beliefs that we hold as real, disallowing them to continue to affect our lives. Overall, humans were seen as living in illusion, failing to perceive reality as a result of false projections. It was agreed in one way or the other that the projections had to be broken and replaced with what is real.

Nature has always been so alive to me, and life itself such a "trip," that I never felt the need to use recreational drugs. As a youngster I surely could have used major mind altering, but recreational drugs quite often have unforeseeable destructive effects, and apparently I was "protected" from that.

Nevertheless, I have always been fascinated by the recounting of drug experiences that ostensibly result in positive transformation. So on a trip I made to Peru in 2000, when I found myself alone with Regner (the truly wise chief of a remote Peruvian jungle tribe I appreciate), I asked him to explain to me, if I were to undergo an Ayahuasca ritual, what would be the proper way for it to be administered. Also I asked him if he knew anyone that he could recommend to perform it.[1]

He smiled, and I could see that he was searching for a way to be tactful. He explained that most of what was being done in Peru with Ayahuasca was a "tourist variety" ceremony, and he could not recommend that. He said he knew of one man in the region that would do the ritual correctly, but he warned me that it was not for the faint of heart. The shaman administering the ritual has a great responsibility, he said, and when he recounted his own experience with that shaman years before, I understood what he meant. He described the process briefly from beginning to end.

First, the shaman has to find an Ayahuasca plant (Banisteriopsis caapi) that "has not been seen by human eyes." He must ask the plant permission to do a healing and entreat the spirits of the herb to bring awakening to the intended ritual participant whose name is spoken to the plant. Upon "agreement," the Ayahuasca plant is then harvested as well as other companion plants that are brewed with it to enable visionary communion.

[1] See Doc's Photo Journal (p.325), second page of the Jungle Collection. Regner is crouched in the center bottom of the group photo with Doc, children, and the head of the Tribal Women's Council.

At the appointed time, the participant is brought alone (never in a group!) to a clear spot in the forest that has been specially prepared. A firm post has been driven well into the ground. A fire pit has been constructed a few feet in front of the post. A ways away, a shelter with blankets awaits. In the dark of night, deep in the forest, the participant is seated on the ground with his back against the post. His hands are bound firmly behind the post, "or he would surely try to escape and run before the ceremony is complete. That could be very dangerous," said Regner.

The fire is lit. The shaman administers portions of the Ayahuasca mixture to the participant until the desired mind-altered state is reached. Then the participant begins seeing visions. First, he will experience either a giant python that will wrap around him and the post, crushing him until his life is extinguished. Or, he will see a jaguar leap from the forest and feel his body torn until death.

Spirit guardians appear and resuscitate him to guide him through a process of life transformation. A "screen" appears in the air in front of him. On it are innumerable small moving images, each a small "movie" depicting pivotal encounters or experiences throughout the existence of his soul. The shaman has taken Ayahuasca and sees the screen as well. The guardians and the shaman review each incident ("movie") asking the participant in relation to those encountered if he will either forgive them or kill them. The decisions are difficult, and the shaman provides energetic support for the process. When all the images have been reviewed and decisions chosen, the candidate is exhausted and is moved to the shelter to recuperate into the next day. "His life will never be the same and will open to new possibilities after this ceremony," Regner commented.

The gravity with which Regner described the ritual was spellbinding. It was easy to see why this type of Ayahuasca ceremony had been nearly lost to antiquity.

The part about "killing" did not make sense to me, so I asked Regner to explain. Apparently, what was meant by "killing," was that a decision would be made by the participant to eradicate ("kill out") memory and to completely terminate all association for evermore, so that no part of perpetrators from the past would ever be encountered or thought of again.

I was enormously impressed by the powerful processes of forgiveness or final disassociation that Regner had just described. Nevertheless, there was not enough time for me to undergo the Ayahuasca ceremony he mentioned. I also felt that there would be a more gentle and more appropriate way for me to positively re-orient my mind and extinguish unconscious negative memories.

That sentiment came from the fact that I had been a recipient of and was a practitioner of the powerful and gentle chiropractic method called Bio Energetic Synchronization Technique (BEST). For years I had been observing its remarkable ability to, in essence, "erase" negative thoughts, feelings, and emotions from the minds of my patients.

What few realize, and I am eager to point out, is that right here in the U.S. powerful forms of "new shamanism" have arisen and have been successfully proven. They employ muscle testing and self-referential statements (instead of hallucinogenic plants and ceremonies) to help locate obstacles of stored memory in our mind and spirit. Then hands-on reflex techniques such as those of BEST and PSYCH-K facilitate thought transformation by reversing the polarity of the register of thought obstacles, essentially overwriting them.

PSYCH-K is concisely described as "a user-friendly way of rewriting the software of your mind in order to change the printout of your life." It creates a receptive state of mind that dramatically reduces resistance to changing at the subconscious level. Then, the subconscious mind is accessed in a way similar to a personal computer. PSYCH-K works like a "mental keyboard – a user-friendly method of communicating with and changing the subconscious mind that is simple, direct and verifiable."

Since performance of the different forms of energy psychology to which I alluded in Chapter One requires focus and clarity while muscle testing, I assessed the attendees quickly to select suitable candidates to serve as workshop partners.

I identified three people who seemed to be quite stable with pleasant energy, and I ended up working with two of them especially throughout most of the seminar. It is rather amazing that even neophytes in a first time workshop can administer deep level transformational healing if they do the process correctly, and that is what happened. We each were able to help the other by identifying limiting beliefs, then using the PSYCH-K physical process we "erased" the limiting beliefs, and finally we retested to make sure they were gone.

Barbara was a bright and attractive woman in her later fifties who owned several massage schools in the southeastern U.S. She had an administration team in place and therefore had a lot of free time, and she intended to "recreate her life" so that she would be able to attract an appropriate life partner and play.

Thomas was a strikingly fine looking man not only because of his features but because of an aura of integrity. His desire was to eliminate obstacles in his subconscious that he felt were interfering with his ability to make a living as a drummer and move out of carpentry work.

My own intention was to break personal patterns and the energetic deadlock that had kept me in an unproductive marriage and that I knew were negatively affecting a lot of collateral areas. I hoped to become attuned in a way that would make my wife's separation process less stressful for her. Once that was accomplished, I intended to find an energetically aligned life partner and delight in more aliveness as I sought to discover the healing frequencies hidden in special flowers.

Each of us in the workshop experienced unclear areas of testing, and when that happened Rob Williams would take over and show us how to proceed. In a couple of instances, he intervened to clear some particularly stubborn beliefs I had. He had a very coherent and steady healing presence, and I am grateful to him because he undoubtedly helped me significantly at a time when I really needed it.

Since I was quite familiar with energy psychology I knew that if I took off for a while to go to the auditorium next door to listen to key areas of Dr. Lipton's lecture, I would not fall behind in learning PSYCH-K.

Dr. Lipton discussed emerging insights in new era biology that help explain how thought and belief, the vibration of thinking, trigger physiological events in our body. He presented information that later appeared in his 2005 ground-breaking book, "The Biology of Belief."

The practical applications of PSYCH-K were married perfectly to the conceptual framework presented by Dr. Lipton, and it became clear why I had to encounter Lipton's work that previous to the workshop was unknown to me.

The mechanisms of cellular "energy" detection that Lipton taught helped me understand the science that can explain how subtle energies within flowers are able to initiate rapid mind changes in the person consuming them. Examining, in some detail, how uncut flower frequencies can produce powerful shifts in our life is the subject of the second part of this book. For now, the simplest explanation of how this can occur is as follows:

Flowers behave in one way similar to satellite receiving dishes. Their geometry, colors, and spatial relationship to the earth determine the kinds of frequencies they can "download." Frequencies they absorb – huge amounts of coherent information that are influenced by where the flower is growing – are stored in semi-crystalline moisture in the surface of the petals. In the uncut flower extraction process, highly coherent transformational frequencies are collected in the extracting water and are then transferred to the consumer who adds drops of extract to drinking water. The "chaos" in the consumer (emotional imbalance and disruptive memories and beliefs) is then transmuted under the influence of the newly incorporated harmonic flower frequencies.

I feel blessed by the vision I received, allowing me to understand how to create an apparatus (now patented internationally) to collect floral frequencies in a unique and new way without cutting the living flower, maintaining its vibrant connection and spatial orientation to the earth.

The next two chapters provide examples of the whole process that enables special flowers to protect, transform, and uplift us.

Madame Fate
copyright © 2004-2014 Brent Davis

8

Madame Fate

Ever since the movie *The Secret*, a great deal has been said and written about The Law of Attraction. The positive functioning of that law, however, depends first on the alignment of many, many factors in our life (what I call "The Law of Alignment") and the union of subtle dimensions of pre-manifestation so that what has been conceived actually appears on our physical plane.

Starting just after the turn of the millennium, my life has been a "study" in alignment. Little shifts, small signs of change, movement away from fixed points of view, and then… unexpectedly, part of a fulfilling dream appears. It has been a wonderful experience for me to witness this happening. (For the past decade, a high priority for me has been to find flower frequencies that accelerate positive alignment for us all.)

An uncanny type of alignment that eventually resulted in my meeting "The Madame" had noticeable points of origin related to my attending the PSYCH-K workshop (and Dr. Lipton's presentation) mentioned in the last chapter. A long string of serendipitous occurrences began there.

At the start of the noon break in the PSYCH-K workshop described in the last chapter, I was standing with Barbara discussing the work we had just done, and I felt a powerful energy enter the room from the hall that led to the lecture room where Dr. Bruce Lipton was speaking. I could not help but look over to see to whom the energy belonged.

The "emanation" came from a Latin woman who walked directly over to Thomas, looked him intently in the eyes, and with considerable animation described the "unbelievable" information that Dr. Lipton had just delivered. She was so excited and delighted. She gave Thomas a warm hug and a kiss, turned, and left the room.

I cannot recall what I was doing during the time of the short scene I just described, but I suspect that to any onlookers I must have looked dazed. I realized after the woman left that somehow I had a deep knowing about who she was and that she represented the feminine essence that I had always been seeking but had never encountered. What does one do with a realization like that? Since I was still married, and she was obviously delighted with the fine fellow I had just gotten to know, there was nothing for me to do except forget about it.

About four weeks after the seminar, I noticed that Thomas' name was on my schedule as a new patient. Turns out that he had a shoulder problem that just was not healing. I treated him three or four times, and everything returned to normal. He was happy with his care, so he proposed that his partner, Maria, (the one I saw at the seminar) should observe the specialized therapies I employed because he was sure she would want to inform some of her clients about my work. He asked me if that would be OK and if I would like to meet her. (Internally, I experienced an upheaval, "Ohh… Uhh… Hmmm" as I stuttered to myself within.) "Sure" I said, "that would be fine."

In a couple of weeks, Maria showed up in my office, doing what some Latin women have a knack for doing – looking strikingly attractive without even trying. Maria was warm, genuinely interested in what I was doing, completely respectful and professional, AND had no interest in me personally whatsoever. That certainly made things easier, for I was experiencing considerable strain as a result of my stagnant marriage (that I knew would have to be dissolved) and due to challenges of internal transformation.

Months passed, and an eventual routine was established once a week where Maria and I exchanged treatments. I did structural, nutritional and herbal work on her, and she gave me shiatsu massage treatments. I noticed each week that Maria was carrying a lot of tension because she gave so much of herself to her clients and was spread rather thin. Thomas was always present to assist, but somehow that didn't seem to be enough to relax her. (She was a woman with a life mission, and I inferred over the time I worked with her that that characteristic was wearing Thomas out.) I was generally able to help her calm down quite a bit, and after she worked on me I always felt renewed by her vital energy.

Then one day something alarming and unexpected happened. My office assistant informed me that Maria was on the phone in an emergency situation. I took the call, and her voice was shaky. She explained that she was driving her car, and it had just spun around several times on the edge of the interstate. It was totaled. She asked if a family member could drive her to my office and if I could treat her immediately. I told her to come on, and she arrived about 20 minutes later.

Maria is an incredibly strong woman, and it really upset me to see her crying. Soon, I learned that her pain was not coming from physical injury in the accident but rather from the emotional pain that led to the accident. She was trying to deal with the news from Thomas that he would be leaving her, dissolving their relationship, and moving out of state. This was unbearable for her to hear because Thomas represented her ideal – she was "so happy with him."

I performed a procedure on Maria called "injury recall," which is a hands-on reflex technique to reverse polarity on the shock response registered in the brain from her car wreck and thus remove it. I then did "emotional recall" to remove the brain memory of the emotional trauma that occurred when Thomas announced he was breaking up with her. (I derived the basic method of both these techniques from the BEST procedure, which employs an ingenious combination of simultaneous breathwork, cranial nerve activation, polarity therapy on the skull, and utilization of key words and numbers to "erase" physical or emotional shocks that register in the brain as spikes of unhealthy polarity reversal.)

I felt the procedures would be helpful, but I suspected they would not be enough. At that time I had not discovered any flower essences to reduce the heartache of losing a relationship. Maria continued to be in a funk. She appeared to be emotionally dead, and there was no telling when she would come out of it.

About two weeks later, I was inspecting fields that lie on open land in the middle of the FlorAlive forest, and as I was walking on the access path to the greenhouse I felt a "tug" of energy. I had to stop to see where it was coming from. I felt directed to walk a few feet to my left to reach an embankment off to the side of the path.

I could feel something pulling at me, and as I searched the area I saw a small, fuchsia-colored wildflower. It seemed to be pulsing with an intense glow, beeping a code at me. I had to bend down to see its beautiful texture more closely. All of a sudden an amazing thing happened. The face of Maria rapidly emerged from the stigma at the center of the flower as if a pressurized vapor shot out her image. It really got my attention. Not very subtle, eh? Could it have possibly been telling me that Maria needed its essence? I lost no time in beginning a photographic session with the most energetic of its flowers. Then I prepared several of them and began the extraction process. A couple of hours later I was done. I wondered if I had been given a magical force to repair Maria's broken heart.

I was so enthused that I could hardly wait to tell Maria about my unusual experience, but then I realized that in her state she would not be excited and that she had no interest in shifting her condition for me or for anyone. I asked if I could come over to her house to speak with her, and she agreed in a rather resigned way.

I got to her house as quickly as I could to recount what had happened, and all she could do was look at me quizzically. It took a bit of nudging, but she agreed to take the newly prepared essence of "Heartmend"– that seemed a most logical name for the new essence (and an optimistic one). After a few days, Maria called me with an entirely different tone. " I feel much better," she said. I was overjoyed.

Maria opened to the possibility of receiving help from other flower frequencies I had prepared, and she began taking them. Months passed and eventually Maria warmed to the idea of developing a personal relationship with me once my marriage was officially dissolved. The divorce process was finalized in the summer of 2003.

During those months, I focused rather intensely on characterizing the new flower essences I had prepared in the previous year. On one patient or another in that time period, almost every week, I had the eerie feeling that some sort of invisible "force" was obstructing clean and rapid recovery of my patients.

I had read enough in cross-cultural anthropology studies of indigenous peoples to be familiar with their ideas concerning the negative influence discarnate spirits can exert, the destructive influence of generational curses, and the hindrance of various other intangible malevolent forces. I reasoned that the troubling energetic disruptions many patients were experiencing had to be associated with negative components operating in the invisible realms of "space" around us.

Once again the "heavenly gatekeepers" seemed to be directing a particular class of patients to me so that I would take note of a serious problem. I did notice, and I began a process of questioning, "What would it take for this to change?"

When we ask a question with clear focus, it seems the fabric of the universe starts to shift so that the question can be answered. The answer relating to eliminating the influence of negative forces that we may encounter from time to time came with the awareness that there must be special flowers somewhere that could help to this end. I pondered, "Where could that be?"

I began to receive an answer that it was a tropical flower, probably in the Caribbean. As time passed, quiet "suggestions" began entering my head on a fairly regular basis. I finally decided to call the kindly assembly responsible for sending me ideas related to healing flowers my "Steering Committee"!

Well, I have always loved beaches, and I was quite familiar with Hawaii, but where to go in the Caribbean? "Ahh… Jamaica" I said to myself, "I will find this wonderful flower in Jamaica. It will come from a tropical area on that island." I had been in Jamaica about six months before to visit my holistic practitioner friend, Gertrude, who ran a healing retreat in Montego Bay. That was just a short trip, and I didn't have time to see any other areas on the island. But at that time I had a sense I would surely return.

With a bit of research I found that, as one might expect, there was a large variety of flowers on Jamaica. I would need help to find a special one to dislodge negative energy.

Even though the metaphysical community in Nashville is generally far behind and smaller than one would find in West Coast cities, we have been blessed with some high integrity individuals that have the appellation the Christian community here prefers, "the gift of prophecy" – people who see into the non-material universe and receive guidance from spiritual forces. (Misguided individuals, unfortunately, can tap into non-constructive energy that is anything but helpful, and that is certainly to be avoided.)

Out of several of these bright souls I knew, I had the sense that I should speak with Liz. Liz was a powerful gal who had left the film industry in favor of using her God-given talent of seeing into the non-material world to help people find solutions to vexing health and other problems.

Liz was quite busy when I called to set up an appointment to visit with her. She kindly fit me into the earliest spot that was available, and she didn't have much time. So as not to be distracted and waste time, I carefully wrote down a clear set of questions. I was pleased and sure that would be helpful.

I rapped on Liz's door, she greeted me with a smile, offered me an herbal tea which was already prepared, and we sat comfortably in her living room. We caught up a little bit on what each of us was doing. I thought I would then inconspicuously pull out my little list and pose the first question.

As I was looking down at my paper, Liz said in a pleasant but forthright voice, "Brent… you won't be needing that… I got it already." I looked up from the list with a sort of quizzical "huh?" Then I saw her smiling face and her head playfully bobbing from side to side.

" You know," she said, "my guides and your guides get along really well! Let me tell you what they're saying."

"Oh, sure… please do," I said.

Liz continued, "The flower you are looking for is white, and it has something to do with women." Her voice dropped; end of message.

I looked at Liz, startled with the brevity of the message. I was constructing some sort of retort, like, "And… what more can you tell me… a bit more detail, perhaps??"

But before I could formulate the words, Liz said with finality, "That's the message, Brent, that's it."

"OK," I said, "well then… that'll do. Thank you, thank you." Liz and I spoke about a couple of other topics for a few minutes, and then I left.

"So let me recap here," I said to myself as I was driving away from Liz's house back to my office. "The flower is somewhere on the entire island of Jamaica, it is one of hundreds of white flowers, and it has something to do with women. Yeah… right." With a big grin, looking up to my "Steering Committee" – presumably in the sky – I uttered quietly, "Guys, I'm going to need a little bit more information here." Then for the first time (and now something that occurs nearly all the time), I simply knew that I would find the flower, and… it was going to be really fun. In fact, it was going to be marvelous.

My divorce had been finalized for a while, and I was really quite spent after that process. I hoped that I had honored my ex-wife's path as well as mine and that the pain of the divorce would find its way to peace in both our hearts. Maria and I had grown close in the months following, and she seemed to be a gift in my life. She had still not moved on completely after Thomas, and I felt she needed a real shift as well.

"OK. I got it." I thought to myself. "I feel so energized when I am with Maria that I will ask her to accompany me on a trip to Jamaica, and we're going to have a blast. It'll be mostly vacation, and in just a couple of days of focused work, I'll find that flower." How things proceeded after that were strikingly aligned.

One night after the epiphany above, I sat down at the computer and began a search for planners of customized vacations in Jamaica. For some reason, I clicked about ten pages into the Google search results, and bing… a name of a small tour organizer jumped out at me. It was around seven p.m. my time, and the number of the agency was back East. I called, eight p.m. Eastern time, and an upbeat woman's voice answered my call. I mentioned to the gal that picked up the phone, Jade, how I found her name, and then I took a leap by launching obliquely into what I intended to find in Jamaica.

I told her I was an herbalist and that I needed to locate someone on the tropical side of the island who could serve as a guide to help me find a particular herb for which I was searching. Amazingly, she didn't hesitate a bit and responded by saying, "That's great. I know several herbalists in the Port Antonio area [the tropical side of the island], and I'll set you up with them."

Then I explained that I was particularly looking for a native Jamaican who had grown up in a setting where herbs were used. She thought for a moment and said, "Oh, that would be Samuel. He is a general guide in that area, and his family has land in the foothills of the Blue Mountains. But he knows herbs, and he can help you."

"Wonderful," I said, "I'll send you the dates that I would like to be there, and we'll create the itinerary." I spoke with Maria, and we set up the dates in the late spring of 2004. We would be gone for a week – five days of relaxation and two days of work.

Maria and I were both tired and really needed a break by the time we actually boarded the plane for Kingston, Jamaica. Little did we know what we were about to encounter once we landed. I am afraid I was a bit cavalier when I arranged transport from Kingston to Port Antonio. From distance on the map, I figured it would take about three hours for the drive. We would be landing at four p.m. and I figured I could handle driving in the dark for about an hour. Problem was, I forgot that Jamaica had been British in colonial times. That meant driving on the opposite side of the road. "Well, I adapt quickly," I thought to myself. "No problem, I can handle that." Maria and I loaded our luggage into the strange little car that was available at the rental agency and set out from Kingston to Port Antonio–on the left (wrong) side of the road!

It was the most grueling drive I have ever made in my life! And here is why. The road had potholes that could swallow a car. The speed limit was 50 mph and, because of numerous blind corners and other "obstacles" one could never even wildly imagine, the posted speed was one that should not have been surpassed. Paradoxically though, it simply was not safe to drive at fifty miles per hour (or less) because a ceaseless stream of Jamaican "Mario Andrettis" were continuously pulling in behind me and riding my tail UNTIL we reached completely blind hairpin turns at which point they would pass!!

As to the other obstacles, there was something even more harrowing in the dark of night than all sorts of living creatures that would shoot out into the road from behind brush cover. It was the Jamaican men with truly black skin, walking on the edge of the unlit roads with no shirts, wearing black shorts, dark flip flops on their feet. They were invisible until nearly hitting them.

Poor Maria. One of her least favorite things was wild driving. And though I truly did not want to taunt her by the way I was driving, I could not help but feel real amusement because of her body language. She was always low key without a hint of drama queen in her, so her gesticulations and uncomfortable squirming were of the minimalist kind. It was the manner in which she made them that was hilarious to me.

Maria's hands were clenched on the seat and on the door handle, white knuckled.

She would emit small, brooding noises punctuated by occasional squeaks. Sometimes I could not restrain myself from laughter, and it got to the point where Maria joined me, laughing as well. She knew that I was stuck in a no-win situation that wouldn't end until we got to our hotel. She has eagle-eye sight and was the official lookout because she could see farther ahead than I.

As quick as she saw a potential hazard that could jump in the road, she would blurt our warnings quickly such as:

"Chicken! … Goat! … Maaan!! ……BABY!!!!!!" After three hours of driving in the dark (and five hours after we started) we arrived at our hotel, unpacked and quickly went to sleep.

The next morning we found that Jade, who had arranged our lodging, had done a great job. She got us a private bungalow on a spectacularly beautiful forty-four acre seaside estate for which, all things considered, I paid very little. It was a place for nurturing and a true joy for my soul. Maria was also able to deeply relax in the sensual beauty of this tropical paradise.

On the day appointed for my flower expedition, Maria made us a picnic lunch, and I packed up all my photo and flower essence gear. We headed out to the center of Port Antonio town where we picked up Samuel. He directed me where to drive into the Blue Mountains. We were headed toward the Rio Grande River which at one time had been a freight avenue for a large portion of the world's commercially supplied bananas. When we got to the edge of that river we boarded a banana flat boat and were ferried to the other side.

Once out of the boat, I thought I should have a chat with Samuel to let him know my intentions and some details about the goal of our day trip. I didn't know what to say, though, because the idea of searching for some unknown white flower (in the midst of a verdant tropical landscape filled with flowers) might seem preposterous. I chose to say the least necessary and to see his response.

I said to him, "I am looking for a particular white flower. Something about it has to do with women. It may have been used traditionally to protect against negative energy. When I see it, I think I will recognize it." I was astonished by Samuel's simple and direct reply.

He looked straight into my eyes and said in a measured voice, "Don't worry. We will find your flower before the day is over." He seemed completely confident of this, and it was uncanny. How could he be so certain?

After inspecting about twelve or fifteen white flowers – none of which were "it"– I was stretching to remain optimistic. Then, as we walked at the end of our hike up a long canyon that led to a waterfall, something unbelievable happened.

Samuel motioned to Maria and me that we should stop. We did, and he slowly walked forward, perhaps 60 feet in front of us. Ahead was a tall rock face that formed the right hand margin of the beautiful rock step waterfall that lay to the left. There was a Jamaican native wearing a straw hat sitting with his back up against the rock wall and his legs stretched out in front of him. It made no sense to me, but it looked like he was holding a burning ember close to his face. Maria, with her keen sight, saw something different, and I noticed that she slowly developed a bemused expression.

Samuel approached the man whom he apparently knew and began a friendly conversation. I walked closer because I wanted to hear (over the roar of the waterfall) what was being said. Maria followed just off to my right. Then, when I got close enough to see clearly, I realized why Maria was smiling. What initially looked like a large ember glowing was actually a massive roll of ganja (the ubiquitous local Jamaican marijuana) in the process of being smoked by Jomo, who was apparently taking a break from cultivating taro plants. He was completely stoned.

He had made a valiant effort to stand to greet Samuel as he approached, and was only able to slide his body slowly upwards, inching up the rock wall behind him. Jomo's eyes were so bloodshot that it was medically upsetting.

I heard several "yah maaans" in the conversation as I approached nearer to Samuel and Jomo, and finally I was close enough to hear the dialogue clearly. After some small talk, Samuel explained that he was assisting me in attempting to locate a white flower that was probably used in folk medicine and had something to do with women. He asked Jomo if he knew of such a flower. There was a lengthy pause, and one can only guess that, as a result of the hashish, Jomo's neurons were having a mighty hard time with any sort of meaningful firing. "Ohhhhh, ya maaaan," Jomo finally said, "I know dat flower."

Then leaning against the wall, he slowly reached out until he grasped his walking staff leaning against the rock. He beckoned us to follow. Astonishingly, he began staggering toward the waterfall, catching himself repeatedly with his staff before entering a trajectory that could only end in a heap. In amazement, we all followed behind.

Aghast, we watched him step into the water about six inches deep that was rushing over the rocks of the step waterfall. He intended to cross and motioned us to walk behind him. Maria grabbed my belt at the back of my pants and held on as I bent over with arms outstretched to balance myself so that my lowered center of gravity might prevent my feet from sliding on the slippery stone. By the grace of God, Jomo did not drown himself, and listed, swayed and stumbled his way across the waterfall. Just as I stepped out of the other side of the waterfall and pulled Maria beside me, I saw a spectacular sight.

A beautiful mist was blowing off the waterfall passing through where we were standing. A dazzling, luminous brightness was directly in front of us. Leaning on his staff, Jomo turned to us and gestured toward the brilliant white flowers with his free hand. "We call this flower 'Madame Fate'," he said.

With chills up my spine, I looked at Maria, shaking my head in near disbelief, repeating silently to myself the guidance given by Liz, "white" and "something to do with women."

Samuel said to Jomo, "So what is this used for in folk medicine?" Without hesitation, as if anyone would know the answer to that question, Jomo replied, "Well, maaan, to protect themselves… warriors rubbed the flowers over their body before going into battle." Then he nodded his head in an affirming and proud way, as if to say, "You see, I know my ancestral roots."

We thanked Jomo and congratulated him on knowing the answer to Samuel's unusual question. Jomo fortunately didn't cross the waterfall again and instead started up a path that led into thick overgrowth beside the falls.

After spending some time visually inspecting and sitting in the company of the flowers, I had a strong sense that they possessed the protective force I was seeking. I asked Samuel if he would mind leaving me and Maria alone to perform a sacred ritual with the flowers. He said he would leave us alone for a couple of hours and take a break for his lunch. He disappeared a ways away into a taro patch.

I began my normal process of photographing the flowers and was soon lost in the internal world of Madame Fate. Maria sat very still, watching me, 30 or so feet away. I then set up my equipment and left the flowers to deposit their healing frequencies into the extraction vessel. We ate lunch in stillness, as if mesmerized by the force of the "wall" of Madame Fate flowers stretching out in front of us. An hour or so passed, I bottled the finished uncut flower essence, and packed up my equipment. Following the tradition of native peoples worldwide, Maria and I gave thanks for the blessings given to us from Nature in a few moments of silent prayer.

As if on cue, Samuel soon appeared, and we began the return journey of a few hours, this time crossing the waterfall without fear of losing a member of our party.

Samuel transmitted to us a wealth of information about the "real" and unvarnished Jamaica. He spoke about its poverty and about hopes that a vastly wealthy Jamaican entrepreneur living in Canada (who made his money selling "pot" and other drugs) would be investing in hotel development around Port Antonio, which he thought would be a great help to the local economy. We ferried back across the Rio Grande and directly returned Samuel to the center of Port Antonio.

We thanked him for his great assistance and speedily returned to our beach hide away for a swim before dark. I was jumping for joy inside. Mission accomplished! And now three more days to play before returning to the U.S. We wouldn't need the second work day I had planned.

That evening Maria and I became lost in the enchantment of a full moon over the small bay of a strikingly beautiful sheltered beach at Frenchman's Cove (which has appeared in several movies, most recently in *Knight and Day* with Tom Cruise and Cameron Diaz). We took a swim, gazed into the sky, and returned to our beachside bungalow.

The following day, we had a lazy morning and eventually got to the next door beach called San San at about nine a.m. We were the only two people there for over an hour. What a joy![1]

We returned to the property where our lodging was and spent the afternoon in Frenchman's Cove. It's not hard to understand how time escaped us, and how we ended up packing so late that afternoon that we would – heaven forbid – be driving again at night, this time to arrive at Montego Bay for the last few days.

The road to Montego Bay (running parallel to the beach) was in a better state of repair and much straighter that the road that led to Port Antonio. That was a great relief. Nevertheless, we were truly startled one more time.

Dark as before, it was difficult for me to see far ahead, so once again I appreciated Maria's keen eyesight as a bit of extra "road security." As we sped along, we noticed over some distance a sort of strange, skittering movement in shrubbery off the edge of the road on the beach side. We went up a small rise in the road that blocked sight in front of us, and when we were at the crest of the rise we saw an odd shape in the road ahead that we could not identify. Even though there were no other drivers in sight, in a voice reminiscent of our first night drive, Maria called out a warning and shrieked … CRAAAAB! We both went into hysterical laughter. A huge land crab was directly in the center of my one lane. It was easy enough, however, to swerve around "him."

The rest of our drive was uneventful, and we arrived late in Montego Bay. Gertrude had arranged wonderful accommodations for us in the villa of one of her clients. In typical third world style, shacks and shanties were sprinkled between sprawling properties with huge (10,000-plus square foot) houses. Very strange setting but a comfortable place to stay.

Since I enjoyed the first time I met Gertrude, I felt that if I should return to Jamaica I would surely visit her again. She was doing great work in natural healing, spanning a practice ranging from economically disenfranchised native Jamaicans to wealthy visitors staying at the Ritz Carlton or in private villas. Honestly, she was more interested in the former. So she arranged for me to give a lecture to her Jamaican clients about the work I had just done collecting flower energy, and to describe rudimentary concepts of energy medicine. I knew before arriving that I would have a chance to test any flower essences I might have prepared on members of the audience that Gertrude would be assembling.

Maria and I arrived at Gertrude's center in the afternoon about two p.m. There was healthy food being served in an open courtyard, and after everyone had snacks and refreshments, chairs were set up for my lecture and demonstration. I explained a bit

[1] Some months before, a crime involving harm to a tourist was committed in the Port Antonio area and it was publicized internationally. The result was virtually no tourists, and literally no one on the beautiful half-mile long white sand beach.

about how my flower essences work, and then I described how I would be testing people to show their effects.

There were 12 people attending the function, and I asked a couple of them to come up and let me demonstrate the screening process using self-referential statements. I was able to show with some of my essences (commercially available) that the disabling influence of harmful beliefs lodged in our subconscious mind can be reversed and eliminated by consuming particular flower frequencies.

Finally, I just had to pull out my newly prepared essence of Madame Fate flower, to see if someone might have the kind of problem it could possibly eliminate. As I scanned the audience, two Jamaican women immediately commanded attention because they looked so beleaguered. Both were in their fifties or sixties.

Javina was the first of the two women I asked to come to the front and sit so I could test her. I asked if she was feeling weary. She looked up at me with kindly and sad eyes, replying in a near whisper, "Yes." I then asked if she could please share some reasons why she was so tired. She described, sadly, what must be a common scenario among poor Jamaican women of her age. As the matriarch of her family, she spent a great deal of energy trying to hold together the broken families of her children. She mentioned numerous problems she was facing, but the one that stood out was her description of the challenge of getting her daughter to leave the "evil" man to whom she was married.

For the Madame Fate flower, I created the test phrase, "I am free from the influence of negative thoughts and beings." A healthy response would be the normally strong (facilitated) test muscle staying strong after the subject makes that statement. In other words, in a person who IS free from the influence of negative thoughts and beings, they would not lose muscle strength upon being tested immediately after making that statement.

When Javina spoke the "I am free…" statement, her strong test muscle collapsed in weakness. In other words, she was NOT "free from the influence of negative thoughts and beings." I administered to her several drops of Madame Fate, first under the tongue and then topically on head and facial acupuncture points. Within a couple of seconds she sighed noticeably, sat more upright in her chair, and generally appeared energized. Her voice had a greater volume when she repeated the "free from the influence of negative beings" phrase, AND her test muscle now did not weaken. She was apparently freed from negative energies to which she had been linked. "Wow!" I thought to myself internally, "something good just happened here."

Members in the audience were smiling in appreciation of what they had also noticed – the lightening of the load of a long-suffering and kindly woman. (In actual practice, consumers of my uncut flower essences take one or two bottles of a formula, sipped in drinking water throughout the day, which lasts in the range of three to six weeks. Over the course of that time, they are exposed to hundreds of sips, each one containing a transformational "blast" of highly coherent positive energy.)

Malene was the second audience participant that came up front for me to test. She was the eldest of the two women and appeared to be afflicted the most heavily. She recounted to me and the audience that she had been seeing Gertrude for several years, and that she always felt relief when she was worked on. But her problems that resulted in great tiredness would generally return quite rapidly.

I asked Malene if she had any ideas as to why her chronic problems kept returning. She felt perhaps it might be related to where she worked as a live-in maid. She was not comfortable going into detail.

I stepped behind the chair so she could twist around to whisper to me privately. She then stated, "The house where I am living is not a good place" … "The man there does bad things to people." Obviously, I could not pursue the line of inquiry further, but I surely wondered what the "bad things" were.

Malene weakened, as did Javina, when she stated the test phrase. With her facing forward toward the attendees, and me on her right side, I administered drops as described above. Then I witnessed something I shall never forget. As soon as the first drops hit Malene's tongue, a "wisp" or a "faint breath" of air blew by me from her body. Tension left her, and her face showed a nearly instantaneous transformation to a state of less stress. I was astonished at what I had just felt. What had just "blown off" her body I wondered?

When she uttered the test phrase again, she stayed strong. Apparently she was "freed from the influence of negative thoughts and beings." Malene looked up into my eyes and with a faint smile said, "Thank you very much." The audience seemed to be aware that something quite striking had just happened, and everyone remained still and silent for a few moments. Gertrude soon came up to the front, thanked me for my presentation, and invited everyone to mingle and sample health snacks and beverages.

Maria and I were conversing with each other when we noticed Malene approaching. I saw that she wanted to speak with me so I walked toward her. When we were standing next to each other she said, "Dr. Davis, I just wanted to let you know what happened when you gave me the drops. For the last ten years I have had a disabling headache that never goes away. Even Gertrude's treatments and herbs do not help it. … Now… my headache is completely gone! So again I just wanted to thank you." What could I do but smile.

I was so happy to hear that. I repeated the story to Maria who was pleased to hear it too. What a wonderful experience we just had, and the day wasn't over yet. Gertrude had a special evening planned for Maria and me that included dinner and drinks first, and then a visit to the best nightclub and casino in Montego Bay, Coral Cliff.

Gertrude has a very pleasing personality and manages to combine kindness and genuine caring with a rather sharp entrepreneurial flare. I learned that she had built a rapport with operations managers and executive staff of virtually all the resorts in Montego Bay, from Sandals to the Ritz Carlton. Gertrude mentioned to me that most of the "all inclusive resort" managers had given her free passes enabling her to bring guests to dine and have drinks at no charge. A nice perk indeed!

I had visited Coral Cliff months before with Gertrude when I first traveled to Jamaica. For professional reasons she wanted me to meet Beulah, the manager there, and an icon of true Jamaican female elegance.

Beulah grew up in a poor family and had risen from the "ashes" of poverty to obtain her management position. Out of economic need and regional tradition, Beulah's family was very familiar with and depended upon local medicinal plants to stay well. For that reason Gertrude thought the two of us would enjoy meeting, discussing herbs, and local healing traditions. And we most certainly did. At the time I realized I would never forget Beulah, but I had no idea I would be seeing her again so soon.

After dinner we headed to Montego Bay's mile and a

half long hotspot of nightlife called the "Hip Strip." In the middle of it on one side is Margharitaville and on the other side, Coral Cliff. After parking, Gertrude led us deftly through the crowd of people waiting to get in until we got to the entrance where the door attendants let us pass inside. We wound our way up a curving ramp taking us through a jungle-like setting until we arrived at the bar of the Rum Jungle, the night club spot that features a variety of live shows every night such as cabaret acts and calypso bands.

Maria and I stood poised between the expansive bar on our left and the nightclub stage and tables on our right. Gertrude momentarily disappeared through the crowd, then I saw her reappear at a closed door to the left of the bar. She knocked and was soon inside. A couple of minutes later she was back with us to report that she had found Beulah who would be coming out to greet us momentarily. I leaned over to whisper in Maria's ear, "Wait until you see this amazing woman. Seeing her here is what one might imagine it would have been like on the set of a glamorous 1940s or 1950s movie."

After a minute or two, for some strange reason, we all synchronously turned to face the door at the side of the bar. It was as if Beulah's enormous energy caused us to turn and then burst the door open as she stepped through. She stood for a moment as she scanned the crowd until she saw us.

And then came what I was waiting for and hoped Maria would have the pleasure of seeing. It was Beulah's smile. To me, it was more than a smile. It was a history of triumph of the human heart in a single expression. I could only imagine it was her heart that took her to the top.

Her eyes lit up with recognition as she and I locked gazes. She gracefully glided through the crowd toward us in her beautiful evening gown of midnight blue satin and sequin trim. Queen Latifah could not have looked more elegant. She stopped a few feet in front of me, tilted her head down just a bit, eyes still fixed, and then all at once began her rich laugh as she lifted her chin, threw her head back and opened her arms wide.

"Docta, docta. How youuu doin' ?" Nothing left to do but hug her.

"Great," I said.[2]

"Sooo," Beulah continued, "Gertrude says you're doin' some special work with flowers. Tell me."

"Oh yes," I said, "I have had an unbelievable experience, and I think I found what I came here for. Do you know about a flower that is called Madame Fate?"

"Yes, I know dat flower," Beulah replied

"Can you tell me what was it used for traditionally?"

"Ya maan," Beulah said, "It had a very unusual and specific application. When women were sterile and could not have children due to scars and adhesions closing the fallopian tubes, we would take a flower from Madame Fate and let it soak in water. Then the woman would drink that water, and she have babies!"

I shook my head in astonishment. "That is amazing that it was used for such a specific problem."

"Ya maan, but it works," she replied.

Then I recounted my experiences that afternoon with Malene. As I was speaking, Beulah seemed to be listening more and more intently, and she drew her head closer to my face.

At the finale of the story I said, "...then I opened my dropper bottle of the Madame Fate flower essence and placed drops under Malene's tongue. As soon as I did that, I felt a wisp of air blow by me from off her body. It was eerie, but it had an amazing effect because her headache of years vanished very soon."

Beulah quickly moved her face within inches of my eyes, and for emphasis she raised her eyelids until the whites of her eyes became enormous, highlighted by her black skin. When she had my attention riveted she said boldly, "Ya maan, dat's the REAL use of the flower! 'Obeah'… in Africa that mean 'bad omen', 'spirit possession.' Madame Fate take that away."

All I could do was smile.

Internally I was astonished as my brain quickly assembled all the degrees of unlikelihood of my quest, starting from the first awareness in my office that a protective

[2] One of the things that was striking about Beulah's smile was its sheer size and beautiful form: perfectly aligned large white teeth set in an expansive and strong jaw structure that is hardly seen any more due to deterioration of jawbone formation over generations from the use of modern era, devitalized foods. The seminal research of dentist Weston A. Price demonstrated how the jaw has become compressed and small, with an elevated and jammed palate, as a result of low quality food in the industrialized era. The poor man's diet of dark greens, beans and rice or taro with fish when available had certainly served Beulah well.

flower energy was needed, to receiving very accurate, concise clues from Liz, to finding a vacation planner that set me up with just the right guide, to the odd process of discovering the flower as a result of being led through a waterfall by a Jamaican taro farmer high on hashish, to select attendance of just the right test subjects at Gertrude's gathering, ending with validation by Beulah.

I had just experienced the "long tail" of serendipity – one improbability stacked upon another that somehow manifested the desired outcome. I have found out since, on my quest for healing flowers, that "serendipity" has become the norm rather than the exception.

For others and for myself, this experience inspired me further to seek out flower frequencies that help to align us by removing thought obstacles in the subconscious mind, so that the positive law of attraction can manifest in all areas of life.

Two years later I was guided on another extraordinary flower essence adventure, this time half way around the world. For reasons I describe below, I had to make this journey alone.

Dancing Goddess
copyright © 2007-2014 Brent Davis

9

Encountering the Dancing Goddess

Every week in my practice, I have the opportunity and the privilege of seeing deeply into the psyche and the subconscious patterns of numerous patients. Fundamentally, I am asked by them to "fix" parts and pieces of their lives that are not working.

After a certain amount of time in practice, and with the proper training in modern, holistic chiropractic (and applied kinesiology), it is relatively easy and fast to remove musculoskeletal pain or discomfort. What causes recurring structural problems and other chronic health complaints can be quite another matter, however, and good investigative skills are required to determine the real origin of a symptom and to remove it. Very often the deepest causes are unconscious mind stressors – buried beliefs or memories that cyclically reactivate imbalance.

At a fundamental level, most current life stressors result from issues relating to either money or love (relationships).

When one feels better physically, one can often work with more diligence or greater creativity, and frequently that will solve money concerns. Matters of love – concerns of the heart and relationships – are much more complex. If there are relationship problems with difficult family members, they can often be solved by forgiveness, surrender, and acceptance, and if that doesn't work, by creating distance!

The question of whether one does encounter – or never finds – a deeply aligned life partner ("soul mate") can be monumentally significant. In the latter case, it can be enervating and truly vexing, because ultimately we cannot control, on a soul level of affinity, who shows up in our life.

Misaligned relationships and absence of fulfilling relationships are an enormous cause of chronic health complaints. From the time I began practice, I have seen hundreds of patients caught on the horns of the dilemma of no partnerships or mismatched partnerships.

Ever since I discovered and began utilizing uncut flower essences, relationships for my patients and my own relationships have incrementally improved.

> *I have often wondered if there were flowers that were integrated into the non-local field grid system – the mind of God (encompassing the earth) – that would locate and draw ideal partners together. What an intriguing idea!*

I eventually arrived at the belief that surely such flowers must exist or could be called into action.

A movie titled, *The Adjustment Bureau* (released in 2011) helped me understand why, from 2006 to the present, I have been so impelled to discover flowers that can not only improve relationships but that go far beyond. The movie raises provocative issues relating to the conflict between free will and predestination. In a truly original and thoroughly entertaining way, it examines a profound subject.

David Norris, the lead character played by Matt Damon, is a charismatic, young populist congressman who has a real shot at winning a New York senate seat. With precise timing, the tabloids publicize a dubious college prank of Norris that discredits him sufficiently so that he loses the race. As Norris heads for a bathroom to find a private place to practice his concession speech, little does he know that by an odd quirk of fate one of the stalls is silently occupied by Elise (Emily Blunt). She is a beautiful and irreverently amusing professional dancer who took refuge in the men's bathroom to escape security guards chasing her from a wedding she had just crashed.

In a muted voice Norris repeatedly rehearses how he will rise above humiliation. Finally, Elise can no longer tolerate that she is surreptitiously eavesdropping, and she emerges from one of the stalls. Presumably, she has been charmed by Norris' authentic character, evident in his monologue, because she walks to within inches of him and envelopes him with completely engaging, irresistibly seductive energy. He is momentarily bemused then realizes quickly he is mesmerized by her. Their "chemistry" is off-the-charts, they embrace and passionately kiss.

Norris' campaign aide enters the bathroom, which breaks up their encounter, and Elise is forced to run off (before they can exchange phone numbers) as she is pursued by security guards once again. The rapturous encounter with Elise infused Norris with such inspiration that a few minutes after that meeting he gives the speech of a lifetime. He wonders if he will ever see this amazing woman again.

Then some very clever filmmaking takes place in which multidimensional time frames are depicted intermeshing as we witness the actualization of probabilities of manifestation in peoples' (Norris' & Elise's) lives. We witness a smartly designed anthropomorphized representation of the action of karma and fate at work – percentages of probabilities of manifestation moving in lines toward or away from one another visible on notebook-sized master "control" logs. The logs are scrutinized by a cadre of black-suited, fedora-wearing enforcers of "the plan" (the Adjustment Bureau), who do their best to make sure the changing life scripts of selected protagonists unfold the way they are supposed to. But what or who controls "the plan," and what does it take to change how it unfolds?

We are given only as much information as we need to know at each turn to follow the twists in the plot. At the end of the story, what we have learned is as follows: The first meeting of David and Elise was written into the "master plan." The encounter with Elise was supposed to inspire David to make a great speech so that he would not disappear from politics, and so that he could, at a later time, fulfill his destiny to become president of the United States. But that was all that was "allowed." (It was believed by the creator of the "master plan" that each of them had bright futures so long as they stayed apart, and that each would never achieve his or her potential if they united.)

David was so smitten with Elise that he could not get her out of his mind, and he was hoping she would reappear in his life. Elaborate roadblocks were set up by the "Bureau" to prevent David and Elise from ever meeting again, but despite the Bureau's best laid plans, David randomly encountered Elise on a city bus. This time, he made sure to obtain her telephone number. That act signaled a higher authority in the Bureau to authorize an "other dimensional" assault on David so that Elise's phone number could be taken from him and destroyed. He was told that his mind would be "wiped" of all memory if he ever tried to reconnect with her. The Bureau felt that would end the problem, and David would never encounter his beloved again.

Despite the threatening warnings, David simply will not give up on his hope of finding and uniting with Elise. Three years pass, and somehow the improbable occurs. In a city of nine million people, David spots Elise from his bus seat as she is walking around a corner. He stops the bus and runs to catch her. When he does, he is so earnest in his explanation of how he has been kept from her that she lets him into her life. They have a long-awaited intimate encounter that is an extraordinary communion. David not only feels that Elise will never be a hindrance, but instead that she will spark his creative fire and be a great asset in his life.

Finally we witness an even higher level of effort made by the Bureau to separate the couple. Yet David's determination is so ardent, and his will to stay united with Elise so powerful, that it eventually draws the attention of the "Chairman" (God, presumably) who grants a rare dispensation, rewrites history, and essentially sanctions the union of David and Elise. They apparently will be able to achieve their destinies together.

We see that huge effort can remove obstacles by changing what appears to be predestiny. We get the message that a pure heart and unyielding belief is what actually earns us the right to self-determination and to create the manifestation of our heart's desire.

The "Adjustment Bureau" has many fanciful parts, but the representation of how obstacles in our path (that are generally never identified by us) regularly alter our life outcome is, to me, brilliant. I have seen that very phenomenon many times in the lives of patients and in my own life as well.

> *That observation, at the core, is what inspires me to keep finding new flower frequencies that act as beneficent "agents" in the "plan," delivering dispensations that can rapidly make our life so much easier and more joyful by providing nullifying frequencies that cancel disruptive forces, and inspirational frequencies that upgrade and align us with God-Source.*

We are told by teachers of great stature that when we are integrated and whole within ourselves – when our anima and animus are equally balanced – we can be entirely self-fulfilled beings whether we encounter a "soul mate" or not.

At certain stages of evolution, and with certain individuals, that is undoubtedly true. But look a little deeper. It is not true for everyone. There are unions and partnerships so powerful that the sum is much greater than the parts. For those that do not feel and sense on many levels that this type of soul union exists, no framework for understanding it exists for them either.

Given the choice of being happy or being dissatisfied depending on whether we do or don't find a profoundly compatible partner, it would obviously be wise to choose solo happiness. The interesting question is, "how happy?" Just "happy" or radiantly happy? Why not choose happy with an option for radiant happiness in all cases where the fabric of the quantum universe can be nudged in our direction by Divine dispensation whenever it is possible so that we surely find our beloved? Isn't that one definition of a miracle?

Our world really needs miracles at this time.

Hold your hands in front of you. Extend a finger for each couple you know who have remained radiantly happy with each other after years of partnership.

There are several tell-tale signs associated with radiant happiness in partnership, some being: a greater proclivity to laughter in each others' presence; the unflagging desire to affectionately touch each other; a twinkle in the eyes upon beholding each other after an absence (of even one day); the ability to differ in opinion or strongly disagree without hostility, the holding of grudges, or spitefulness; the arising of an enlivening energy in each others' presence that results in the automatic lifting of weariness; no hint of domination, manipulation, or control.

Do you need both hands for your fingers that are extended? Most people I have asked must think carefully to come up with even a few extended fingers on one hand.

It occurs to me that this is not right. There are obstacles interfering with what should normally be a more prevalent alignment of compatibility. What would happen to this planet if radiantly happy partnerships abounded? Isn't that worth aiming toward?

For several years, I have been searching for "holy grail" flowers that are woven so deeply into the energetic fabric of the universe that they touch the "source codes" of each light being. I have the impression that as part of Universal Intelligence such flowers can receive "signals" from the Divine that are a type of frequency dispensation, so that those who "qualify" can more easily encounter their beloved when their own radiance is enhanced by this specific floral activation.

The idea that certain flower frequencies can improve relationships is not without precedent, because several flowers whose transformational abilities I discovered and have been using for years definitely change and improve relationships.

A great deal of evidence that attests to this is presented on the FlorAlive.com web site.[1]

Well proven examples of frequencies from extraordinary flowers that consistently perform the above-mentioned duties are:

Blue Eyed Grass (prepared in the FlorAlive forest in central Tennessee) for removing memories of emotional pain and trauma; Flor de la Luna (prepared in the high Andes) for enabling the ability to receive love; and Flor del Oso (prepared in the high Andes) for acting as a powerful conduit to link us to God-Source for empowering the Higher parts of ourselves.

Before I set out on a quest in 2006, described following, the best example I had of a "relationship flower" is one that grows abundantly in the wild in the FlorAlive forest where I live. It is called Maroon Bethroot. Its frequencies have the remarkable ability of stopping women (and men too) from attracting into their life troubled or unavailable partners. One might say this is a "defensive" flower helping to protect us from trouble.

From 2004 to 2006 it struck me numerous times that personally I would really benefit from finding proactive flower frequencies (quite different from the "defensive" ones) to draw more highly aligned relationships into my life. And, of course, such flowers would be enormously helpful for the population at large. But where in this world would I find such flowers, I asked myself.

I have referred to my heavenly "steering committee" before, and they seemed to have their fingers in my "flower soup" once again! I kept getting the strongest sense from them that I would find the flowers I sought in the Land Down Under. "Australia?" I asked. "Are you sure you want me to venture all the way down there?" The answer was clearly yes, so I began researching the flowers of Australia. I compiled a list of about 15 flowers that I intended to "meet" and get to know once I got there.

I was astonished to find that in Western Australia – basically a desert – there are an estimated 12,000 different wild flowers that bloom in September, during the short season when there is moisture. In March of 2006 I decided that I would go there, so I had some time to prepare before the next bloom cycle. And lots of preparations were needed because I didn't know a soul in that country.

I decided to write an open letter to the natural health practitioners in Western Australia letting them know of my intentions to explore their homeland for special wildflowers. I included the list of the wild flowers I was interested in studying, and I asked for contacts who might know something about those flowers and who might help me locate them. It was a great "fishing trip." I received a wide range of responses. I primarily encountered genuine interest and support for my venture, but there were a

[1] The basic model described there states that creating balance in our life depends sequentially on three steps: first, removing subconscious memories of emotional and physical trauma and abuse; second, reversing the shutting down that occurs after trauma and enabling the ability to receive and especially to receive love; and third, enabling empowerment of the Higher parts of ourselves.

couple of characters that thought I had (as the Aussies say) "lost the plot."

There was one response, a silent one, that was truly ominous, and I was never intended to discover it.

About three months before my scheduled departure to Australia I began noticing an odd malaise. I experienced unwarranted tiredness, and I perceived a low-level inflammatory response beginning in my system. I have all the tools and therapy that normally restore balance and eliminate those types of symptoms. I applied them and did not obtain relief. As time progressed, I realized that my health was being seriously eroded by an energetic source, but I could not determine where from. I knew that if I could not reverse what was going on in my body, I would not be able to make the rigorous trip I had planned.

I called Natalia, one of my trusted clairvoyant friends, and described to her the odd phenomenon that I was experiencing. I asked her if she could please energetically trace from where the disruptive influence affecting me was coming. She said she would look into it. By the time she contacted me a few days later, I was already aware that the disruptive force was slightly diminished. So you can imagine, I was truly curious to hear what she had discovered.

By tracing the energy backwards to the source, she discovered that it led to an aboriginal elder who was a board member of a natural healing community in Western Australia. Apparently, my letter had gotten into his hands, and when he saw the list of flowers I was going to investigate, his full wrath was aroused.

Little did I know that among the list of flowers I had chosen was one particular flower (an exceedingly rare one) that, to some of the aboriginal people, was among the most sacred of living things. On the spirit and soul level, that flower's frequencies had protected the native peoples from the unconscionable abusive actions of the "Whites" that colonized and exploited Australia. It prevented the extinguishing of their heart energy and defeated some of the colonialists' annihilating intentions. From reading the energy of the flower, I knew without ever having seen it in person that it was very powerful. It was the number one flower on my list that I intended to study.

Well… if the board member and the aboriginal spirit elders that he called in had anything to say about it, that was just not going to happen. They clearly intended to psychically and physically keep me from ever setting foot in Australia.

Natalia is profoundly non-confrontational (a true practitioner of non-violent communication), spiritually gentle yet powerful, and clear in motive. Those wonderful qualities allowed her to communicate (on the inner levels) with the aborigine board member and to hear his concerns. She allayed his fears about me and explained my loving relationship with flowers. She let him know that under no circumstances would I ever exploit Nature. He acknowledged hearing what she communicated but did not yield with his directive about the one sacred flower. I was not to work with it. She let him know that she would deliver his message to me.

Natalia has a straight-forward, unadorned way of communicating. After listening to my description of how enthralled I was with that particular flower she said, "Brent, I know you would really like to work with that flower, but don't! There are too many aboriginal spirits involved now, and it would simply not be wise. They're pretty powerful, and you just don't want to mess with them."

I asked Natalia why, if these aboriginals were so energetically advanced, could they not read my motives and understand that I would do no harm to the plant. Could they not read my history and see the non-exploitive body of work I had produced, I asked her? She then explained to me that the power of these particular individuals was at a lower level "earth magic" frequency, and that their response to me was entirely instinctual. It was enough that I was white, and they didn't care to look any further, she explained. "O.K.," I said, "let them know that I will respect their wishes, and I will leave that flower alone." She said she would. She did, and the "spell" was lifted. My health returned to normal within one week.

As soon as the disruption from the elder was cleared, I began to experience a harmless yet truly unusual phenomenon. Once or twice a day a large, strange looking flower with a vivid red color would flash in front of my face. I soon checked Australian flora manuals and found that the image I was seeing was the official territory flower for western Australia, red and green Kangaroo Paw. My intuitive mind sounded up, "That flower is just not from this planet!" Whatever the case, it is a striking flower with a very unusual design.

As time went on and my departure date grew nearer, the frequency of appearance of Kangaroo Paw kept increasing. In the two weeks before I left for Australia, the flower was appearing in front of my face several times per hour. I let it know that "I got the message! When I land I will visit with you immediately."

I did advanced research before I left to find out where the flower grew around Perth, and determined how long it would take me to get to this location on the first morning after my evening flight into Perth from Sydney. The first morning I was in Perth I got my equipment together and immediately drove to the region where Kangaroo Paw was growing. I had to explore for a couple of hours to find just the right blossoms to extract, and it was a delightful experience.

Once the extract was finished, I collected and bottled it and made good use of the extra extract that was left over. With considerable ceremony that involved my communication with the flower, I thanked it for its great attention and for the benefits I imagined it would bestow on me though I didn't know what they would be! I proceeded to drink some of it, then drizzle a substantial quantity of the water extract on the top of my head so that it ran down my face and back and quite soaked me. The flower and I certainly became one.

It wasn't long before I realized what the Kangaroo Paw had done for me. Simply, it removed all obstacles from the trip, and I was able to accomplish something that otherwise would not have been possible. There was grace at every turn. I met every person I needed to meet (except one, which I shall explain). When I returned to my practice I soon found the astonishing test phrase for red and green Kangaroo Paw: "I have the means and the power to restore paradise on earth."[2]

Never having been to this region of the world, I nevertheless found rare flowers (unknown to me) in hours rather than days and was able to peacefully prepare extracts of twelve different flowers, driving over a range of about 1000 miles in ten days. The wildflower bloom started about 200 miles north of Perth and extended about 200 miles below Perth, and that was the range I explored.

The one objective and desire that was not fulfilled? Meeting the woman of my dreams – my life partner.

Interestingly, several of my seer friends independently predicted that I would encounter my beloved on this trip. A locational astrology reading I had done a few months before I left showed that for me the one place on earth where there were the strongest planetary conjunctions for romance and partnership was Perth, Australia – out in the middle of nowhere! "Crazy!" I said to myself.

I found that prediction hard to believe because I knew on this trip that I would have no time to socialize. Western Australia is about the size of western Europe, yet it only has a population of around two million people, and one million of them live in Perth where I would not be "hanging out." By and large I imagined on this trip I would be meeting sheep, kangaroo, and "road trains" (huge three trailer freight trucks 140 feet in length, driving way too fast to ever stop for anything).

I had no idea that I would have to drive such distances when I planned the trip, but had no choice if I wanted to encounter, photograph, and prepare the flowers I had chosen before commencing travel. I fell into an apparently insane quest, yet there was great stillness as I sped (at 70-80 mph) from location to location, highly focused and at the same time in a waking dream state.

In mid-day, as I was driving a particularly barren stretch of road, with a type of hypnotic focus, I had a truly memorable experience.

Just a few inches in front of my eyes there suddenly appeared the face of an Australian Aboriginal elder. He had a very warm and comforting energy, and I knew it was not the elder that initially tried to prevent me from traveling to Australia. There were no discernible words, but he sent me a very clear message.

He let me know that the Kangaroo Paw ritual I undertook brought me into a resonance that was appropriate for my intentions to collect healing flower energies in his land, and that he (and elders associated with him) would help and guide me

2 Several Australian flower essence companies manufacture Kangaroo Paw essences and, upon testing by myself and others, it is clear that they do not have these extraordinary characteristics.

whenever possible. He told me that I would be protected and need not worry about interference from the lower frequency encounter I'd had with the practitioner of negative "magic." He communicated that I could investigate the special flower I had originally sought, but that I would not find it in a state that I could extract, though I should explore the region where I knew it was growing. He intimated that I would find other flowers in that area that contained important transformational frequencies.

I truly appreciated his kind blessing, thanked him, and let him know I would do my best. From time to time on the rest of that trip, his wise and cheerful face would pop in through another dimensional plane, and I could feel his presence for just a moment.

At the farthest northern reach of my trip I found lodging with Russell Watkins and his wife, Emily.

At first glance, Russell appeared to be, from my stereotypic image gallery, the quintessential Aussie farmer. He was stout with enormous hands of blunt-tipped fingers, a ruddy face, and a heavy accent. According to him, he had an "average" farm (5,000 acres!) where he grew "a bit of wheat" (300 acres!), and "mostly grazed cattle with a few sheep."

Russell, however, was hardly an average farmer. He was a self-educated genius with an encyclopedic mind in the areas of habitat ecology, botany, animal husbandry, progressive farming technologies, grain and farm-related commodities markets, and much more.

His brilliant mind could only be satisfied by communicating and corresponding with top-level university professors in different parts of the world. They apparently found him so engaging that many of them came to Australia to conduct research in his bio-region with his assistance. Once they were staying in his home, experiencing Emily's congeniality, intelligence, and great cooking, Russell was able to "mine" them for a wealth of information. He just kept getting smarter.

Russell graciously gave up one day from his busy schedule to help me locate several flowers over a large area extending from coastal reserves to a few miles inland. I made notes of the roads we traveled and marked areas next to each of the flowers with brightly colored surveyors' tape so that I would have a good chance of finding them when I returned the next day on my own. And return I did, later in the morning, on a day that began in a truly memorable way.

I awoke early, before day break, eager to explore an area perhaps half a mile from the Watkins' farmhouse. I had noticed it the night before because it rose above the flat plains, in a way signifying that it was an aboriginal mound. In all directions around the rise, it was flat as far as one could see.

I set out with my camera, already mounted on a lightweight tripod, but I didn't get far because of a breathtaking scene that was developing in front of me.

The dim light of the coming sunrise was rapidly giving rise to a horizon of rose and orange hues that served as a backdrop to the silhouette of kangaroos traversing the landscape. I was dumbfounded by the beauty of this scene and didn't even try to catch it on film. The lighting was changing too quickly, and I didn't want to miss the magic of the moment. Most of my walk towards the aboriginal mound was similarly enchanted, and I was only able to snap a few photos.

Half way up the mound I abruptly halted when a really big kangaroo jumped into the middle of my path, seemingly out of nowhere. At that moment I realized that I had failed to inform myself about potential confrontational habits of large marsupials! He (no pouch) at about 6 feet tall, stood motionless perhaps 25 feet in front of me and felt rather intense.

I did not flinch and held the prayerful wish that the kangaroo should jump away just as quickly as he had appeared. After about fifteen seconds he did, and as I was startled by the incident, I looked for a place to sit down for a moment. I noticed an open spot in the middle of flowering plants on the edge of the path and seated myself there while I regained composure. I scanned the area on all sides around me, and seeing no other potential "visitors," was able to relax.

Then a special occurrence took place for me of the sort that gives rise to the message on an inspirational poster: "Life is not measured by the number of breaths we take, but by the moments that take our breath away."

Nearby, I spied a flower. She was truly feminine, a rare beauty and so distinctive – gorgeous pink blended with dove gray. I had to move closer to gaze at this magnificent creation. This flower indeed took my breath away. The pink and grey components of the flower gave me the sense of a feminine, poised, elegant princess. Moving in the breeze, the brilliant yellow and red adornment at the lowest part of the flower reminded me of the tassels at the bottom of a seductive, dancing gypsy's skirt. To me this seemed a marvelous combination – wild, raw abandon combined with poise, elegance and grace. That is how I thought of naming the flower Dancing Goddess.[3]

It felt as if I could photograph her endlessly, but I stopped when I saw the position of the sun was nearing time for extraction. I put away my camera gear and sat for a few minutes in meditation with this beautiful presence. Then, all of a sudden, I was struck by a wonderful thought. What if this flower were MY "dancing goddess," the female my friends had predicted I would meet? And what if she emanated the attractor field that would help to draw my beloved to me? It was a wonderful thought. Surely it could work for many.

When I returned to my practice with the essence of "Dancing Goddess," it did not take me too long to characterize how it worked. I found several test phrases on my patients that demonstrated how this flower re-patterns the unconscious mind.

[3] The colloquial flower name "Pixy Mops" just didn't seem right to describe this grand flower.

I found that Dancing Goddess possesses frequencies that really liberate women to be more fully feminine – that is, IF they wish that to occur. The purely male part of me said, "Well, why wouldn't ALL women want to be more feminine and attractive?" Then the clinical part of me recognized why many women choose to largely abandon an admirable feminine power of attraction.

First, what if a woman attracts the wrong man (as she has before), and has to endure again the hardship of a bad relationship? Second, many women in the Western world have never been exposed to the "culture" of the feminine – the tribal grandmothers, wise-women, and the sisterhood of extended families of women who naturally train each other in the art of being what is truly feminine.

For women, the two principal test phrases for Dancing Goddess are:

(1) "I am being the goddess energy that draws the ideal partner into my life now." When a woman repeats this phrase and a previously strong indicator muscle weakens (becomes inhibited), it means she is <u>not</u> being that attracting "goddess" energy.

(2) "I fear abandonment." That is such a huge theme for many women. When that phrase is found to test true in female subjects, nearly always they nod with the recognition that they already knew that was an issue within them. Astonishingly, Dancing Goddess can remove disabling feelings of abandonment rather quickly.

For a man, as I suspected, Dancing Goddess can initiate the attractor field which draws "goddess energy" into his life. That test phrase is: "I am emitting the attractor field which draws the ideal woman I desire into my life."

During the period of years since 2006 that I took Dancing Goddess and numerous other flower essences, I was graced by the additional presence in my life of three beautiful and spiritually attuned women.

Each, coming at a different time, possessed wonderful and rare qualities that helped rid me of some illusions and spurred me in my evolution. But each also possessed an unalterable force that was a "deal breaker" – deep memories of failed relationships with men, a profound fear of being dominated or controlled, and a guardedness and prohibition against vulnerability.

Women often don't seem to realize that such memories form a palpable wall around them, indicting decent men with good intentions before they even have a chance to build trust. It is a very negative self-fulfilling prophecy, and the poor fellows that encounter that affliction in women are shipwrecked before they get aboard.

Each of these women served to "hold a mirror" in front of me. I adopted a resolute commitment to identifying in myself and removing whatever unhealthy frequencies I could find that were making it necessary for me to encounter potential partners with the same troublesome characteristics, and to miss encountering my beloved who I can feel exists.

I realized that nearly all of my dreams have been granted to me (though it has taken quite a while for some of them to materialize!), and for that I can only feel gratitude. For me personally, the biggest dream is yet to be fulfilled.

For some time I have been aware that the loving and transformational energy of flowers has been helping me to prepare a field of wholeness for a truly extraordinary woman – a place of tranquility for my beloved where children of a whole different order can be conceived and raised in peace in the company of Nature's aliveness.

That is a dream I see, wish, and work toward for everyone.

We cannot bring a dream to completion until we can fully grasp the scope of it. As I prepared for another trip of a lifetime in May of 2011, serendipity provided me once again just what was needed. It was a book (a series of books) that explains how we expand our field of awareness so that our light-filled dreams can come to pass. The significance of this book is soon explained, and how it is perfectly aligned with the most astonishing flower frequency collection trip I experienced until that time – one that I had to wait nineteen years to take.

10

How Dreams Become Real

– Flowers From The Stars –

The following unusually written chapter may seem obscure at first. There truly is a reason for mentioning larger-than-life movies that depict the play of Light and Dark Forces, for that subject has a real relationship with the protective and transformational frequencies of flowers. And...I will get to the point!

It is curious that in early 2011, a few months before I was to take an "epic journey"– high into the Andes mountains to search for super-forces of Light resident in flowers there – that I should feel impelled to view two movie trilogies again. It seemed they had a message reinforced by powerful images of which I needed to be aware.

When we carry the resonance of a specific awareness, it can act as an "attractor field" that will draw to us the experience, necessary encounter, etc., associated with that awareness. In this particular case, I speculated awareness of certain themes in the movie trilogies might help me find important flowers associated with those themes.

I enjoy certain science fiction and fantasy movies for many reasons, but principally because they allow us to escape the confines of normative, restricted thinking, sometimes stimulating a closer look at who we really are and how we are responsible for the world we create.

Movies can fulfill the role that morality plays have served throughout history, and in recent years, two such examples are the epic trilogies of the *Lord of the Rings* (based on J.R.R. Tolkien's *The Lord of the Rings* novels) and the *Star Wars* prequels conceived by George Lucas. Both these trilogies depict the age-old theme of a duality: the struggle between the Forces of Light and Darkness. One might ask why it has been necessary – from the *Ramayana* to *Faust* to the present time – to continue presenting to audiences depictions of that duality. Apparently, this theme is still necessary to present because the bulk of humanity has not fully appreciated that we are constantly subject to the play of Light and Darkness in our life; that we are always free to identify and choose the Light (love, kindness, humility, forgiveness, integrity) and that it is always a good idea to do so!

Certain of the characters in each of these trilogies beautifully depict the traits and choices that either support manifestation of good dreams or prevent it. Whether or not we choose the Light must bear strongly on whether our dreams that are purely motivated actually materialize.

In *Lord of the Rings*, the embodiment of evil, Dark Lord Sauron, created a talismanic ring associated with his ability to remain unchallenged in his plan for world domination.

As long as the ring exists, Sauron with his array of dark powers that destroy Light will prevail. The wizard of Light, Gandalf, and other counsel see that Sauron can only be defeated in his campaign for domination if the ring is destroyed by throwing it into the fires of the volcanic Mount Doom where it was originally forged.

To destroy the ring is deemed to be virtually impossible unless someone could be found with undaunted courage, trust, and a completely pure heart. Frodo Baggins, a Hobbit, small in stature, with no magical powers volunteers for the extremely dangerous mission of destroying the ring, knowing he might lose his life in the process.

Frodo's closest friend, Sam, has such a deep fraternal love for him that he will not allow Frodo to go on a virtual suicide mission alone, and he accompanies him for support. Sam is the embodiment of devotion and selfless love.

Frodo and Sam need a guide along their perilous journey and attract a malicious being named Gollum who poses as a helper but is actually motivated solely by the prospect of stealing the ring for the purpose of personal power. Gollum is the embodiment of guile, ambivalence, treachery, and selfishness. He is an exaggerated personification of what is called in some spiritual traditions "the lesser self."

Sam's unwavering love and loyalty to Frodo is such a strong force that it buoys Frodo when he is exhausted to a point near death and allows him to prevail in destroying the ring and Sauron – the Force of Darkness – along with it.

Contemplation of honor, loyalty, steadfastness, dedication to the light versus the flip side of guile and deceptiveness, and indifference to the genesis of massive destruction and suffering would apparently be necessary for me to carry as an active resonating energy in my field so that I could discover and prepare blessed flower frequencies to enhance the former characteristics while canceling frequencies to diminish the unwelcome latter characteristics. For me, the most important meaning of the entire Ring saga distilled into: the heart that is entirely pure becomes an immense power, able to draw support from the far reaches of the universe (the mind of God) to prevail against enormous odds and great darkness.

The *Star Wars* prequel trilogy (the second trilogy conceived by Lucas) offers a different (but related) message. It helps us recognize through the great visual imagery of the story how latent destructive traits within a person – especially pride and arrogance of an untamed ego – can become activated to the point of becoming a profoundly negative force.

Over the course of the three movies we see the development of the main protagonist, Anakin Skywalker.

It is immediately evident in the first movie, showing scenes of his early years, that Anakin is a child prodigy. He has lightning-fast reflexes, advanced problem solving skills, and a strong air of confidence. Even as a child, when he encounters beautiful Queen Padmé Amidala (Natalie Portman) who is several years his senior, he fancies that she should be as smitten with him as he is with her. His irritation is evident when she treats him as the child he is. When the spiritual master Qui-Gon (a Jedi Knight played by Liam Neeson) closely observes Anakin, he suspects that Anakin is the rare being predicted in a Jedi prophecy that would "bring balance to the Force" (Light vs Dark).

In the second movie of the trilogy we encounter Anakin ten years later (now twenty years of age), well underway in his training under the tutelage of Jedi Master Obi-Wan Kenobi to become a highly revered Jedi knight, a force for righteousness. Anakin is handsome, powerful, and… arrogant.

As he interacts with Obi-Wan his ego is constantly on edge, feeling humiliated that he should still have to listen to the advice of a teacher that he feels he has already surpassed.

When we observe Anakin, who has become a man, interact with Senator (Queen) Amidala, it becomes clear that she has been an obsessional fixation of his from childhood. By force of will, he intends to seduce her, violating the chasteness that is an important part his Jedi oath, all the while rationalizing his actions at every step down the slippery slope of self-justification. Senator Amidala tries to discourage Anakin's seduction, but she cannot withstand the force of his personality, and he prevails, eventually causing her heartbreak that leads to her death.

In the meantime another subplot is concurrently developing that carries into the third and final installment of the *Star Wars* trilogy. Supreme Chancellor Palpatine is introduced as an important political figure in the Galactic Republic that Senator Amidala serves. We have seen him previously in the first movie, and he always appeared to be thoughtful, just, and even caring.

In the second movie of the trilogy, he begins by maintaining that persona, but as opportunities develop which allow him to seize power, intermittently we see flashes that reveal his true character. We eventually discover that he is actually a supremely evil Sith Lord by the name of Darth Sidious (insidious) who has cloaked himself and his intentions in the respectable figurehead of Palpatine. (The Dark Lord masquerading as a servant of the people strikes me as a theme that is profoundly important in our times. Darkness masquerading as Light is at the core of modern politics and technocracy, preventing the expression of the Paradise that is our Earth.)

With his true identity cloaked, having adopted the image of Palpatine, Darth Sidious recognizes that he can ensnare Anakin to obtain his power and allegiance by taking advantage of a fatal flaw: Anakin's rapacious ego, always on guard against the prospect of being slighted, ever preoccupied with the annoyance of never receiving sufficient adulation.

If Anakin's love of Padmé were true, it might have saved him from Darth Sidious. But Anakin's love was a vain love and became more tainted when he had a dream of impending doom (Padmé dying in child birth) that bore a strong resemblance to a horribly unsettling and prophetic dream about threat to his mother. When he went searching for his mother, he discovered her just before her death, and found that she had been brutally beaten. He became insanely enraged at the loss of what he loved and went on a killing spree, annihilating the perpetrators and all the nearby innocents.

As a result of his mother's death and the dream of Padme's similar ill fate, Anakin became completely vulnerable to Darth Sidious' lure: the prospect of gaining even greater power – the power over death. Darth Sidious suggested that if Anakin were to pledge to him complete allegiance, he could teach him the Sith Lord Darth Plagueis' technique to prevent death, an ability only gained through the dark side of the Force.

With the prospect of learning how to avert death (to save Padmé), and remain immortal (to fulfill his own agenda), Anakin abdicated all allegiance to the Jedi, abandoned his alignment with the Light, and pledged to serve the forces of Darkness as Sidious' new apprentice, who soon became known as Darth Vader. Ironically, he never had the opportunity to save Padme who died in childbirth while he was recovering from near fatal wounds he received when dueling Obi-Wan Kenobi.

I looked at each of these trilogies and questioned how they might relate to me and how I could potentially benefit by reflecting on them before embarking on what I felt would be a truly momentous flower essence "mission". Themes that stood out for contemplation from both movies were:

1. How one naturally accumulates the power of Light by maintaining a pure heart, faith, hope, and trust;
2. Delusion and erosion of Light that is a consequence of identifying with the feeling of being diminished, not receiving what we believe is rightfully due;
3. Learning how rage, anger and associated destruction can arise from deep hurt or a sense of entitlement, and learning about the folly of justifying those feelings and expressions (especially when they derive from the defeat of personal desires);
4. The importance of learning to identify the signature of Darkness and to sense its premonitory signs.

This is heavy stuff: the subject of forces of darkness and light at play within each of us. One reason why people don't shift more quickly toward self-realization and enlightenment may be that they are afraid to look at that subject. But I hope that you will take heart because what will become clear by the end of this book is that there is a wonderful updated easy way to rapidly increase the power of goodness – Light and God-source wisdom within you and at the same time reduce attractor fields that draw to us Darkness. I shall explain in Part III how to apply certain flower frequencies for that to occur.

Whether a dream manifests or not seems to involve several conundrums. It is a complex matter and a phenomenon that is difficult to penetrate clearly because there are so many invisible factors at play. How can we elucidate what those factors are?

First, let's look at how we choose.

Behavioral economics is a specialized discipline that analyzes the factors that come into play which prompt an individual to choose one way or the other when making a purchasing decision. Dan Ariely of the MIT Media Lab, an expert in behavioral economics, explains how "relativity" is a critical issue in the selection process. He states in his best selling book, *Predictably Irrational*, that people generally don't know what they want until they see it in context. He writes, "We are always looking at things around us in relation to others. We can't help it. … We always compare jobs with jobs, vacations with vacations, lovers with lovers, and wines with wines. …Relativity helps us make decisions in life. But it can also make us downright miserable. Why? Because jealousy and envy spring from comparing our lot in life with that of others."

In order to make a selection between two objects we have to assign more value to one than the other, and that is fine for choosing a toaster. But what happens if we want to weigh the value or merit of one of our dreams? Do we compare it to someone else's dream? That could be pure folly, a misguided version of "keeping up with the Joneses."

If we care to lead anything more than a superficial life, we have to look at our motives. What is the reason for our dreams, and from whence do they spring?

> *Is the field of creativity and potential awareness from which our dreams arise bursting with joy and gratitude for the love of Creation which sustains us even as we have made very poor choices which hurt us and our Earth, or is it contaminated by discontent? Is that creative field selfish?, resonating with Darkness, or is it altruistic?, seeking alignment with the Light.*

In order to evaluate the motive of our dreams, we cannot be controlled by the sway and illusion of our own ego mind and the ego minds of those that have defiled our current society and defined its norms. But how do we avoid that? Simple. Just by embodying all the principles and teachings of the world's most enlightened Masters and whatever representative of God is the focus of your religion. Are you smiling? I hope so, because the last sentence is obviously written in jest.

What is true and heartening is that frequencies in special flowers remove many of our illusions so that we can more easily encounter our real life purpose, begin living it, and move one step at a time closer to fulfilling our dreams.

Sometimes it can be just plain difficult to know honestly and in depth what motivates our choices and our dreams. We naturally seek guidance and instruction from the best sources to which we have access for the purpose of gaining wisdom in this area.

From the non-denominational standpoint, there are a number of "thought transformation" educators and "spiritual teachers" in the public eye at this point in time. Some of them have audiences in the millions. What I find truly interesting about the most popular of these teachers is that they studiously avoid mentioning "forces of

Darkness," "powers of evil," etc. Why is that? Is that because:

A. They have created a paradigm that excludes existence of "Darkness," for they believe recognizing it would remove individual power and authority to be the architect of one's own future?

B. At a core yet subtle level, they themselves do not feel, observe, or believe in the influence of malevolent energy and forces?

C. They feel that to mention the existence of destructive forces for which there are no simple means of control would create fear, render them susceptible to being labeled a "fringe lunatic," dilute their useful instruction which can proactively help people, and, importantly, erode their base of followers?

I believe the answer is primarily C and secondarily A.[1]

So who are some of the groups that DO discuss "forces of Darkness" and how to overcome "powers of evil"?

1. Christian splinter factions that speak a great deal about "spiritual warfare," and approach the removal of Darkness through prayer and specific types of ceremony.
2. The "lunatic fringe" (UFOlogists, "conspiracy theorists," etc. who are definitely fringe but not necessarily "lunatic." Many of their observations are certainly worth noting.[2]
3. "New Age" thinkers who are well versed in the tenets of "energy medicine" and who know from experience that distortional frequencies ("Dark energies") exist and have negatively affected the body. These individuals are among the constituency prone to study shamanic practices that address straight-on how to manage unwanted destructive influences that may touch us.[3]
4. A free thinker by the name of Anastasia who defies categorization, and perceives the world in a radically simple (yet profoundly deep) way without distraction, living as a recluse in a remote Siberian forest. Her biography/ autobiography is written by Vladimir Megré, and consists of nine books, the

[1] In recent years that I have worked with patients, I have become much more aware when destructive forces and energies are "attached" to them, and I am able to measure when those unwanted energies leave. Although I have absolutely no interest in becoming an "exorcist," I take note when "distortion fields" are negatively influencing my patients, and I apply flower frequencies to remove the distortion, accentuate the Light, and restore balance.

[2] The real conspiracy seems to be the mainstream power brokers perpetrating crimes–primary and secondary– who are able to cover them up and remain free from censure and out of jail!

[3] As long as the shamanic practices come through a highly evolved lineage, such as the teachings of Don Miguel Ruiz or Alberto Villoldo, my impression is that they are very useful.

first titled with her name.[4]

Little Dreams/Big Dreams: Challenges to Manifestation

A major purpose of this chapter is to help you appreciate commonly overlooked reasons you may need help (and can truly benefit from divine dispensations resident in certain flowers) so that your "big dreams" especially, but little ones too can become manifest.

I am not using the term "dream" in the normal way, that is: visions or images some people see during sleep that are often vague, confusing, or senseless. What I mean by dream is aligned with the aboriginal view of "dreaming the world into existence." This most often occurs when we are in a harmonious waking state and intentionally "tune into" streams of energy that flow as a consequence of our beneficent thoughts or actions or those of others resulting in the crystallization of form as an image that physically embodies in life.

Following is my effort at defining/describing three types of "dreams" as points of reference for understanding the relative degree to which they may be challenged or blocked from manifestation:

1. A big dream has an objective that is selfless and altruistic with the capacity to influence many people in a positive way.
2. A "combo dream" has personal desires associated with it but may have the potential to influence others or many others in a positive way.
3. A little dream is something we personally desire that helps us feel more comfortable, safe, stronger in self-esteem, etc. Its influence generally does not expand much beyond one's self or one's family (though from the perspective of our quantum universe, the tiniest choice affects everything).

As we stairstep up in our evolutionary development (hopefully toward the Light) all levels of dreams may be important for us to fulfill.

"Little dreams" (e.g. obtaining a new car) have the least likelihood of drawing fire from "oppositional forces" because their fulfillment has neither far reaching implications nor the ability to tip balance of power in the world domain of light vs. dark, love vs. manipulation/domination/control.

A relatively recent and good example of a very large "combo dream" is the creation

[4] *Anastasia* is the first of many books in the *Ringing Cedars Series*. It is written as though it is the true life present day story of a mystical recluse (with superhuman abilities) named Anastasia living in the remote Siberian taiga. Megré claims to have met her, fathered children with her, and learned esoteric secrets from her about society in ancient Russia. Despite the fact that Megré is reportedly a scoundrel of an entrepreneur – an imposter – he has written a very interesting series of books that carry an inspiring message about lost knowledge from ancient civilizations to serve as a guide for reestablishing agrarian culture in our modern times.

of Facebook.

"Big Dreams," for example furthering and completing the work of inventor genius, Nicola Tesla, to perfect and bring into use a non-internal combustion engine that works by tapping into virtually unlimited ambient energy that exists in the earth and above the earth so that neither fossil fuels nor nuclear energy need to be used, would likely draw huge "oppositional forces," and would be very dangerous for any individual or group to undertake. Existing structures for economic and geopolitical domination and control would be toppled if such a power source were disseminated. They would be loathe to let that happen.

Who or What Are "Oppositional Forces"

(and how to avoid a visit to your local insane asylum)

> *When we once acknowledge existence of the most common (ambient) obstructing energies – described following – and hierarchically more potent Forces of Darkness that have an agenda, it is profoundly important to recognize that we must always assess our self FIRST to see if we are the source of obstruction – the cause of our dreams not manifesting. Otherwise, if we initially attribute our failure to outside influences, we abdicate our divine birthright of creative ability and power, and run the risk of inhabiting a delusional world.*

There are two common sources of obstructing energies (which we might interpret as "oppositional forces.")

First is our soul's past history of actions/choices resulting in accumulated frequencies that are imbedded in our being and influence our birth and the life thereafter (known as karmic inheritance in Eastern religions or trans-generational influence in the Judeo-Christian tradition.)

Second is the realm of humanity's "collective unconscious" described by psychiatrist Carl Jung, that we can unwittingly enter psychically and erroneously interpret as our own.[5]

After a period of time where we give focused attention to "cleaning up our own house" (in New Age jargon, "doing our shadow work"), we are more likely to sense and see clearly outside our self to ascertain if we are being influenced by unwanted or malevolent energies/forces.

Cross culturally (and over a long period of history) there are well-established

[5] Part III of this book has been created with the intention of guiding one through personal evolutionary steps, and with the aid of special flower frequencies, help remove energetic disturbances that have been holding us back, allowing us to become more clear in our ability.

precedents that point to the existence and influence within humans of unwanted or malevolent energies/forces.

In the Spanish-speaking countries of the Americas for example, two words are commonly used in the practice of spiritual healers (shamans) to describe unseen causes of feeling poorly: susto (translating as "scare," "fright," "shock"), and daño (translating as "damage," "harm," "hurt.")

An example of "susto" is driving a car and experiencing an inattentive person rapidly and unexpectedly turn in front of you, nearly causing a severe accident. That could very easily cause a shock to the nervous system resulting in disturbance and brain depolarization that leaves a distortional field within us which can cause ill health symptoms.

An example of "daño" is being the recipient of words used carelessly or words that have been crafted to be hurtful by someone of ill intent, such as "I know you have lost weight, but to me you are still fat!" Simple words have a profound ability to cause lasting damage in others (and to the one responsible for them.)

There is another form of daño that real shamans deal with – addressed forthcoming – and that is the projection of mal intention through fearsome illusion.

As I have mentioned previously, there are wonderful new methods in energy psychology (a modern, clear, and very efficient form of "shamanism") to remove both the influence of "daño" and "susto". But they require finding someone who is gifted and well trained in these specialized techniques.

My mission in the high Andes on the upcoming trip was to find exceptional flower frequencies that anyone can use on their own to remove the types of shock and hurt just mentioned, and also to remove obstructive energies at a much deeper level than humans can normally access. I am delighted to report that my dreams with respect to finding astonishing flowers there for those purposes were realized.[6]

When we move into the realm of trying to understand potent forces of Darkness, those that have kept the majority of our world in an enslaved state, preventing the natural expression of the paradise that is this Earth, we face a daunting conundrum: Darkness has been able to prevail precisely because of its great skill at "covering its tracks" – keeping its origins and methods of operation invisible.

I was soon to discover information that was really heartening – information that exposes an example of "sleight of hand" of disruptive forces that is actually meagerly powerful, but that causes us great disturbance because it projects the illusion of the real "dark side of the Force." I learned how we could end up losing energy by fearing what is an energetic mirage, or at least not materially very substantive.

[6] A remarkable blend of flowers from that region are combined in a product named Pure Potential.

With a proper perspective, one can arrive at a point of psychological and spiritual solace so as not to worry about personal vulnerability to attack from the forces of darkness.

If one has a light-filled dream that is so powerful and positively evolutionary that it draws the attention of real Darkness and forces of evil, one only could have achieved that vision by the grace of God, accompanied by legions of light and angelic protectors that can prevail against any challenge. In the rare instance of such a dream, the intelligent choice is to hand over the details of fulfilling the dream to our Creator, the only one possessing complete enough sight to bring it safely into manifestation.

It would appear that the vast majority of light-filled dreams attract oppositional force from the servants of Darkness – not from the Masters themselves. As we shall see in the following chapter, it is often within our personal ability to deal with such mettlesome underlings because they commonly operate through illusion. If, from a point of stillness, we learn to see what is real, and if we take advantage of the profoundly coherent and Source– aligning frequencies of special flowers, the illusory challenges of Darkness can vanish.

11

A Flight of Revelation

Just as I was preparing to leave on my flower essence expedition to South America in the Spring of 2011,[1] I was gifted with two sources of profound information to accompany me on my trip and to fill the hours during the long flight there with lay-over time in Miami. One was a copy of the book, *Anastasia*. The other was an article by John Lash dealing with an analysis of sources of negative influences that have affected earth's inhabitants for eons, described ages ago in the Gnostic Nag Hammadi Codices (discovered in Egypt in 1945.)

When we look at the state of the world today – the division between people, the suffering and sub-human brutality that exists – does it make sense? Were humans designed to treat each other this way?

The newborn babe suckling at his mother's breast enjoys an energetic exchange with her of love, caring, security, and adoration. Isn't it reasonable to assume that those characteristics should define human interactions throughout life? Since a state of harmony is not occurring for the majority of Earth's inhabitants, it is only natural to ask what has caused such a distortion of balance. Whole libraries could be filled with books exploring that topic. But I do not sense that question can be answered at the level of our individual, rational mind.

To understand the human dilemma in which the light of love is often extinguished, one may gain insights as to how that can be happening by reviewing codices from early Christianity – later in the chapter.

Or, for a very select few – the highly advanced seers – there is another option. By virtue of a specially bestowed Gift, they are able to leave the personal mind and enter into the Universal Mind where, in another dimension, exists an energetic matrix holding a record of all activities that have ever taken place. It can be viewed just like we view a digital video image on a surveillance camera that runs continuously. I have known two people in my life that I believe can do that accurately.[2]

In Eastern traditions this complete historical recording is called the "akashic record." In early Christian times certain advanced seers were able to access this information, and their findings were recorded in the Gnostic spiritual order.

[1] See Doc's photo journal p.321.

[2] In chapter 7 of this book, the shaman's description of the review of all the events in the ceremonial participant's life came from accessing that very same source.

Little did I know that Anastasia's book and Mr. Nash's article both addressed critical issues (related to what is written above) that would help me understand the activities and illusions of Darkness that can influence, distort, and eventually remove our opportunities.

With that new awareness, I was able to create (outside of my personal mind) a field of light with unlimited possibilities, open to receive and be filled with flowers possessing massively powerful frequencies to remove distortion and help restore balance and freedom in our life. My heavenly "steering committee" was at it again, providing me just the information I needed, and a full day to digest it, before I began my arduous journey into valleys at an elevation of 15,000 feet to find and collect enormously protective and transformational flower frequencies. On this trip, I truly was searching for the miraculous.

The problem with "invisible forces" is, well ... they're invisible! If we were to allow the existence of a paradigm potentially assigning motive power to unseen forces capable of buffeting us about in life, jeopardizing our free will and the power of self-determination, such a possibility would be unnerving. We can easily see why our current transformational thought leaders would avoid mentioning the influence of unseen forces. Hence such topics are not discussed, and focus is placed on giving all manner of excellent instruction in "abandoning mental content," learning to be fully "present," "loving what is." In other words, they are teaching spiritual self-sufficiency, allowance, and surrender. "Do not blame others or look outside of yourself" is their message. "Operate from a point of true stillness." "You are the master of your own destiny if you can only get in touch with the the 'real you'."

If we do not believe we are the masters of our own destiny and act accordingly, we are working against life to great disadvantage. My friends and I and many of my patients have been enormously helped by the teachings to which I refer above. And those teachings will always be valid.

The use of powerfully transformational flower frequencies in my patient practice each week, however, has caused me to naturally expand my view of how we may speed the evolution of consciousness. I regularly encounter patients who ardently believe in the teachings of our best transformational thought leaders. They practice those teachings to the best of their ability, and they know such practice is beneficial. Yet, by using the scanning process I developed,[3] I can rapidly find the flower frequencies that their being (and soul complex) is seeking, and the words (test phrases) that define the energetic blocks or mind obstacles still resident in them, stalling their evolution.

[3] Please refer to Holographic Scanning Appendix 7, p.315.

Within days or weeks of consuming liberating flower frequencies in drinking water (or using a topical spray), one's "arresting frequencies" that have been preventing forward movement are generally removed. Quite often my patients make large evolutionary leaps in a short time. They have essentially received "Divine Dispensation" through special flowers. Or to put it another way, they have received a miracle. And similar miracles can be repeated again and again.

At this time in our evolutionary cycle, we truly need miracles.

Part of what makes a "miracle" seem miraculous is that we cannot normally see or sense (and hence comprehend) how it operates. So it is very beneficial for our understanding if we should encounter those rare beings or teachings that shed light on what has heretofore been incomprehensible. I believe that is why my "heavenly helpers" made sure I had Mr. Lash's information and Anastasia's book. I shall attempt to summarize the valuable insights they provided me after I digress (quite a bit!).

If one could possibly define the purpose, character, and scope of Evil or Darkness, it would surely be helpful because it would give us insight into how "distortion fields" arise that limit our opportunities and very often spoil sweet dreams. Since I was a youngster I have had the opportunity of listening to many wise teachers discuss this subject, and I have had a few of my own insights, so I'll give a shot at that definition.

The struggle between Darkness and Light is represented mythically innumerable times. The consensus message from all those tales is that when this universe was created, the evolution of consciousness could only be propelled forward if there were an opposing force to Light, so Darkness was essential and was constructed so there would be just a little bit less of it than Light. The Hindu religion especially teaches the importance of understanding the balance between the forces of destruction and creation, and destruction is not considered inherently bad or evil.

It is heartening if we believe that Light will always prevail, and I believe that eventually it always does. It is the period of time during the "eventually" that concerns us.

Once again, the imagery and descriptions from a particular piece of science fiction come in handy.

I seem to remember there were six episodes on the television program, *Star Trek: The Next Generation,* that were the most popular in the entire series that extended over many years. They were the episodes that dealt with the profoundly destructive cyborg race called the Borg Collective. The Borg traveled at high speeds in very large cube structures that were impenetrable to even advanced weapons systems. The sole purpose of the Borg was to "assimilate" entire planets and all the people on them–destroying life entirely. They had no "heart," no moral compass, no scruples. They made no judgments about what was good or bad, what should be destroyed, and what should be preserved. They simply destroyed everything.

Just before perpetrating annihilation they would tell their victims, "Prepare to be assimilated. Resistance is futile." Their "consciousness" grew by incorporating the totality of what they assimilated. One could argue that the Borg were not evil, rather they were just massively destructive. They did not selectively destroy the Light. They destroyed everything.

I have understood from the wisest teachers and seers I have encountered that such beings as the Borg do in fact exist, but because the planet Earth was created to be the jewel of the Universe and the grandest experiment concerning the development of free will that has ever been devised, Earth is actually protected from such massively destructive beings as the Borg. The "Higher Powers" have essentially created a "no fly zone" around the Earth to protect against harm from that type of destruction.

Dropping down a notch we find a zone in which Earth's inhabitants experience spiritual testing via contact with destructive energies. In that model, we encounter the realm of Darkness where Evil operates in contrast to the Light.

The Light serves all of life, is magnanimous, and illumines everything. Under its influence all creatures have the possibility of expanding the reach of their luminous field and ascending into a higher stage of union with God. That individuated expansion in Light is what enlarges the mind of God.

Evil seems to exist for the purpose of accumulating power, driven on a willful path that is bent on separation from the whole of life in a vain effort to prove that by separation it can gain sufficient power to equal the light, then surpass it, gaining supremacy. Since this constantly proves futile, rage, anger, and a firmer commitment to domination arise, causing collateral damage everywhere.

Evil gains strength by expanding the field of duplicity and obfuscation, creating shadows wherever possible to hide its trail. It masquerades as the Light whenever possible. In the previous chapter, I mentioned the movie character with a dual personality, Senator Palpatine/Dark Sith Lord Darth Sidious. The three parts of the Star Wars prequel brilliantly show how a destructive monster (Sidious) can successfully masquerade as a caring citizen, and I recommend everyone see those movies, if only for that amazing and instructive depiction.

Before we go any further, I would like to emphasize an enormously important point:

> *Now it is safe, wise, and advisable to look directly at the characteristics of Evil and the shadow world where it operates because for the first time in a very long time, it really is beginning to crumble, AND there are now simple*

measures that can be taken to disengage its entanglement in our life.[4] *The more people become aware of how it works, the faster it will disintegrate.*

How Can Humans – God's Pinnacle of Creation – Fail In Their Humanity?

There is an interesting practice among certain advanced holistic healers and a small group of chiropractors called "following the energy." It is a process where one steps out of and above the rational mind to enter a larger field of awareness. In that space one simply "feels" what the point of origin is for a particular physical or emotional complaint. There are often threads of energy in the patient that can be traced back to a primordial cause.

Practitioners of this art over the years have noticed, for example, that areas where the spine is out of alignment and muscles are in spasm often have causes for physical pain that are not physical. In other words, an energetic influence outside the body apparently is influencing the body. The body's innate consciousness senses this outside disturbance and develops a state of defense – spasm– as a result. Muscle spasm can pull vertebrae out of position, cause pressure on spinal nerves, and contribute to all manner of physical maladies beyond structural discomfort.

I have concluded that some of the same sources responsible for generating disharmonious or distortional fields that our body tries to reject (evidenced by pain and spasm) are most certainly also generating distortional fields that contribute to us failing in our humanity.That is to say they interfere with our normal and humane proclivity toward loving kindness.

There are many interpretations and theories of what these "external influences" are, and unfortunately they do not fit into any models that are acceptable or understandable to current, institutional science. However, that does not mean that these phenomena, visible independently to thousands of practitioners worldwide, do not exist.

These energetic disturbances that cause physical manifestation of dis-ease are classed in different ways, including: "energy cysts," "implants," and "devices." (Energy cysts can include implants and devices.)

Most popular transformational thought leaders believe and teach that thoughts are "things," that thoughts become physically real, or to put it in another way, that thoughts precipitate matter. What do they teach after that?

Nothing.

[4] Seers that I respect envision that what has been a relatively free reign of Darkness on Earth will be over by 2035! Wouldn't it be great if it were even sooner.

Our famous and most respected transformational thought leaders leave the inquiring mind hanging. What happens when beings use the mind and the power of creation unwisely and to selfish ends? How does it materially affect our physical existence?

In this vast universe, could humans be subject to the influence of destructive thought from the collective unconscious of this world and possibly from elsewhere? Well… if those questions lead to people fearing the murky realms of the supernatural, you can see why it would be a topic to avoid.

I believe we are at a point now where the population that believes in the possibility of change on this planet–the possibility of creating the paradise that can be our Earth–must probe the realms of the "invisible" to find the real causes of our problems so they can be removed.

So how to answer the question of the above heading, "How Can Humans Fail In Their Humanity?" We are being influenced by thoughts (and precipitated thoughts such as implants and devices) that displace or block our channels of connection to the Divine. When that happens, all manner of problems ensue.[5] I have been able to clinically test this premise many times. Negative thoughts, beliefs, subconscious memories, implants, and devices can be removed by specific flower frequencies. I will explain how to achieve this in Part III.

So… if we are being influenced unwittingly by precipitated thought, implants, and devices, I have asked myself many times who is doing the influencing, and for what reasons?

There are many answers that apply to that broad topic, most of them leading us into the realm that has been labeled by detractors (and undoubtedly by perpetrators wanting to evade detection) as "conspiracy theories."[6] There is both extraordinarily valuable information in this realm as well as a good measure of individuals afflicted with neurotic and delusional disorders. I certainly desire to avoid the latter.

To understand "who is doing the influencing" and for what reasons, please follow with me in the ensuing train of thought. Please open your mind to unlimited possibilities.

Think about the origins of crime. Why does it occur? Someone wants to accumulate wealth and power. How is it perpetrated? An entire deceptive and destructive team is organized from street level thugs up a hierarchy that eventually arrives at the crime

[5] The theme that I will repeat again and again in this book is that flowers specially touched by the Divine have been placed on our beautiful planet precisely to remove the fields of Darkness that keep us from our humanity.

[6] There are many websites that offer information and news that has not been predigested and homogenized by the mainstream. You have to listen to your own intuition to discover what may be true. Some of the topics are waaay out there.

family boss,[7] who has a boss, who also has a boss, and so on. Where does it end, or does it end? Important historical records indicate that there is a continuum of devious manipulation involving the earth that does not end on the earth.

Finally, I am able to return to a point at the beginning of this chapter, Mr. John Lash's article mentioning astonishing information in Gnostic cosmology recorded in the Nag Hammadi Codices (NHC), dating from the third and fourth centuries A.D. (Twelve of the thirteen codices are housed in the Coptic museum in Cairo, Egypt, and the remaining codex is in the Jung Foundation in Zurich, Switzerland.)

By now many people have heard about the early Christian, non-canonical New Testament apocryphal book, the Gospel of Thomas. However, most people know very little about the rest of the Nag Hammadi Gnostic writings. What I was amazed to learn is that "perhaps one-fifth of the intelligible information in the NHC concerns the origin, methods, and motives of the Archons… [who] appear to be identical to the extraterrestrials (ET's) of modern ufology." In Gnostic cosmology, the ultimate purpose of Archons is to act as a test for humanity. Mr. Lash continues:

> "Although Archons do exist physically, the real danger they pose to humanity is not invasion of the planet but invasion of the mind. The Archons are intra-psychic mind parasites who access human consciousness through telepathy and simulation. They infect our imagination and use the power of make-believe for deception and confusion. Their pleasure is in deceit for its own sake, without a particular aim or purpose. They are robotic in nature, incapable of independent thought or choice, and have no particular agenda except to live vicariously through human beings. Bizarrely, they are able to pretend an effect on humans which they do not really have. For instance, they cannot access human genetics, but they can pretend to do so in such a way that humans fall for the pretended act, as if staged events were taken for real. In this respect, Archons are the ultimate hoaxers. This is the essence of "Archonic intrusion," as I call it. The trick is: if humanity falls under the illusion of superhuman power, it becomes as good as real – a self-fulfilling delusion."

To me this was profound information. It helped me understand how one possible

[7] *Inside Job*, a disturbing and informative documentary narrated by Matt Damon, shows how a whole new breed of white collar "crime bosses" has evolved in recent decades. These criminals no longer need thugs to carry out their bidding. They use the cover of carefully crafted special interest law to protect themselves from the largest theft and destruction of human welfare ever perpetrated. To wit, the financial theft of billions (trillions?) of dollars from the public, culminating in 2008, whereby the guilty have accumulated vast wealth from theft of others' financial life blood, and remain free instead of serving a life in prison, or worse. On a financial news network, I heard a statistic that by 2013 Americans had only recovered 40% of the total wealth lost in the theft I just mentioned.

additional source that is hard to trace could be responsible for the installation of self-defeating beliefs that I consistently find in the unconscious minds of my patients. And it makes sense to me that highly coherent God-source frequencies that I have been able to discover in certain flowers could remove that interference responsible for unproductive behavior, unwitting self-sabotage, and lack of manifestation.

If we inquire a little deeper into the odd phenomenon of the Archons, doesn't it seem logical that behind the scenes manipulators could be making use of these beings to carry out their agenda?

After looking at many books, personal testimonies and other information, I realized that I would not be able to find a conclusive answer. There were just too many confounding variables. So I did what I often do. I took the question to what I envision as a "Higher Authority," what we might call God Source. In a still state, I asked to be given an answer that would help me understand the simple overall picture of a very complicated subject: the evolution of human consciousness, why it was necessary for it to be challenged and tested, who is behind what seems to be truly unnecessary human suffering, and what is the "pecking order" of the exploiters of humanity. All little questions… yes?

I did not get a complete answer to those huge questions, but what I was given, parceled out bit by bit, had a lot of meaning for me, and I will pass it on to you. I received the answer, reaffirmed over time, when I was alone in remarkably still locations surrounded by powerful forces in Nature: the Amazon basin, the high Andes mountains, on an aboriginal mound in the dry desert of western Australia, in a canyon of waterfalls on Bali, in an extraordinary meadow in the San Juan Mountains near Telluride, Colorado, and various times in the enchanted FlorAlive forest in Tennessee where I live half of each week.

The information condenses into the following narrative given to me:

> "As easy as it would be for the tallest giant to carelessly crush the tiniest ant, so there are crude forces in the universe that could annihilate you without notice or care. But such destruction of Earth's inhabitants is not part of its planetary destiny. Though Man is physically fragile in comparison to many other life forms in the universe, he is magnificently powerful from the standpoint of his direct access to the Divine. He has been asked – and soon he will be forced – to awaken his spirit, to assume his great power as a co-creator with the One.
>
> "Suffering is only necessary on your planet when few bother to deeply investigate why suffering arises there, and even fewer act in unison to stop it.
>
> "Earth is a jewel planet with greater diversity of life and material resources than any other planet in your universe. Do you not realize how valuable your earth is? It has been noticed, and for eons of time, many of its precious resources have been removed. Following the sources of power that control the earth's resources will lead you to the beings—existing both on the earth and in other

> dimensions—who are responsible for the manipulation, domination, and control that result in suffering.
>
> "As far as ending the thievery that exploits the Earth? No force that could challenge your planet is capable of withstanding the power of the activated human heart and the Light of love from the human soul."

Not long after I received final "transmissions" that coalesced into the simple message above, I had a very interesting experience in my office while treating Jeanette, a patient I have assisted over the years who is genuinely dedicated to self-awareness and the evolution of consciousness.

I performed a screening test called Holographic Scanning (see Appendix 9) to locate probable sites of primary bodily involvement underlying her chronic health complaints. She had pain in her sacrum, and I tested neurologically associated muscle strength (such as the important pelvic stabilizer, the piriformis muscle, which was weak bilaterally).

The Holographic Scanning process I developed is an intuitive medical technique that easily allows a practitioner to dialogue with the super-consciousness of the body/being so that it can direct the questioning process to a single answer. What I found was that the muscle weakness was probably caused by an energy disruption that had its origin outside the body. "Outside?" I thought. "Where? ...What? ...That's weird!"

Then I quietly sat with that observation for a few moments until I felt the inspiration to visualize the obstructing energy pulled from the dimensional space it was occupying into a vortex that took it back to Source for dissolution and absorption. When I re-tested the piriformis muscles which initially were weak, they had normalized to full strength. Jeanette had received an "adjustment" without any manually applied force. It really surprised both of us.

That experience opened an entirely new understanding for me. Thereafter, I began to search in my patients for symptomatic areas in the physical body that had "off body" sources of energetic disruption. I then began testing for flower frequencies that removed external causes of bodily weakness, and that is how I became convinced that the right flower frequencies remove "implants" and "devices" that are associated with "energy cysts."

As time went on, I received more information from my "steering committee" relating to "interference" that is stalling the evolution of consciousness on our planet and its ordained return to a state of paradise. I was told:

> "When a loving human being has a break-through revelation or a powerful happy thought that opens the heart and enlivens the spiritual mind, it initiates a burst of a particular form of light that radiates into the universe. For eons of time, various extra-planetary life forms have coveted the energy of that light. Since the middle of the twentieth century, a particularly sophisticated electronic grid system was installed around the earth that operated on an auto-responder basis. The system, devised by advanced technology beings, automatically

detected any burst of light from spiritual illumination and sent an "other dimensional harpoon" (corded into their collection grid system) that penetrated the human field emitting the light, allowing the "harvesting" of light energy from it.

"To those beings that could not emit light themselves, this harvested light was a valuable energy commodity. The "men behind the black curtain" (the true controllers of your planet and the real bosses directing your political figureheads) knew of this damaging practice as well as theft of resources from your earth, and, for their complicit allowance, were rewarded with energetic and material shielding to hide their own exploitive and nefarious practices. There was free reign with this type of abuse until around 1992. At that time the rights to further "harvesting" practices were forcibly revoked by advanced light beings that have taken over guardianship of Earth as a result of the expiration of an ancient extra-planetary treaty.

"The damage to human force fields from this practice still persists, and in the majority of humans must be repaired,[8] but the auto-responder system itself, and its grid, is being rapidly dismantled.

"Look for flower frequencies that will repair the human energy field distortion (caused by that practice) that still afflicts most of Earth's Light beings."

So… after that long digression I am back to this chapter title, "A Flight of Revelation," referring to both John Lash's article and parts of Anastasia's book that particularly struck me as I read it in flight to South America. The book was really a powerful source of inspiration and illumination which I soon realized could help me attract the transformational flower frequencies that I sensed humanity truly needed.

After I had just gone through the process of trying to understand the significance of the Archons and their energetic incursion into our unconscious mind, I began to contemplate how protective fields might be developed to prevent such incursions or remove their influence if they had already taken place. Thus when I encountered Anastasia's account of how she had to devise a method to circumvent the destructive influence of Dark Forces, I was intrigued.

Anastasia seems to be a highly evolved Light being[9] who, in order to bypass the real

[8] Young light beings born in the new millennium are largely immune to this type of manipulation.

[9] From her biographer's initial descriptions, one might playfully imagine Anastasia to be a combination of the goddess Athena for her wisdom; a twenty-six-year-old Russian version of Christie Brinkley (supermodel) for looks; and Angelina Jolie's Tomb Raider character, Lara Croft, for her athleticism and daring.

or imaginary energy of negative resistance, devised a system, in her words, to move herself and others "across the Dark Forces' window of time." Her abilities felt like attributes from another star system, or perhaps, I thought to myself, she was employing the stars to help accomplish her task. From reading her account, it seemed as though she was altering the space/time continuum by shooting her consciousness and energy body at (faster than?) the speed of light to the farthest reaches of the universe, and then quickly "ricocheting" back to earth in a way that couldn't be accessed, giving her time to set in motion whatever her intention was, free from any sullying influence of Darkness.

As I pondered the amazing Anastasia, it occurred to me that her system to dislodge the mettlesome influence of the shadow world could possibly be emulated by a divine dispensation that would encode transformational field energies into the semi-crystalline matrix of water that is contained within the bodies of flowers. The challenge would be to find specially endowed flowers (with the help of my "steering committee"), and extract that protective energy which would aid manifestation in the world of Light.

On this expedition, when I finally arrived at the particular high mountain valleys I was seeking in the Andes (the margins of which I encountered originally in 1992), I was amazed at the serendipity. The shamanic appreciation of certain highly protective and transformational flowers there arose from the flowers' purported ability to transform and restore humans by bridging them between earth and distant stars in the heavens, thereby freeing them of disruptive influences!

Over the two weeks that my team and I combed the remote Andean mountain ranges from bottom to top (at elevations reaching thirteen to fifteen thousand feet), I discovered and collected massively transformational flower frequencies. After I returned and put them to use clinically, I witnessed the extraordinary and inexplicable way that the enchanted flowers were able to restore balance in my patients' lives.[10]

I had to wait nineteen years and make a total of three trips into the Andes before I was able to locate the hidden and protected "Shangri-La valleys" I was eventually able to explore. The flowers there seemed to be "tuned" to our human evolutionary needs and to update their frequencies continuously for our benefit. I have the impression that the uncut flower extracts I collected there will be automatically updated continuously as well. That would be quite an interesting trick, wouldn't it?

I witnessed an unbelievable but true event at a health conference (in Chantilly, Virginia, 2007) that called for the type of clearing and protection I had just recently discovered (mentioned above.) The extraordinary scenario I encountered is described as follows...

[10] I created a combination of these flowers' frequencies that I named Pure Potential. Its applications are described in Part 3.

[illegible]

[illegible]

[illegible]

[illegible]

[illegible]

[illegible]

[illegible]

12

In The Company of Those Who See

By the time 2007 arrived, I had been working clinically with my flower essences for about six years. When I received an invitation to the annual conference of the Association for Comprehensive Energy Psychology (ACEP) that year, it struck me that I should attend. I was looking forward to sharing my findings with respect to a new way of removing energetic disturbances that negatively affect the unconscious mind, disturbing many areas of one's life.

There were two particularly noteworthy things that took place at that ACEP convention related to the topic of this book. The first concerns what I found when I performed brief evaluations of the attendees; the second relates to something extraordinary that I saw.

The conference was set up in the usual way. There were several "tracks" of speakers presenting workshops throughout the day, and at certain times there were key presentations in a large lecture hall, attended by everyone. There were morning and mid-afternoon breaks, and one around lunch time to allow attendees to visit the vendor section where there were booths displaying items for sale: equipment such as biofeedback devices, stress reduction paraphernalia, books and especially educational seminar information. My flower essence company had a booth there with literature describing how to use the flower essences to clear unwanted information from the unconscious mind, and tester bottles of all the individual products.

In my excitement over the prospect of sharing my findings with an audience that was used to working with the unconscious mind, I failed to take note of the fact that most psychologists and mental health professionals are prohibited or discouraged by their license from dispensing any type of supplementation to their clients. So it wasn't really a good venue for my company to attend. As the spokesperson for this new approach to healing, I nevertheless had a lot of fun. I also had the opportunity to test an important experimental question. Here is how I did that:

At one side of my company's booth I had set up a portable adjusting table that served nicely to allow me to perform a brief diagnostic screening on visitors who wanted to learn about what I was doing.

In my office, before I see new patients, they fill out a short but rather comprehensive set of questions about their history, chief complaints, etc. Here, of course, that was not done, so when an interested person wanted to be evaluated to see how the process worked, I had no knowledge of any of their complaints or history. It was basically blind testing. I used the screening method I had developed called Holographic Scanning.[1] That procedure works in the following way:

The participant lies down face up with feet slightly over the edge of the table to allow access to the examiner who is seated at the "feet end" of the table. The examiner performs a specific type of leg length check originally developed in the chiropractic profession by a very intuitive doctor. The legs are positioned so that the leg length is even, and the feet are held in such a manner that the heels of the shoe can be brought together so they touch. At the beginning of the test, the bottoms of the heels should be even, right and left. A silent questioning process is then begun that takes place between the examiner and the participant. The examiner poses questions to the super-consciousness of the participant, whose leg length will change in response to the questions posed. The participant has no idea as to the nature of the examiner's test questions and therefore has no way to interfere with the outcome of how his leg length changes. The examiner "calibrates" the test initially to find out where the "yes" and "no" responses lie, that is to say, whether the right leg shortening signals a "yes," or whether it is the opposite. Most of the time, a right leg shortening signals a "yes" response from the body/mind complex of the individual being tested.

The original way this method was used by the chiropractor who developed it was to screen the body to find out in which way the patient's body might be experiencing spinal distortion. For example, the examiner would picture each cervical vertebra and project the image of a right rotational distortion, asking the body to indicate "yes" or "no" and then the opposite of a left rotational distortion. The participant's super-consciousness knows exactly the physical status of its attached physical body and will signal that information to the examiner if he can access it clearly. In this example, we would find out if the particular vertebra was rotated to the right, to the left, or if it was properly positioned. With that screening information, one can then proceed to a manual exam and other methods of confirmation if desired. It is a brilliant screening tool that saves a great deal of time.

I adapted this test for screening of the flower frequencies I have developed. I teach this method (in an instructional DVD) to health professionals as a rapid way to initially match potentially needed flower frequencies to each individual patient or client.

The procedure consists of projecting the image of each flower onto the super-consciousness of the recumbent participant.[2] His leg length will change in a manner to indicate "yes" if the body has a positive affinity to the totality of the flower's frequency (represented in the image), or the leg will remain neutral if the particular flower in question has no benefit. Very rarely do we see a "no" reaction in response to a given

1 See further description of Holographic Scanning Appendix 9.

2 There is an incomprehensible amount of information encoded into the geometric design, color, and fragrance of a flower. We can approximate that totality of information within a flower much more fully by using the image of the flower rather than words describing it.

flower.

> *What still amazes me to this day is something that initially I did not expect. I discovered that this flower frequency matching system is astonishingly diagnostic. In other words, without knowing anything about a person, and by "blindly" finding the flower frequencies that the participant's higher consciousness or "soul complex" chooses through a "yes" response in terms of compatibility, we find a great deal of information relating to specific internal blocks that, when removed from an individual, lead to progress in his life.*

One of the first participants that I screened at the ACEP conference was a senior member of the organization. He was a psychologist with considerable clinical experience, and he had mastery of several different techniques for removing unwanted subconscious "programming" in his clients. (He had been treated with numerous clearing techniques by colleagues attending this very conference.) I explained to him how the holographic scanning process works, and soon he was lying down on the exam table for me to begin.

In just a couple of minutes, I found the flower frequencies he needed. Out of the 38 Basic Level 1 flowers for which I screened him, he only needed two. That indicated to me that he was pretty "clear," and that is unusual. I assumed that many of the clearing techniques he had been treated with had helped him. I remember that one of the flowers he needed was Heartmend (the one I mentioned using on Maria). I told him that I found he had a "hole in his heart" from the loss of a loved one, and I asked him to whom that might be referring. Whom had he lost? He looked straight at me with a pained expression and quietly said, "My mother… it's my mother." And then he said to me, "How did you know that?" I replied, "It is the flower that told us."

The point is, I was not employing some psychic technique. All I was doing was matching the resonance of the flower to his unconscious mind, which was linked to his soul need. When we then used the second part of my protocol, muscle testing with the test phrase, "The loss of my mother leaves a hole in my heart," his muscle stayed strong (facilitated) indicating that his unconscious mind was coherent with that statement. In other words, it was true that the loss of her was causing a "hole in his heart." That "hole in the heart" phenomenon is a very common hidden problem and can really weaken and disable a person. When I administered a couple of test drops of Heartmend to him lingually and had him repeat the test phrase, the statement was no longer true. There was an instant quantum transfer of restorative frequencies. That is to say, the Heartmend flower frequencies had energetically closed the hole. I told him that one bottle of the product would likely clear the problem, which all previous therapies and therapists had not detected, and he shook his head in amazement, assuring me that in fact he did sense that it would relieve him of this great burden. He had felt an instantaneous shift after the drops touched his tongue.

During the course of the conference I had the opportunity to perform the fast Holographic Screening on about 30 highly informed and well trained health professionals. Many times I heard the refrain, "How did you know that this is the ONE area that has been so resistant to change?" or, "How did you know to create this particular and very specific combination?" (referring to the flowers that showed up to assist). The whole event was a heartening experience of confirmation. I knew that with my beloved flowers I was "in the company of those who see."

In the vendor area of holistic conferences there are always people who are fun to meet. I noticed that in the booth next to mine were two women who were demonstrating how to balance the energy field of a client using a type of "light wand." There was an aura of integrity that shone from their display, and I had the impression they were earnest in what they were teaching.

There was a lull when no one seemed to be around our two booths, so I took that opportunity to go "next door" and introduce myself. And I am so glad I did, because it was a pleasure to meet Frances and Marie. Frances was the inventor of the light wand therapy device, and Marie was her most advanced student who had come from across the country to assist her at the convention.

Frances was truly congenial when I approached and began speaking with her. She mentioned that she had observed what I was doing from her booth and hoped that the participants to whom I had administered test drops would fully realize the power of transformation that was taking place from the flowers. Since I had not performed the flower screening process on her, I wondered how she had come to that conclusion. I was soon to find out.

Frances demonstrated on me how the light wand works, and I was quite astonished at its action. In her hands it was so powerful that it was able to make deep corrections in cranial compression within my skull. I could feel it acting. Later, Marie used the light wand on me, and although I felt its benefits, it was not working as deeply.

Time and time again, I have witnessed the phenomenon of the same instrument delivering different therapeutic outcomes in the hands of different therapists. That is why holistic healing will always be an art in addition to a science. That is also why it is foolish to try to establish rigid controls in energy healing experiments, because though we may be able to control the physical framework, we cannot nor should we try to "standardize" the energy of the healer. It is naturally variable, and there is always room for the evolutionary advance in a healer's capability.

While Marie was working on me, I noticed that Frances had a fixed and very focused gaze. She was looking intently to her left across the hall at a booth 30 or so feet away. There was someone lying on a massage table with an "operator" busy at work running energy patterns over the female participant's body and occasionally vigorously massaging and pressing areas on her back. Frances did not waver in her concentration and continued her focused gaze for a couple of minutes. I wondered what she was seeing.

Then she looked away, shaking her head with a disgusted expression. "Do you see what he is doing?" she asked me. I looked over to the booth she had been observing and noticed three or four people lined up to register with an assistant for a session with the "operator." There seemed to be "dull" energy around the whole area, quite different, for example, in comparison to Francis' booth. I wasn't drawn to go nearer to the therapist to observe any more closely, but initially I didn't intuit anything more than that.

Frances continued, "This fellow has been at conferences before, and I have watched him at work. He is really quite talented at what he is doing. He doesn't have any formal training, and yet people are lined up to pay six hundred dollars per session. Can you imagine? Six hundred dollars. If you don't notice what he is doing, let me tell you.

He really has quite a bit of "animal vitality" to his energy field, and people feel substantially different after he works on them – for a while! Little do they realize that he must have quite a background in magic – and I do not mean the good kind! I can see that he is constructing energetic devices (by the concentration and intention of his mind) that he is strategically placing in their spinal column to tap into their vital energy which then feeds into his. Not only does he gain more power of the most dubious kind by this approach, but he also maintains a hook into his "hosts" so that they are likely to keep calling him and paying him for his work. He is stealing from them, and he is keeping them happy at the same time. Quite an accomplishment – if you want to call it that!"

Ever since that experience I have paid much closer attention to what might be core causes of energetic disruptions in patients that are frequently associated with spinal imbalances and discomfort. As I described in the last chapter, I was finally graced with flower mixtures that often undo the kind of damage that this fellow was inflicting.[3]

"Teachers," Amulets, and Consciousness Technologies

There is another type of energetic damage I often find in patients that is almost always a surprise and generally quite upsetting when discovered.

When we do not see clearly and entrust our spiritual wellbeing and evolution to someone whose real motives are masked or who is just plain lacking in spiritual virtues,

[3] There are two flower essence blends for energetic shielding and protection: Pure Potential (Combination#2, p.232) and Freedom Flowers (Combination#4, p.240.)

i.e. someone representing himself as a trustworthy guru or teacher who in actuality is not clear and therefore should not be giving direction to other's lives , we can find ourselves dealing with real problems. Just because someone has a convincing personality and may possess energetic or supernaturally strong abilities, it does not mean he/she has beneficent spiritual authority.

This point is well illustrated from one of my patient case files. Carla sent me a digital image of her face along with her history so that I could consult with her by phone to try to get to the bottom of what might be "cutting off her life force," and find some lifestyle changes and flower frequencies that could get her back on track. She was one of the most beleaguered and energy-deficient people I have ever seen.

Over a period of about four months, Carla received many custom blended flower essence formulas from me, and her progress was amazing. Before each consultation she would send me new digital images (always with a non-smiling, resting expression as I request), and her positive energy (evident in the photos and confirmed in our interviews) just kept building. She was so pleased with her progress that she referred Joan to my office when she happened to be passing through Nashville. She was a new acquaintance whom Carla had recently met at the spiritual retreat of a guru guy in California. For reasons I shall describe, I checked this fellow out and found that he had a highly commercial website. He seemed to me, unfortunately, to be a shameless self-promoter, representing himself as a "manifestation of God."

Guru Guy (GG) worked closely with a group of Tibetan monks (All monks are not created equal! Can you say "*dugpa*?"),[4] and presumably that gave him legitimacy. One can only hope that the kind of picture of him I am painting comes from awareness and not judgment. You'll see why I think that it is the former.

When I started to examine Joan I found that something was seriously disturbing the harmonious flow of bio-energy in her body. Her nervous system was in a state of reversed polarity, her adrenals were being drained, and several important immune reflexes were "blown." She was surely at risk for more serious illness.

When I noticed that she was wearing a large chain around her neck, I asked to see what it was holding. Joan reached down and lifted from under her blouse a truly impressive piece of hardware! It was a massive crystal and gemstone amulet meticulously made with carefully designed geometry, held together by gold and silver wrapped wire. It was clearly not a Dollar General purchase. (When I asked, she told me that she had paid $1100 for it.) I asked her where she had obtained it, and that is how I found out about GG.

It turns out that one of the "guru's" primary operations is to produce what he describes on his website as sacred jewelry (amulets) to promote the rapid evolution of spiritual consciousness. They are purportedly specially charged and blessed by him and

[4] *Dugpas* are a class of Tibetan monks within which are members highly trained in the "dark arts."

the monks with whom he associates. I thought to myself, "O.K., maybe so."

Then Joan allowed me to remove the amulet, place it across the room, and retest her using some advanced applied kinesiology muscle testing of reflexes. When the amulet was off her body and far away, all her previously weak reflexes returned to normal. I then repeated my testing for her benefit, showing her that when the amulet was on her body, she was essentially being short-circuited. When it was off her body, important physiology returned to normal. Since I have seen this type of phenomenon many times over the years, I addressed the issue in a tactful way, letting Joan know that some energy devices are tuned to frequencies that some peoples' bodies cannot incorporate. My own response internally was more volatile, wondering how many other people were being harmed by the powerful objects available from GG's website.

There really wasn't much more I could say. I simply hoped Joan would choose wisely. We finished a productive session, and she went on her way, returning to California.

I did not hear from Carla for a longer than normal period of time, but eventually she did send in a new photo of her face. When she did reconnect with my office, she mentioned that Joan had briefed her about my findings with her amulet. Carla then went on to explain what a powerful influence GG was in her own life and that he was helping her recover from her very traumatic past. She found comfort in his spiritual community. She was using his "spiritually attuned and consciousness accelerating jewelry."

Carla's new photo was truly alarming. Her eyes that had been growing in clarity and light now radiated a dull emission from hollow sockets. It immediately called to my mind the Tibetan term, "hungry ghosts," which are purportedly a type of negative entity living between earth and hell. Something was really stripping her energy. Nonetheless, I had no option but to honor Carla's choice. It did not feel reasonable to try to oppose the humanly created energy emanating from GG's devices and organization with the utterly pure God-force that comprises the frequencies in uncut flower essences. I told her that she should contact me again in six months to reevaluate.

It is worth noting that there is a huge and growing number of "frequency healing technologies" producing many types of hardware and processes that are supposed to help us break through our limitations and more rapidly progress in our evolution of consciousness.

My advice is: Please do not use any of those technologies or processes unless you have had them tested by a practitioner who is trained and competent in the ability to measure subtle energy changes of your body when wearing the device or using the frequencies generated. Have at least one impartial observer test the way given invisible fields are influencing you.

Vibrational technologies also include numerous methods of treating water, energy bracelets, geometric forms such as special pyramids, sound CD's, products taken in liquid form, and a long list more.

So... what are safe and effective ways of clearing oneself and enhancing one's spiritual awareness? Initially, it is essential to practice what many of the best transformational thought leaders are espousing, that is: learn to be present and grounded, in the moment, without projecting into the future or ruminating about the past.

Then, it is helpful to understand and apply the practice of "Neti Neti" a doctrine deriving from the Hindu philosophy meaning, "Not this… Not that." It is an awareness practice designed to help us avoid labeling things, so that we remain free from judgment which creates a polarity distortion in the field of our mind. It is especially valuable when we do not "see" as deeply as we might like.

Once perception is more highly developed, then it becomes more a matter of balancing awareness versus judgment. In the example earlier in the chapter, Frances described what she clearly saw (and others generally do not see), so it was a matter of awareness, not judgment. It is understandable that she did not appreciate the energetic thievery that was surreptitiously taking place to the detriment of trusting conference attendees.

It is surprising and wonderful that we can achieve a boost in the evolution of our consciousness (and move closer to joining the company of "those who see") by using entirely pure, powerful, and rare flower frequencies. They can safely clear our negative unconscious mind and cancel or eject the energetic disturbances lodged inside our body and around our energy field.[5]

We shall explore in the next chapter the unassailable integrity of flowers that instills them with pure transformational power.

[5] The flower frequency blend I was guided to find in 2011 in the high Andes (named Pure Potential) has been used in inner shamanic traditions for centuries to clear malevolent attachments from our body and being. More recently developed "Freedom Flowers Blend" was created especially to break negative attachments.

13

The Incorruptibles

The healing power of certain extraordinary flowers, vibrantly alive and rooted to the earth, is totally benevolent. They are steadfast. They follow their innate design that impels them to give fully of themselves with no expectation of anything in return.

They are utterly incorruptible.

Such flowers are complex receptacles of divine light coded into physical form in an incomprehensible way. I have often described amazing flowers I have found as "saints among herbs."

As I was contemplating the content for this chapter I encountered an interesting call for papers to be presented at an international conference hosted at the Sorbonne University in Paris, September 7-9, 2011, titled, Forms of Corruption in History and in Contemporary Society: Origins, Continuity, Evolution. The following is an excerpt:

> "The etymology of the word "corruption" (lat. co-rruptum) indicates either an alteration, or an act of seduction, but in any case it leads toward a rupture. In a broader meaning, corruption is understood as the behavior of a person who derails another one from his/her way, customs or duties, through the promise of money [reward], honors or security. History shows that this phenomenon has generally been manifesting in different kinds of cultures and societies starting with the most ancient times. Today corruption is still a reality, generated by the particular economic, cultural and political conditions in both developing and developed countries.
>
> "We are seeking contributions on different forms of corruption and on special aspects of corruption in different cultures, historical times, and juridical systems. The major questions which will be discussed during this international conference are: Do phenomena of corruption evolve over time, or remain as primitive as in their first manifestations? What is the impact of these phenomena on forging the identity of certain individuals, communities or nations?
>
> "Is the ideal that corruption disappear one day utopian?"

From the Wikipedia entry on "corruption" we see:

> "In philosophical or moral discussions, corruption is spiritual or moral impurity or deviation from an ideal."
>
> The word *corrupt* (Middle English, from Latin corruptus, past participle of

corrumpere, to abuse or destroy : com-, intensive pref. and rumpere, to break) when used as an adjective literally means "utterly broken".

What really stood out from these two entries was the question, "Is the ideal that corruption disappear one day utopian?", and the concept of corruption signifying "utterly broken."

In the last chapter, Francis stood midway between two opposite poles. On her right hand, twenty feet away, she observed the ineffable at work: Divine and pure power from uncut flower frequencies causing transformation of the mind and elevation of the human spirit. On her left hand, thirty or so feet away, she observed an "utterly broken" state of trust as darkness was woven into the fabric of unsuspecting people who believed they were receiving healing, and who paid dearly for that deception.

Over a period of years, I have observed that energy from the right flowers can help humans to become less corrupt.

It only takes a few times of witnessing events similar to those described in the previous chapter to realize how much the protective and powerful forces found in special flowers are needed. I used to wonder often why only few and very select flowers have a profound ability to transform us. Then all of a sudden one day I was struck with the notion that flowers, just like humans, must be in different states of evolution. That is when I coined the term, "saints among herbs."

The concept of saintly people exists in all cultures. These are individuals who:

- Act as intercessors
- Model exemplary character traits, especially selflessness
- Possess benevolent powers with which they work wonders
- Have a revelatory relationship to that which is holy

Highly evolved flowers seem to possess the same attributes as the list above.

So how does a flower become "evolved?"

There is no single answer to that question, but I believe that one of the most important answers is by co-creation with humans. I can explain what that means by some examples.

Before I was led to move to rural Tennessee, I worked with medicinal plants for several years in Los Angeles. There I had a manufacturing facility to produce fresh-plant extracts of the highest quality herbs that I could obtain from organic farms and herb gatherers around the country. After a while, the calling for me to obtain a tract of land that I could tend personally and from which I could harvest wild herbs and build an energy within Nature, became an impelling force.

The 160-acre forest with an open field of about seven acres in the middle (where I built my house in rural Tennessee) was a godsend. There I found the tremendous stillness that I had long sought. The land, the trees, and the diverse flowering plants had much to communicate, I imagined, and I was eager to hear their "voices."

In the first two or three years that I owned the land, I ended up traversing just about every square meter of it. I noted in my mind and catalogued where wild herbs grew, and made an effort to keep track of their population density. I was elated each time I found a new wild herb growing that I had not noticed before. I resolved that my land would be a sanctuary where herbs would flourish, and that if I needed a quantity of one of the wild herbs, I would not deplete it in the wild, but would transplant wild stock to a specially constructed shade cover structure I envisioned. After a couple of years I was able to build that structure with 63% shade cloth to mimic forest sun exposure.

I discovered "hills" of tremendously rich soil derived from rotted hardwood tree bark in an abandoned sawmill that had not been active for over 30 years. I brought in about 200 tons of that soil to spread in the 12 long rows of my new "forest" under shade cover. Herbs that I knew and particularly valued were planted there, as well as several herbs that were new to me.

From 1993 to 1999 I spent a lot of time "conversing" with the herbs, and we became well acquainted. I felt they knew my hopes, celebrated with me my victories, and understood my frustrations and failures. Most of all, I think they knew how sad I was at the way humans were treating our great Mother Earth, and how I aspired somehow to contribute constructive energy in the midst of so much man-made suffering and hardship. I believe the plants were aware that I ardently wanted to create a new possibility for an improvement in the condition of the human mind and spirit, and I believe that led to our ability to co-create.

As I sat in the woods in stillness, sometimes it felt as though there were consciousnesses there reading my mind. It is as if the plants saw the most common deficiencies and afflictions that had affected me and a majority of my patients for the years I was in practice in Los Angeles and afterwards when I arrived in Tennessee.

It is an unusual notion (and one that can never be proven), but I believe that herbs can communicate what they witness about their human companions to something like a governing board of the Flower Kingdom that is one of many hierarchies in Nature. (This would simply be one component of the vast mind of God.) I had the sense on numerous occasions that there were assemblies of herbal consciousnesses akin to an electoral body. It felt to me that certain species of flowers were "chosen" in angelic committee to undertake a mission for humanity, and would finally be confirmed for that role at a point when they had evolved to take on the responsibility for developing transformational healing frequencies to transmute human afflictions.

The larger the healing challenge, the greater the power and dedication required of the particular flower. It seems there is an evolutionary framework that produces "saints" among herbs, and that I have had the pleasure and opportunity to work with and collect the essence of several of these astonishing "beings." On the one hand, they help alleviate human suffering, and on the other, they amplify the joy that is our birthright, creating greater opportunities for positive manifestation.

What is splendid about my collaboration with plants is that my soul request for particular healing dispensations from flowers takes place from the eternal part of my being that resides above the level of my personality and its shortcomings. So when a particular flower is activated to fulfill the request, and I am able to locate the flower and extract its living transformational frequencies by the uncut flower process, healing of a high and pure order is already mandated. It does not carry my personal limitations. This is a very important point, because it relates to a core issue to which I have already alluded in other chapters.

When healers are using their own physical magnetism, mental constructs or "quantum techniques" to shift the energy of a patient or client, it will always carry their personal signature of energy. If they are highly evolved beings or are particularly pure or kindly in their motivation, generally all is well. Humans certainly can bestow blessings and great healing and we do well to remember Christ's words, "he that believeth on me, the works that I do he shall do also; and greater works than these shall he do..." (John 14:12)

However, if healers are operating at a lower level of devotion, comprehension, or sight, then the practitioner can unwittingly create problems at a deep level of spirit in the recipient of therapy. An example where this could take place follows.

Let us imagine an aspiring energy-healing student encountering one of several of a "new breed" of energy healers/teachers that have come into prominence since the turn of the millennium. These teachers are typically born with an enormous power of magnetic influence and physical powers of manifestation (powers described in India for eons as "siddhis"). They are able to perform physical miracles such as rapidly healing fractures, straightening deformed bones, instantly closing wounds, and, in some instances, purportedly passing their hands through solid matter. This obviously sets them apart from others, and it is easy to see how they could develop a following of students who ascribe to them advanced spiritual characteristics, and who study their techniques to emulate them.

There is a consensus among a few of the pure and deeply sighted practitioners I know that some of these teachers are abusing their powers for the purpose of control, for developing a following, and for fame and fortune. Physical miracles do not necessarily correlate with what is highest and best for one's spiritual core. Physical healing can be forced, and that is always to be avoided.

When I see the miracle of a profound subconscious mind shift (and spiritual enlivening) occur in a patient after coming into contact with special uncut flower frequencies, I am overjoyed. That is because I know those results derive from transformation that has occurred deep in the spiritual realm, AND… flowers never force that.

Whatever healing occurs in that manner is as pure as the mind of God.

Year after year I have greeted particular herbs at the time they begin flowering. In certain instances, unexpectedly, the herb would all at once communicate that it was "ready" to do its healing. Before it had achieved that maturity, it was just a beautiful flower. Once necessary evolution and preparation had taken place, the flower contained powerful transformational forces.

Confirmation of this type of process was communicated to me clearly on a trip I took in 2009 to the San Juan mountains in Colorado not far from where I had the wonderful experience at Chama mountain in northern New Mexico many years before. My "steering committee" told me that I was to go to this area to find herbs that would enliven the human heart and renew life in those whose hearts had been crushed and closed.

I was accompanied on this trip by Serena, who had been a partner to me two years before, but was now solely a trusted platonic friend with a love of flower healing. She is half Native American Indian and half Mexican. Understanding of the destruction of the native heart ran deep in her blood. She is a skilled doctor and natural healer, and was the ideal companion for this trip in honor of re-awakening the heart.

At one point we stood together on the rim of a bowl-shaped meadow at 11,000 feet, opposite a huge red rock face across a wide valley. I could feel the rock face reflecting powerful energy from the heavens into the meadow below us. In front of us was an amazing spectacle due to the density and diversity of flowering plants ablaze with color.

Before walking into the incredible variety of chest-high herbs, I scanned the meadow for several minutes. One area "lit up," and I imagined that was where a special flower was located. When we got closer, I saw an "old friend" awaiting me, but one whose flowers I had never seen before. The herb was Green Hellebore, and its inflorescence was spectacular. Over the years I had seen and admired this plant in many areas of the U.S., but never once had I encountered it in the flowering stage. It let me know that it was "ready."

As Serena and I prepared Green Hellebore flowers to collect their healing frequencies, it was as if there was a chorus of flowers singing so sweetly to accompany our work. There was a communication of gratitude from dozens of different flower species around us, all praising this moment when the first of their sisters was able to undertake her healing mission.

There was a clear communication to me that in a few years' time several more flower species in this special place would be "ready" for their healing work, and that I should return then.

14

Life Change: How Long Does It Take?

Norbu was a valued student, earnestly devoted to the path of spiritual awakening. One day as he and his teacher, Tenzin, were walking alone in the forest, Norbu began to inquire about the path to self-realization, and wondered why he had not made more progress. Tenzin, who was known for his patience and kindness, explained to Norbu honestly what he saw were the obstacles that needed to be overcome.

He chose tactful language so as not to hurt Norbu's feelings, and he did his best to communicate a difficult observation. He explained that Norbu seemed to have fallen prey to a type of listlessness and that he needed to awaken much more spiritual zeal. Tenzin heard from Norbu's continued questioning that his message had not been understood or was being resisted.

As they continued walking Tenzin saw a stream ahead, and he asked Norbu to sit with him on the bank for meditation. When they were both seated at the water's edge and Norbu had entered into meditation, Tenzin, with the speed of a martial artist, plunged Norbu's head under water and forcibly held him there to a point near drowning. He then quickly pulled him from the water and left him gasping on the bank, horrified, and in a state of disbelief. Tenzin all the while had maintained his spiritual intention, flooding Norbu with love so that he might understand the teaching.

When Norbu was finally able to speak he said, "Master, you are known for your kindness, and I have been your devoted student. What could I possibly have done to cause you to nearly drown me?" Tenzin replied, "When you desire spiritual illumination as much as you wanted air, then you will progress to the state you wish to attain."

Ardent desire. Willingness. Those are the keys to rapid and meaningful life change that lead to fulfillment. But we still have to find the right locks for those keys to open. The locks we must locate are in the subconscious mind.

Lack of willingness to change at the level of the unconscious mind is perhaps the greatest reason that people initially stay chronically ill or chronically stuck in an unhappy life condition.[1]

The great benefit of the best self-help/motivational teachers and transformational thought leaders is that at the level of the conscious mind they can stimulate willingness.

[1] (In Part 3 we will explore deep insights from flowers as to hidden core beliefs in the unconscious mind that are responsible for a lack of willingness to change.)

Their personal power of persuasion, and, in some cases, vibrational clarity and coherence, inspire the desire for change. It can be a foundational first step. Only **rarely**, however, do vibrational frequencies derived from a lecture, a seminar, a book, an audio track, or even a meditative experience, have the ability to re-pattern the unconscious mind – and that is **essential** for real, lasting change and evolution in one's life.[2,3]

Although many more pages and books could be written to examine the evolution of consciousness and how one can personally progress, what it boils down to is this:

> *All obstacles in life essentially stem from the loss of our native, deep-feeling state and the resulting inability to creatively know as real what is channeled to us directly from the mind of God. That is what confers upon us the greatest wisdom as well as a vast power of positive manifestation.*

The enormously common experience of physical and emotional trauma and abuse, which shuts down our feeling state, coupled with living in the artificially constructed technocracy of this era and experiencing the hypnosis it induces through highly controlled channels of information and frequency broadcast, has cut down our access to the largest body of useful information in the universe, i.e., invaluable knowledge that is freely available in the multidimensional fields all around us.

In coming chapters, we will examine those areas where hidden obstacles may lie in sufficient depth to shed light upon the ways in which special flower frequencies can assist us in re-establishing a harmonious, coherent feeling state. Once such a state is achieved it re-awakens our ability to perceive directly into the heart of Nature (Source, the mind of God). When that option for our enlightenment exists, life becomes easier and more joyful.

I have had a lot of experience over the years in analyzing chronically "stuck" patterns, both in my patients and in myself. From that experience, I have compiled the following brief core guide to the easiest and fastest ways I know for breaking through to our true identity and our greatest spiritual and physical potential.

As an exercise, it is very useful to:

1. Assess your pre-birth, birth, and early childhood conditions, especially relating to mother/father and sibling relationships.

2. Assess your levels of willingness, truthfulness, vulnerability, surrender, joy, patience, forgiveness, gratitude, harmlessness, and kindness (the latter of which is substantially defined by the preceding four attributes.)

3. Assess the status of your personal ego.

[2] Please refer to the "LA 100 Phenomenon" study that comprises Appendix 7.

[3] Some exceptions to that observation have emerged in the last decade as a result of teachings that instruct how to personally access and utilize transformational quantum thought fields.

4. Create a plan for your personal transformation WITH benchmarks for measurement.[4]

It is my intention that all people, regardless of their religious background or ethnic heritage, shall be able to use the information and tools in this book. However, my logic and rationale for a safe and fast new way to improve ourselves, using transformational frequencies from special flowers, is associated with a conceptual framework that not everyone recognizes: That is, we are strongly influenced by the distant past. From my perspective, one's current birth life never fully explains all our behavioral or unconscious memory patterns.

The Judeo-Christian tradition attempts to explain these patterns by the theory of trans-generational inheritance. Eastern religions accommodate them through the doctrines of rebirth and karma. Here it should be noted that early Christians of the Essene and Gnostic traditions believed that the doctrine of reincarnation was part of Christ's inner teachings. Other religions and agnostics might account for the influence of forces outside our present birth circumstances as a result of tapping into what Carl Jung described as the "collective unconscious."

Regardless of your background, I hope you can intuitively understand the validity of past or outside influence in shaping one's life and in the involuntary registering of unconscious memories and beliefs.

1. Pre-birth, Birth and Early Childhood

When I was studying obstetrics, my instructor recounted something he had witnessed several times just after a baby was born. He described that the newborn basically has one of two reactions to birth. Predominant is the expression of fear, uncertainty and crying. But there is a much smaller percentage of newborn infants he had seen that are peaceful upon entering the world, almost jubilant. Some few had gurgled and giggled. What could account for that diametrically opposed reaction to beginning life?

Let us speculate about the type of background and experiences that could give rise to the Uncertain and fearful (U) or the spiritually Jubilant (J) newborn.

Imagine on planet Earth the history of being (U) who has experienced a preponderance of hardship thru past lives or trans-generationally: Lifetimes of poverty, starvation, destructive life decisions, brutality and violence of war, torture, loss of love, the defiling of rape and other sexual mistreatment, defeat of spiritual goals, targeting by

[4] To accompany you as you read on, please visit the following website:
http://www.TheFloralHandofGod.com/tools so that you can download FOR FREE:
(A) Your guide to measuring areas of your consciousness and
(B) Documentation tools to help you measure how or if you are making progress in the evolution of your consciousness.

the forces of darkness if/when (U) had engaged in battles for the light. Imagine a time wherein, with all the being's might, there was an effort to uphold righteousness, and yet (U) was struck down, leaving a sense of deep failure. Alternatively, imagine times when God's grace presented to (U) opportunities to transmute the burden of poor past choices by making a pivotal new choice in alignment with Divine Mind, and upon missing that opportunity, the profound regret (U) would have felt.

> *The permutations of possibilities are infinite. The point is that under the burden of the enslavement forces that have controlled our planet for way too long, there have been far more opportunities for lifetimes of suffering than there have been for lifetimes of ease and joy.*

Once that is understood, it is easy to see how destructive and defeating subconscious memories could be so deeply lodged in our unconscious mind that they would repeatedly carry forward in time until being removed by vibrational countermeasures.

What consistently strikes me as miraculous is that certain flowers have been touched by the Divine so that they carry the frequencies to "overwrite" and rapidly clear from the subconscious mind hurtful memories and beliefs that have persisted within us, reinforcing resistance to change.[5]

When it is time for (U)'s being to enter into physical incarnation once again, in concert with Divine Mind at an imponderable level, U's soul chooses the appropriate setting and birth parents for continuing evolution in consciousness. Astonishingly, that choice and "assignment", in the moment, is in balance with the whole universe.

If (U)'s cumulative memories and life patterns are painful and heavy at the time of parental "assignment," (U) could receive either a special dispensation that offers surcease through the experience of having kind, patient, economically privileged, and balanced parents who are in a position to lift and transmute some of (U)'s past burdens; some lesser degree of those positive attributes; or the opposite, i.e., parents that carry many of (U)'s same troublesome patterns/characteristics. The latter option, parents inviting dysfunction, is the one that has predominated, especially in the industrial era, and the last half of the twentieth century.[6,7]

[5] Marketing consultants often advise that a new product must have a concise slogan or "elevator pitch" that quickly conveys the action and benefits of the product. At the beginning of 2011 I finally found a brief description for my uncut flower essences that was comprehensive, and I coined the trademarked slogan, "Liquid software for the mind that encodes the divine."

[6] It is important to recognize that there is the opportunity for a positive outcome when troubled souls are born into more trouble. Under those conditions (U)'s may be impelled to exercise the spiritual authority needed to finally step out of historical dysfunctional patterns and put an end to a cycle of difficult karma.

[7] There is a belief among the so-called "consciousness community" that beginning at the recent turn of the millennium, children that carry a great deal of "light energy" within themselves are being born more often, and are coming into the world to help rapidly transform societies so that we might experience

We can similarly reflect on the different scenarios that involve the arising and the incarnation of the spiritually jubilant being, (J). What a delightful thing to see a (J), to be a (J), or to give birth to a (J)! How is a (J) created?

(J)'s are most readily created through conscious intention by parents that act in ways favoring the manifestation of light, though on occasion some (J)'s astonish us because they come from such troubled parents.

One way to explain the arising of a (J) is to describe a unique and wonderful association I had with such a being (Kendra) during a FlorAlive internship that she undertook with me on my farm in the summer of 2011. Kendra (then aged 24) is a medical intuitive with a natural ability as an animal communicator. She is able to inform owners of the feelings and desires of their animals, so that their otherwise invisible or non-communicable issues and health concerns can be resolved.

When I met her I noticed she spoke clearly, had no artifice, and was just plain pleasant to be around. We experienced a very warm yet entirely platonic relationship. Many of her qualities reminded me of the partner (and eventually a daughter) I would like to have. I was interested in how she got to be who she is, and so she filled me in on some details.

Kendra is a middle child with an older sister and two younger brothers. She adores her siblings who in turn adore each other, and her mother and father were and remain passionately in love. They were also highly conscious at an early age. In anticipation of enlightened conception, both parents prepared for months with special dietary and cleansing practices, meditations, and sacred ritual. They were preparing to bring in special children, and they did! Kendra adores her father, and that gives her a great advantage in getting along well with men in general. I wish all children had parents that were so mindful. It makes all the difference in the world.

With respect to the conditions around one's birth, it is very instructive to study information from the discipline of rebirthing, formally started by Leonard Orr in 1974 and assisted thereafter by Sondra Ray.

Rebirthing posits (from Wikipedia):

> "... that the trauma suffered during birth, and the specific nature of this trauma, has a deep effect on one's psyche and shapes one's perception and experience of life, self and the world in ways of which one is mostly unaware. (For instance, someone born by forceps delivery might rely on others to pull them out of destructive situations.) Practitioners believe it is possible to gain recall of aspects of birth, gestation and early childhood and to release the accompanying emotions through conscious connected breathing; such release can generate a positive paradigm shift and life transformation based on a change

---

global transformation toward manifesting the paradise that Earth can be within just a few decades.

in the experiences they believe one unconsciously attracts."

Clinically I have observed, over the years, that the emotional disposition of the father and mother before and around the birth is very important. For instance, when a child is not particularly wanted, it can negatively affect self-image of the child and leave him/her with long-lasting, destructive subconscious patterns. In Part 3 we will examine several of the disturbing thoughts that can start during infancy and carry through to the adult mind in the event of this scenario. Also in Part 3, I will describe some of the special flower frequencies that can transform and eliminate negative unconscious beliefs and improve self-image.

2. What are your levels of willingness, truthfulness, vulnerability, surrender, joy, patience, forgiveness, gratitude, harmlessness, and kindness?

Each component of this question is easy enough to understand consciously, but can be challenging and sometimes impossible to answer from the standpoint of the unconscious mind. Why? Because we are often unable to perceive consciously the root causes of limiting, defeating, or destructive subconscious beliefs, memories, and attitudes when they are deeply buried in our distant past.

In discussing this concept with "devotees of consciousness studies," workshop participants, and the like, on occasion I have found a particular type of initial resistance to the notion that the core causes of buried beliefs in our subconscious mind may be inaccessible to us. Self-reliant individuals occasionally reject the idea that something as simple as specific flower frequencies can be powerfully transformational. Certain individuals might be vexed if their pursuit of "consciousness disciplines" were shown to have fallen short of the evolutionary mark or their stated goals. Sometimes a matter of spiritual pride seems to be involved.

I have heard retorts along the lines of the following. "Due to the fact that I meditate [or pray] and do yoga regularly, I am very much in touch with my inner world. Through introspection I know the degree to which I am willing to change, my levels of vulnerability, the degree to which I am patient, and so on, and I consistently 'work on' those areas that need attention and improvement."

Well, of course, self-actuated clearing is outstanding and fundamentally important. What the respondent I allude to above does not know (or may be unwilling to find out) is that there is a new way to discover if one's "inner work" has been effective.

Holographic scanning performed with properly administered muscle testing to measure the influence of self-referential statements sheds remarkable light on the extent to which one's unconscious mind is free from limiting beliefs!

If all of the inner "work" of the millions of people worldwide involved in dedicated religious and consciousness practices were substantially effective, Earth would have returned long ago to the paradise it once was and shall be again.

Presently, we are on one side of an abyss -very deep but not too wide. It faces paradise just across the way, just a short flight or one great leap to its banks, but it is an abyss nevertheless. Despite the great teachings that have been given to us, we all need additional help from whatever pure sources are available.

Here is an example of a representative open-ended dialogue with one of my patients Bernard, that would take place toward the beginning of our treatment session. In this case, as I often do, I opened with, "So… what would you like to improve in your life today? What's on your mind?"

To which Bernard replied, "I have been having a lot of shoulder, neck, and jaw tension, and I haven't been able to sleep very well. That is unusual for me. But I have been under a higher than normal amount of stress. Do you remember the business deal I mentioned that I have been working on for the last couple of months?"

"Oh… yes," I replied

He continued, "Well it was finalized last week, and due to some very clever maneuvering, I was forced into a corner where I had to accept its terms, or the whole thing would have fallen through. My business partner, who I have completely trusted, altered the paperwork so that my percentage of royalties was cut by half. I have been really angry, in fact, enraged. The partnership is no more, and he moved on. I have been clearing my feelings about him with a number of different processes, and that seems to have calmed things down somewhat, but I am still really tense. I hope you can do something, 'cause I'm bottoming out."

Bernard continued, telling me that he knew that the cause of his unresolved stress was the anger and resentment he consciously felt toward his ex-business partner, and he had undertaken specific breath-work and meditations to clear his unconscious mind. He didn't know what else to do, nor did he know if what he had done really made any substantial difference.

I explained the process of semantic screening and self-referential statements[8] to him. It made sense, and so we began the holographic scanning procedure to find the flower frequencies he needed at the spirit and soul level.

In his custom blend (which may contain a combination of up to six flowers), four particularly important flowers (Star Spirit, Claytonia, Golden Seal, and Joe Pye) communicated their ability to assist with providing transformational frequencies from which Bernard would benefit.

The core beliefs discussed below were given to me by the flowers in a variety of ways, and have now been tested clinically and shown to be valid by scores of health professionals over several years.

[8] The self-referential statements corresponding to forty-nine outstanding flowers appear in Part 3.

Even though a given flower may have the ability to remove numerous impediments and may possess frequencies that heal our spirit on many different levels, it often seems to excel and express in one area of focus above others. Those special areas of focus are generally the ones that are communicated to me by the flowers.

We can gain insights into the larger picture of the unfolding of Bernard's life by recognizing what his soul called for from the flowers. His response to self-referential test phrases is below.

"If I step into my power, I will be annihilated." – Joe Pye Flower

Bernard tested coherent with this statement (i.e. His test muscle stayed strong – facilitated– indicating he believed it to be true.) If that belief were broadcasting from his unconscious mind 24 hours per day, every day of every week, wouldn't that be likely to place him at a disadvantage? He would be broadcasting an attractor field that would invite exploitation, because he could never be in his personal power.

Joe Pye flower emanates frequencies to "overwrite" that belief and essentially erase it from the subconscious mind. In other words, Joe Pye's frequencies would impel Michael to step into his power.

Second Joe Pye test phrase: "I am too sensitive for this world."

Importantly, all of Bernard's introspection and "shadow work" never tipped him off to the fact that he was harboring these particular destructive beliefs in his unconscious mind. Considering the second test phrase, just by placing the uncut flower frequency drops of Joe Pye in drinking water and consuming it for a short time would likely overwrite his belief that he is "too sensitive for this world," thereby promoting his empowerment. Really, quite a miracle if you think about it!

"I am an innocent victim." – Goldenseal Flower

Tested true. Bernard similarly had no idea that he was harboring this belief. Once again, given enough time, it is easy to see how this belief would likely create a self-fulfilling prophecy. Taking drops of Goldenseal flower frequency removes this very damaging subconscious register.

"I cannot forgive the injuries others have done to me." – Claytonia Flower

Tested true. What if Bernard, from his birth, had been holding memories of transgressions at the hands of others in his previous existence or from other sources? If that were the case, he would be inviting more transgressions in the present, and perhaps that is what set him up for betrayal.

Forgiveness is profoundly necessary to clear our life path. It is such a joy for me each spring to see the carpet of Claytonia that covers the whole forest floor of the FlorAlive forest where I live. I hear a "song of forgiveness" from those flowers each year as a wonderful reminder.

"My mistakes are unforgiveable." – Star Spirit Flower

Tested true. One hardly needs comment on the deeply damaging nature of this unconscious belief. Taking drops of the quantum frequencies of Star Spirit flower removes this subconscious "error."

This second subject heading deals with the importance of assessing one's levels of willingness, truthfulness, vulnerability, surrender, joy, patience, forgiveness, gratitude, harmlessness, and kindness. In Bernard's case, there was a direct damaging correlation with his inability to exercise forgiveness. (Claytonia is the flower antidote to that affliction.)

What would happen to one's level of willingness if there were an embedded belief cycling in the unconscious mind affirming, "My mistakes are unforgiveable?" Why would one want to be willing if one were forever doomed to condemnation? (Star Spirit flower is the antidote.)

How would the unconscious fear of annihilation affect vulnerability, the ability to surrender and to embrace harmlessness? One is not going to be very vulnerable if he believes he is always on the brink of annihilation, nor would he be prone to surrender, or to the exercise of harmlessness. (Joe Pye flower is the antidote to the unconscious fear of annihilation.)

One of the greatest gifts a person can receive is a routine screening for the self-referential statements correlating with the transformational flowers I have been so fortunate to find. When we take action on the findings, administering the indicated flower frequencies, it is proactive and pre-emptive. Follow-up evaluation clearly shows whether the destructive unconscious beliefs have been removed. Happily, we can often extinguish problems before they fully mature, especially when we evaluate and supply corrective floral frequencies to youngsters.

I look forward to the time when there are many more practitioners trained to perform holographic scanning for the indicated flowers, and to their delivering precise recommendations that will clear limiting or sabotaging unconscious beliefs in their clients.

Without that clinical asset, however, there are very valuable self-help protocols that I have developed for people to use on their own, and those are mentioned in Part 3 of this book.

3. Assess the status of your personal ego.

True evolution of consciousness is surreptitiously opposed by one's own ego, and unless the ego's methods of operation can be understood, the path to honorable contentment and harmonious living may be permanently forestalled. Philosophers and mystics have been writing and speaking about the steps to higher awareness since antiquity. That subject is at the core of all esoteric spiritual studies, and yet only recently has there been a "bare bones" exposé of how our ego stops genuine spiritual progress. The exposé appears in the form of Eckhart Tolle's book, *A New Earth.* If one reads it, the unhealthy ego is immediately disadvantaged. If one practices Tolle's recommendations, it stimulates powerful steps toward awakening.

I was fascinated by a lecture Mr. Tolle delivered entitled: The Flowering of Human Consciousness. In it, he specifically described the elevated and transformational properties of flowers. In his words:

> "Any flower could be your teacher, and you wouldn't need any other teacher if you can truly be with the flower and be alert…
>
> "I recommend you do this: look at a flower. The first thing you notice is how still it is… So when you look at a flower, an amazing thing happens. …You see the beauty – there is the color, and there is the light shining through the petals, it is very beautiful – but it is more than that. …You notice that there is an essence beyond that which you see. It lives in a state of deep stillness. And when you notice that…it means at that moment, that deep stillness is there in you… a state of great sacredness, aliveness, and beauty – but deeper than the beauty of form. It is the formless that arises in you… That is what I mean when I use the word "spaciousness." "

4. Create a plan for your personal transformation WITH benchmarks for measurement

It is important to recognize that there are two basic responses to transformation from uncut flower frequencies. Individuals who have an ardent desire and willingness to change and improve their life, and who have tried many approaches to transformation with moderate or minimal success, are most likely to experience shifts from the right flower frequencies that initiate real evolution. This type of person can often specifically notice what has changed and improved within them, and how quickly the transformation is progressing.

The other common response to uncut flower frequencies is the experience of individuals who wonder if they have changed, for they do not notice signs of transformation. For the latter category especially, I have created the assessment tools available at www.TheFloralHandofGod.com/tools. If you have not already downloaded those forms, please do so now, and it will be a helpful guide.

The 47 Words of God Chant

HI FUMI… YO I MU NA YA… KOTOMO CHI LO LANE

"We are Gods and Creators. We create everything in the Universe for us, and it belongs only to us and forever."

SHI KI LU… YU I TSU WANU… SO O TA HA KUMEKA

"We practice Freedom, Truth, Love, Beauty, Happiness, Advancement and actually becoming God Beings."

U O E… NISALI HETE… NOMASU A SE E HOLEKE

"We live together forever for our happiness and advancement. Thank you, God, for everyone, everything and for me."

15

We Are "Gods" and Creators

– Ours is the life we take the power to create –

At the outset of this chapter, there is an important point to clarify which relates to the words in the chant "We are 'gods' and creators" on the facing page.

I have encountered individuals, professing to be Christian, who are very uncomfortable with the idea of personal empowerment, i.e., owning that we are "'Gods' and Creators." For them it is a perilous concept, because they seem to imagine that anyone committed to self-realization and the strengthening of our individual link to God is automatically rejecting the teachings of Christ, and embarking on a road of personal aggrandizement that will lead to perdition.

I would not want any reader to take that point of view of me. From my perspective, drawing closer to the mind of God is a joint venture. It requires two collaborators: the highest part of our individual God-consciousness, residing within us in our spirit, plus the external totality of the mind of God, the Universal Source we access when we pray or meditate. Christ, a great exemplar of God on earth, provided a unique road map for that grand endeavor.

In my research, I have found that esoteric teachings of Christ (like the subject above) historically were not offered for public consumption for reasons of wanting to keep "the message" to the average person simple, to gain the greatest numbers of adherents, sometimes in order to encourage humanity's next evolutionary step but more often to maintain a certain fundamental ignorance that kept them servile, dependent, and easier to control. Christ's metaphysical teachings were, however, recorded in the early Christian writings of the Essenes as wellas the Gnostics, and differ substantially from what we hear today preached from the pulpits of virtually all Christian churches.

His esoteric teachings align quite closely with age-old approaches to God seen in other religions before his time. And all of humanity's efforts at approaching God consciousness on the deepest level (often hidden teachings) encourage us to see ourselves as divine parts of the mind of God and to act as such.[1, 2]

1 One of the most perplexing questions that can be raised is: Why have the inner teaching of Christ been suppressed? Why were critical parts of his message removed from the Bible at the behest of mortals making administrative decisions about the best ways to create the structural organization of a physical church and minister to souls they felt were incapable of arriving at truth without a great deal of "guidance."

2 I am not sure if Christ genuinely believed in the inherent value of brick and mortar churches, which take a lot of time, politics, and resources to manage. ("For where two or three are gathered in my name,

That is the reason I placed an ancient Shinto chant on the page opposite this chapter heading. I believe Christ fully embraced and taught the core message of this incredibly powerful and ancient chant, which truly holds keys to the unfolding of humanity's next evolutionary step.

At the end of a day-long gathering of healers in Asheville, NC, in 2006, I had the pleasure of meeting Hideo Izumoto who sang the "47 Words of God" chant. It was an extraordinary thing to witness. There were about one hundred people who had participated in the various workshops that several instructors and I had presented that day. We gathered in a small assembly hall, entered into meditative stillness, and awaited what we had been told would be a very special experience.

After a few minutes, a man of small stature in a simple robe walked with great dignity and slow, measured steps to the front of the room. He explained that he was a Shinto priest[3] and that he had been sent on a mission by his spiritual community from a remote region in Japan where he had studied since he was a child. His assignment was to bring to the public the most important of all chants, which previously had never been shared with the outside world. That is what he would sing for us (The 47 Words of God Chant.)

I have never been particularly drawn to most chants that one now hears (generally from India), but there was something extraordinary about this specific chant. That became particularly evident when *sensei* Izumoto sang the last phrase, "Thank you God for everyone, for everything, and for me." Very simple words, but what transpired when he sang them transcended simplicity.

Upon commencing the chant, a powerful resonance began to build in the room, starting from an emanation around him. The note of the last word in the chant, "*holeke*," is held for a long time. When Mr. Izumoto reached that word, all of a sudden a metallic-gold aura blazed from him, and the whole room burst into radiant white light. He was visible, but only faintly. The intense white light diminished gradually after the last note faded.

there am I among them"... Mathew 18:20) Did Christ mean "two or three gathered in my name" in a cathedral, or a church occupying one entire city block; or might he have been thinking more along the lines of "gathered" in a private dwelling, a field, or a forest. I feel it was the latter.
If one tries to drive home any personal opinion on any matter of mainstream religion, he is jumping on a bed of hot coals. Since I prefer warm, sandy beaches to hot coals, I want to defer to the works of religious scholar Elaine Pagels who thoroughly explores the historical record relating to the early Christian church being created by men, in part as an instrument for social control, and why that had to occur.

[3] Shinto, Japan's indigenous religion, originated in pre-historic times and was centered strongly around love and respect for Nature.

Apparently, as a result of the energy he manifested during the chanting, he had entered a highly coherent alignment with God-consciousness, and showed a divine radiance for a short time as a result. It was wonderful and inspired me to obtain his CD of the chant to see if it felt comfortable for me to sing. Now, years later, it is the only chant I use regularly.

It is interesting that I was exposed to this highly empowering chant at a time when I was just beginning to be led to flower frequencies that especially cancel disempowering beliefs. Such unwanted beliefs have been and are still being meticulously installed in the unconscious mind of all human beings who do not have awareness and energetic protection against that type of thought invasion.

> *What better way to fulfill corrupt and evil agendas than to install in the unconscious minds of an unwitting general population variations of beliefs that we are: powerless, meaningless, inadequate, alone, incapable of pharmaceutical-free living, destined to poverty, unattractive, unintelligent, and so on? For the purposes of enslavement and exploitation, if you wanted to dominate, manipulate, and control a society (or a planet for that matter), wouldn't that be a clever thing to do?*

How are these self-defeating thoughts installed? Most obvious, and generally undeniable, is the constant stream of negative news media. Also, there is a lot of negativity in the air waves, and by that I mean the microwaves that are passing through us all the time carrying everyone's phone conversations; huge amounts of violence in movies, and so on.

But there are explanations much more sinister than that, and I will leave that up to the reader to explore the enormous resources now available online dealing with so-called "conspiracy theories," many of which are likely spot-on accurate accounts of what is actually taking place or has taken place on this planet.

Most individuals are not yet capable of generating the intense white light that *sensei* Izumoto cultivated through arduous training as a monk. But what is consistently heartening (e.g., Sara's testimony following) is that anyone can fill himself or herself with a divine light obtained directly from Source, whenever he or she wishes, by consuming special flower frequencies that concentrate God's radiance, and that are available for everyone.

When we are filled with Divine Light channeled through flowers, the unhealthy frequencies of insecurity, self-loathing, disconnectedness from all of life, and many other depressive frequencies are ejected from our unconscious mind where they have been stored, and from which, like a recording loop, they play daily.

When we consume the enlivening frequencies of special flowers by adding drops of the flower essence to drinking water and sip that many times a day (ideally achieving hundreds of exposures within a few weeks), we etch new frequency pathways in our mind through repetition, and we are often permanently elevated to a more highly conscious, luminous, prosperous, and happier place.

During my workshop in Asheville, each of the attendees was examined by me so that everyone could observe the process and learn the flower essence assessment technique in order for them to begin employing it on their own clients and patients.

I noticed for nearly forty-five minutes during the time I was examining the attendees and administering to each the flower frequencies indicated, that one woman in the workshop seemed aloof. She had not introduced herself and stood behind everyone else, nearly motionless with a highly concentrated gaze directed at the exam table and each test subject. She was poised in a way that reminded me of a cat that is intensely focused, looking off into space at something normally invisible to human eyes.

During a break, I simply had to make acquaintance with her. I approached her, said hello, and with a smile asked what had she been observing while I was doing the testing. She spoke with such a steady groundedness and authenticity that it really grabbed my attention.

She said, "My name is Sara, and I am a trance medium. I see the levels of the multidimensional universe, and I have been observing what happens when you administer the drops to each of the people that you have been testing. It is really quite amazing.

I have been doing clairvoyant work my entire life, and I have never seen changes like I am observing occur so quickly. When the flower drops hit the person's tongue, instantaneously a whole series of events begin. I have been able to trace the activity to the highest dimensions of existence. At that level, energetic shifts are occurring which are at a stage of pre-manifestation. Then a cascade of re-organization in the individual's field energy begins flowing down from the deepest dimensions until it reaches this physical plane. Many effects can be observed: radiance and explosions of light, discharge of blocking frequencies, arcing between and activation of the chakras… This is very good."

PART 2

Toward A Science of Flower Frequencies

Changing the Address of Our Quantum Mind

"I am enough of an artist to draw freely on my imagination.
Imagination is more important than knowledge.
Knowledge is limited. Imagination encircles the world."

Albert Einstein Ph.D.
Nobel Laureate Physics, 1921

"If we can recognize that change and uncertainty are basic principles,
we can greet the future and the transformation we are undergoing
with the understanding that
we do not know enough to be pessimistic."

Hazel Henderson Ph.D.
Sustainable Human Development Consultant

"If you think you understand quantum physics…
You don't understand quantum physics."

"Science is the belief
in the ignorance of experts."

Richard Feynman, Ph.D.
Caltech professor of Physics
Joint recipient of the Nobel Prize in Physics (1965)

Introduction

Changing the "Address" of Our Quantum Mind

We are all familiar with what happens when we type a new address (URL) into an internet web browser.

The store of information to which we have been connected (the web page) changes as we are directed to a different repository of information stored on the server that the new address begins to access.

How rapidly we can see the new web page (information) depends in the most basic sense on:

- Network bandwidth,
- The amount of information we are downloading,
- And to a lesser degree, the characteristics of our particular computer hardware – its brain – the brand, processor speed, etc.

Generally all modern computers can switch to an address very quickly. So for the purpose of the following analogy, what is most important in downloading information from a particular URL, for example, is:

1. The volume, organizational clarity, and coding of its information, and
2. The amount of interference in our connection.

Thinking about the everyday experience of switching web addresses and downloading information struck me as the best way to describe what may be happening when a person consumes uncut flower frequencies that cause personal transformation. In previous sections of this book I have described the clinical testing procedure that has allowed me (and hundreds of other health professionals) to witness in patients nearly instantaneous changes of stored subconscious information.[1]

The following finding, for example, is commonly seen in new patients. Upon making the statement, "My self-esteem is strong and balanced," the patient's test muscle that was initially strong weakens immediately after uttering the statement. If the patient's unconscious mind were in alignment with the above screening phrase, the test muscle would maintain strength. The collapse of strength indicates that self-esteem is NOT strong. By administering on the tongue test drops of specific uncut flower frequencies

[1] Chapter 1, p.3.

resident in the Tulip Poplar bud (collected from the FlorAlive forest), immediate re-testing shows a nearly instantaneous change in the information displayed in the unconscious mind. The muscle that previously collapsed in weakness now stays strong. The unconscious recognition of poor self-esteem is completely flipped into stronger self-esteem by this procedure. What is going on? How could poor self-esteem nearly instantaneously change to stronger self-esteem?

Having observed scores of this particular response over a decade, it has become clear to me that such predictable reversal of register in the unconscious mind is not a random occurrence. For me it points to a profound phenomenon for which there must be logical explanations. And those explanations have to include an accounting of why some individuals who clinically show the same response to a specific test phrase (e.g., the strengthening of initially poor self-esteem conferred by Tulip Poplar frequencies) do not notice any change in their subjective feeling state, while others notice profound change. To be clear, two individuals can express the same strengthening of a self-esteem challenge that produced weakness, and one of the pair can report weeks later a clear subjective awareness that self-esteem has improved, while the other notices nothing.

To find explanations, I delved as deeply as a non-physicist could into the fascinating subject of quantum biology and our quantum mind. I would like to share this adventure with you. But before we begin, my short intuitive explanation for the nearly instantaneous change that flower frequencies can initiate is as follows:

Specific uncut flower frequencies, by a "switching effect," can change the "address" to which our quantum brain is connected into Universal Mind. When that happens, in the moment, our reality changes. We are drawing from a different information source. If the "new site" is more satisfying or functional than what we were connected to before, we might just decide to stay for a while!

Why do some individuals notice change and others do not?

It could be because the amount of "interference" to the downloading of our information stream from where our whole history or memory is stored in Universal Mind varies tremendously between individuals.

The mass of personal unresolved emotional issues that we have stored in Universal Mind over eons of time (through trans-generational inheritance, tapping into the collective unconscious, or individual karma–whatever fits your model) has to be reconfigured before change is noticed. If there is a large mass of issues, it takes much longer for the reconfiguration to produce noticeable change. Sometimes there can be an exception to this. If issues are acute in nature OR if there is an uplifted attitude of striving for transformation, it may constitute a large potential energy for change. If the emotional mass is large enough, tangled and stuck enough, it may not produce signs of life change for many years, sometimes more years than are left in the duration of one's lifespan. From another perspective, some individuals just don't want to shift to a different "address," a different mind and spirit space. They have an investment in staying where they are!

To recap:

- **One's "mind address" may be nearly instantaneously shifted to a new location by flower frequencies;**
- **Properly administered muscle testing with self-referential statements can neurologically indicate that the shift has occurred; and...**
- **Depending on the amount of one's individual, stored, unresolved emotional history, and upon one's readiness and free will to make change, the outcome that is seen in everyday life is variably expressed.**

It is not a surprise that as I examine the case studies that have responded very well to the flower frequencies, it is often true that such individuals have previously made an effort to evolve in consciousness. That can provide a "jump start" to the action of transformational flower frequencies.[2]

I have also witnessed individuals who do not have any formal understanding (or appreciation) of new era practices of thought transformation, but whose lives were nevertheless definitely improved by my flower frequencies. In some of those cases, the transformational effect seemed to be enhanced simply by underlying faith, hope, and devotion that alltogether allow the action of grace.

And to add an interesting twist, it is astonishing very often to see in animals dramatic positive responses to selected flower frequencies they have been given by their owners. When the action of a remedy is corroborated by measurable response in animals, we know it is not a result of placebo effect.

To me, how all these variables interweave is intriguing. Please join me in examining the magic of an accelerated path to increasing our potential and happiness…

[2] A core requisite for transformation is intention, and that is a key feature of the quantum information transfer model explained forthwith.

16

The Disappearance of Personal Obstacles

Observing transformation in my patients and in my own life is what prompted me to take the time and energy for scientific study of the flower frequencies I prepared, and to probe the ridiculously complex world of quantum physics, seeking answers relating to their possible modes of action.

I saw remarkable and uncommon clinical response, both immediately in terms of in-office reaction to self-referential statements, but especially with respect to long-term results. Patients that had been stuck in their life process were liberated in an extraordinary way – sometimes very quickly. This caused me to ask the question, "How could this be possible?" And that set me to thinking about all the things that might be involved in the totality of the transformational experiences I have been observing in patients and myself since the turn of the millennium.

I constructed a mental list of the components or processes acting in the frame of reference of daily life that would need to be defined. The crazy thing is that to be honest, the frame of reference would have to be the universe. And how can you put that in a neatly defined box to study it? The best that can be done is to try to isolate some of the largest factors that could account for rapid transformational shifts in stored personal memory, its related biological systems, and life outcome.

In order for a patient to have a documented history of an undesirable trait such as poor self-esteem, for it to be evident upon neuromuscular reflex examination, and then for it to disappear upon re-evaluation after dosing with uncut flower frequencies, significant *information transfer* had to occur from the flower to the patient.

First you see it, then you don't. An enormous change of a human trait is occurring without any of the transformational efforts that are normally undertaken: no requirement for reading of books, repeating affirmations, listening to CDs, special meditations, workshops, etc.[1] How could a particular flower, with its unique geometry and color, have encoded within it such specific transformational energy – such amazing "software for the mind"?

It is particularly impressive that within two to four weeks of dosing with Tulip Poplar frequencies (the "self-esteem flower"), clinical reassessment via neuromuscular

[1] I never suggest that the use of uncut flower frequencies should supplant any purely motivated practice for the evolution of consciousness.

evaluation with self-referential statements shows that the poor self-esteem issue that was present is no longer there. Often the patient notices significant positive change in his or her own demeanor. Others (friends, family, etc.) frequently notice changes even if the consumer does not. Something had to be transferred from the Tulip Poplar liquid drops to the consumer for that change to have occurred. Where did that something– that "information"– come from?

The following are factors to consider:

1. Point of origin of creation and coding of transformational "information".

2. "Information" transfer. Movement of "information" through the vacuum – the vastness of space.

3. Physics of the flower array for "information" capture – and discussion of my new technology for the collection and transferring of coherent uncut flower frequencies.

4. Instrumentally measuring the characteristics of the flower frequencies and modeling their potential modes of action – considering quantum energetic (fast) stepping down to the classical molecular biology (slow) response of the emotion/mind complex.[2]

Number one on the list above will never be able to be proven experimentally because its components are part of the ineffable – God, Universal Consciousness, or whatever similar term is appropriate. It is important to contemplate, however, and I will share my own views on it.

With respect to numbers two through four, I was extremely fortunate to have the personal assistance and significant mentoring support of Dr. William Tiller, a pre-eminent physicist,[3] refined humanist, and life-long student of consciousness, to help me with theoretical modeling, and his "number one," Dr. Walter Dibble, to conduct experimental testing.

I am also truly appreciative of the personal support and mentoring I have received from distinguished researcher, Pier Rubesa,[4] who demonstrates genius in his understanding of the effects of vibrational frequencies as they influence living systems. He has invented a highly advanced form of spectral analysis that can measure and graphically display an enormous time interval not otherwise possible in mainstream

[2] "Mind" will be considered to be "space" outside the physical brain which is the repository of information and core memory from which our bio-computer brain (a peripheral) draws information.

[3] William Tiller, Ph.D. is a fellow of the American Academy for the Advancement of Science and a Professor Emeritus of Stanford University's Department of Materials Science. He spent 34 years in academia after nine years as an advisory physicist with the Westinghouse Research Laboratories. He has published over 250 conventional scientific papers. He was a founding member of the Institute of Noetic Sciences.

[4] Pier Rubesa is the director of research and development at the Center For Bioharmonic Research in Switzerland, and has specialized in the development of biological energy sensors.

spectroscopy, allowing the detection and monitoring of the long wave length (low frequencies) that are so critical for the regulation of biological systems. He was kind and generous in the use of his time to help me characterize what I believe are profoundly important combinations of floral essence blends. In a novel and meaningful way he was able to scientifically measure uncut flower essence frequency emissions from samples I sent him. As a result I am able to report ground-breaking findings here with respect to the manner in which "information" contained in select flowers may be affecting our bodies and the environment we inhabit (e.g., in the event the essences are used as sprays for "space clearing").

I also feel fortunate to have met and befriended, at just the right time, a science graduate student savant by the name of William Brown. We agree that his having taken some of my most potent flower frequencies likely contributed to a shift in his quantum reality so that the opportunity manifested for him to rather seamlessly relocate out of his relatively non-aligned doctoral research at the University of Hawaii, Manoa, into a dream of a setting on Kauai at the research institute of a pre-eminent (older) new era savant scientist, Nassim Haramein.

Additionally I have benefitted from discovering key information about the quantum character of our brain/mind from highly qualified scientists in the domain of consciousness such as Dr. Stuart Hameroff, physician and anesthesiologist, and Dr. Edgar Mitchell, Ph.D. in aeronautics and astronautics from M.I.T. and founder of the Institute of Noetic Sciences after his Apollo 14 mission and retirement from NASA, plus others.

17

Consciousness and Science

A significant challenge in trying to explain consciousness (and how it can be changed) is that average folks normally regard it as an invisible and ephemeral entity. Most people probably do not spend much time thinking about it! Pre-eminent brain researchers, Roger Penrose and Stuart Hameroff, begin a substantive technical article[1] on consciousness with the following statement:

"Consciousness implies awareness: subjective experience of internal and external phenomenal worlds. Consciousness is central also to understanding, meaning and volitional choice with the experience of free will. Our views of reality, of the universe, of ourselves depend on consciousness. Consciousness defines our existence."

They then state:

"Three general possibilities regarding the origin and place of consciousness in the universe have been commonly expressed.

(A) "Consciousness is not an independent quality but arose as a natural evolutionary consequence of the biological adaptation of brains and nervous systems.

(B) Consciousness is a quality that has always been in the universe."
And the third possibility, which is the position they take:

(C) "Precursors of consciousness have always been in the universe; biology evolved a mechanism to convert consciousness precursors to actual consciousness."

In following chapters I will address in detail what I find to be a fascinating idea:

• That special flowers may be a part of these "consciousness precursors;" and

• That certain flowers might be facilitating translation of "Divine intention" into human consciousness, and hence can initiate change and improvement in our life.

Mainstream views on how consciousness could arise solely from brain action fail to explain several key phenomena listed by Penrose and Hameroff related to the process of cognition. (The intricacies of arguing consciousness are too complex and detailed to discuss here.)[2]

[1] Consciousness in the Universe: Neuroscience, Quantum Space-Time Geometry and Orch OR Theory, Journal of Cosmology, 2011, Vol. 14.

[2] A definitive scholarly work on this subject is: Explaining Consciousness – The 'Hard Problem' (1997) edited by Jonathan Shear. MIT Press.

Their article continues:

"In the 1980s Penrose and Hameroff (separately) began to address these issues, each against the grain of mainstream views."

The line "each against the grain of mainstream views" really caught my attention. Why is it that throughout history, inspired, intuitively driven, AND academically qualified scientists have had to fight against opposition from entrenched colleagues who seem to have an agenda against change? In Appendix 2, I explore that important point.

What has science been, and what could it be? "Science" can be described simply as a rational, orderly, and consistent way of investigating an experimental question.

In its earliest incarnations, the practice of science seemed to represent an earnest search for truth (e.g., what is the nature of matter?) in a manner similar to religion's search to understand the principles of universal organization and integration, i.e., the "mind of God." But it differed fundamentally from religion in its commitment to avoid pre-conceived notions and central dogmas. In a perfect world, science would objectively discover new insights into the nature of our environment (near and far, microscopically and macroscopically), and guide us as to how we can optimally interact with it.

When one has a powerful intuitive insight, or a strong sense of knowing (and sometimes just a compelling hunch), the alert and inquiring human mind might naturally ask, "Did I just experience an anomalous "blip" in my mind – meaningless static – or did I spontaneously tap into an "awareness field" that just revealed an aspect of the true nature of reality?"

Throughout most of history, such an inquiring human had a resource to which he could turn for interpretation of his insights and honest assessment of their validity. The sage and the seer, the shaman, the sibyl, the high priest or priestess of the temple, other dimensional beings (called angels by some), and occasionally master teachers of the "Brotherhood of Light" were the main resources that were consulted for their purportedly evolved consciousness that allowed sight into the heart of creation and advanced access to the "Truth."

Clairvoyants who successfully predicted events that physically manifested in the future enough times earned their own degree of authenticity, and often became trusted advisors in the courts of rulers and emperors.[3]

With the exception of that rare class of prophetic "consultants," the status of "wise men" and "wise women" was variable, and the assignment of merit to them was

[3] It is worth noting that in past decades the C.I.A. invested major resources in developing psychically gifted clairvoyants for the purpose of intelligence gathering and espionage ("remote viewing"). (Dr. Harold Puthoff, now director of the Institute for Advanced Studies in Austin, Texas, founded the CIA-sponsored program carried out at Stanford Research Institute with assistance from Russell Targ.)

subjective. However, for each individual that received from such seers the grace of keen metaphysical insights or real-time help in navigating the physical world, whether their insights and guidance constituted "truth" for anyone else was irrelevant.

It can be argued that truth ultimately is always personal and subjective.

"Ah" says the intellectual mind, "There have to be hard-and-fast rules that govern the physical universe, laws that explain, for example, why objects fall with no apparent motive force."

The mystic might reply, "Why do you speculate about falling objects? Can't you see for yourself what makes things fall? I do."

If science has proven one truth, it is that there is no ultimate truth. There is only a progression in the evolution of our awareness. In the loftiest sense, science and spiritual pursuits both are driven by an internal, personal exultation arising out of wonderment when we observe the beauty of our universe; when we feel sheer gratitude for being a part of the breath of life.

Throughout history, scientists and philosophers of science that have left the greatest contributions to posterity often have experienced metaphysical insights.[4]

Scientists with strongly religious views would naturally be reluctant to reveal them for fear of censure. The doctrinal beliefs and dogma of religions religions have, over the centuries, prevented open-minded theoretical modeling that is a hallmark of good science.

In the public eye, scientists by default are often classed as agnostics, meaning presumably that they are non-spiritual. I do not think that is generally the case. Many scientists, I suspect, share Albert Einstein's view that he expressed as follows:

> "I believe in Spinoza's God[5] who reveals himself in the orderly harmony of what exists, not in a God who concerns himself with the fates and actions of human beings."

The great figures in the history of science often possessed an outstanding trait: they were paragons of intellectual honesty. Their earnest desire to pursue the discovery of "Truth" to the fullest extent sometimes seemed to resemble the resonance of the aspiring spiritual seeker. Since the latter half of the twentieth century, however, science has suffered the same erosion of honesty that has afflicted most areas of contemporary society. It would seem that interests of commerce too often oppose the light of truth in scientific discovery in a stealthy manner, when findings from theory and

---

[4] The website of Geoff Haselhurst (www.spaceandmotion.com) very nicely summarizes philosophical views of many leading natural scientists and physicists.

[5] Benedict de Spinoza was a 17th century Dutch philosopher who espoused strongly naturalistic views of God, the human being, and the world. Stanford Encyclopedia of Philosophy-Spinoza (http://plato.stanford.edu/entries/spinoza/#GodNat.)

experimentation could threaten financial gain and corporate profits by disrupting the status quo.

Science is a cyclic process that generally progresses from theoretical modeling, to experimental testing of theory, to repetition of the experiment by the original investigator (producing the same results), and finally ends with the ability of different investigators at different locations to recreate the experiment and obtain results that confirm the original investigator's findings. Sadly, with this process there are many opportunities with this process for creative ideas and their novel experimental results to be lost or compromised. Even worse, great ideas may be barred from ever reaching the light of day.

Scientific experimentation is expensive, and so as we evaluate which material results or social directives deriving from scientific data have the possibility of being based on "truth," we had better take note of who is funding the research and who will financially benefit from the findings. The amusing perversion of the Golden Rule comes to mind, "He who has the gold makes the rules."[6]

[6] To avoid drifting too far afield from the purpose of Part 2, I refer the interested reader to Appendix 2. It explores one stark example of corruption in scientific research that is costing many people their health and wasting untold billions of dollars: falsification of drug studies and perversion of scientific research integrity by pharmaceutical giants bent on profit. It also reveals the potential folly of some "peer-reviewed" science.

18

The Scientific Frame of Reference: Key to Merit and Meaningful Outcome of Experimentation

Sincerity is not a test of truth.
It is possible to be sincerely wrong.

Jim Rohn
Motivational Speaker &
Life Coach Extraordinaire

The Wikipedia entry on "frame of reference" is over five thousand words. It includes formulae, graphs, and extensive bibliographic citations. Yet, as I sort of expected, nowhere could I find discussion of motivation/intention and the implications of choosing what is included (and excluded!) when one constructs an experimental frame of reference.

What one chooses to examine within a frame of reference will obviously define the set of possible outcomes. To me, this has always been the central dilemma in orthodox scientific research. If one looks too far out of the box (because one senses what *might* be operating in the ephemeral reaches of space),[1] one risks encountering doctrinal resistance before research even begins. There is an obstacle even more basic than that – simple logistics.

The cost of scientific research is directly related to the number of variables that one chooses to include and measure in a given experiment. Increasing the number of variables that must be examined, at some point, exponentially increases costs and time requirements to the point of unfeasibility. So, as I mentioned in this book's introduction, it is generally necessary to choose very few variables to include in a given scientific experiment, and this may not at all represent reality either in the space we all

[1] It is interesting to note that the major impulse that inspired Einstein in his discovery of the principle of relativity (that the speed of light is constant in any inertial frame) was the perplexing dream he had at age 16 of running alongside a beam of light.

occupy or in distant space.[2]

One's personal theory of knowledge (epistemology), i.e., what constitutes our own reality and how we justify it – is of utmost importance in defining a frame of reference for scientific study. I would suggest for all researchers the exercise of making a list: write down their points of view, biases, fixed ideas; and if they can find such a region within themselves, determine how in that space they relate to all that is inexplicable around them – all that is ineffable.

In a thoughtful, short article titled "*Effing the Ineffable*", author and philosopher, Roger Scruton wrote the following:

> "Anybody who goes through life with open mind and open heart will encounter these moments of revelation, moments that are saturated with meaning, but whose meaning cannot be put into words. These moments are precious to us. When they occur it is as though, on the winding ill-lit stairway of our life, we suddenly come across a window, through which we catch sight of another and brighter world — a world to which we belong but which we cannot enter." (To that beautiful passage, I would have ended with "but which we *feel* we cannot enter!")

Here is my partial list of biases:

• I have a natural appreciation of cross-cultural traditions with respect to world views, natural healing, and philosophy. Therefore, I have never accepted institutional views of science and the healing arts as being automatically the most valid.

• Since my teens I have always felt there was a "voice" calling out from Nature offering solutions to the stressful and vexing modern problems that we have created for ourselves. So I have always wanted to hear that voice to the fullest extent possible. Perhaps that is associated with intuition. I do not know. What I do know is that in Nature, there is a perfect economy. Huge feats are accomplished with very little energy (that has conventionally traceable origins). With that point of view, it makes sense, if one is looking and maintains an intuitively open mind, that he may find hidden clues that lead to the discovery of systems and mechanisms that operate very efficiently, and can initiate change in remarkable ways.

> *It has been my clinical experience (testing self-referential statements and following patient progress) that the use of uncut flower frequencies as a type of "software for the mind" to "overwrite" intractable, counterproductive*

[2] The sticky point that arises again and again relating to "new age" discussions of progressive science and its presumed "quantum" corroboration of metaphysical concepts is that the subatomic nature of particle physics (which seems to metaphorically align with transcendental views in philosophy) cannot be assumed to relate to activities of our macroscopic life. Little did I know that I would encounter a scientist who had theoretically bridged some of that impasse.

subconscious beliefs (and install positive views) is one of those highly efficient systems. In general it appears unmatched in its ability to rapidly remove historically longstanding mind (karmic?) patterns that are unhealthy.

• In previous chapters I have pointed out, in various ways, aspects of my unconventional points of view as a result of having very physical (albeit sometimes bizarre) experiences. Not only have these experiences occurred in fields, on beaches, in forests, in jungles, and on mountains, but they have occurred consistently, in different ways, in the setting of my clinical practice. It may be worthwhile to list ideas and notions resulting from all these experiences that have served to help me define the reference frame for my research on the action of flower frequencies.

1. Apparently subtle forces and fields that may not be noticeable can turn out to be a vast power. Don't overlook what seems invisible.
2. Ask, "What am I not seeing that may be exerting an influence?"
3. Ask, "Which of my beliefs and intentions may be (visibly and invisibly) altering the outcome of what I experience?"

If it sounds like the above has implications of placebo effects, that is correct. What is not generally recognized is that "placebo effects" – or unaccounted for distant effects – occur all the time. This has to do with the concept of "entanglement" within the discipline of physics, a topic we will discuss later. The extent to which "placebo effects" are disregarded in mainstream science may well be proportionately related to how truly valid the science is, as we are living in what is now posited to be a multidimensional universe that is highly entangled.

19

Physics of the "Invisible"

For a good part of the twentieth century, physicists strove to find a way to somehow unify laws of physics that apply to the macroscopic world in the domain of relativity theory and laws that apply to the microscopic or subatomic world in the domain of quantum mechanics. Since our universe includes both vast and small components, it is reasonable to assume that there is continuity throughout, and that different sets of rules cannot exist for that which is vast (such as the far reaches of space) and that which is small.

Despite the fact that many brilliant minds have undertaken intense efforts to unify rules of physics from relativity theory and quantum mechanics to create what has been referred to as a Theory of Everything (T.O.E.), to date no one has succeeded.

Since I am neither a physicist nor a mathematician, I can only recognize, in a non-technical way, the value of ONE shared model for both "worlds" large and small.

Two of the contentious areas in this whole confusing mess of many different physicists' independent theories center upon questions of (1) whether "information" can or cannot travel through the vacuum of space at speeds greater than the speed of light, commonly written as "c", and (2) whether sub-atomic entities (e.g., positrons and electrons) exist as particles OR waves (so-called wave/particle duality) OR both.

Please be patient, for in coming chapters we shall see how that type of information bears directly upon the floral quantum frequency model I propose which explains the rapid elimination of limiting beliefs.

In 1905 Albert Einstein elaborated the special theory of relativity which predicted the equivalence of mass and energy in the famous equation:

$E=mc^2$ where c is the speed of electromagnetic light in a vacuum.

This theory gives rise to the doctrine that it is impossible for any particle that has a rest mass to be accelerated to (or beyond) the speed of light. Forthwith a theory is presented explaining how, if we are considering movement of "information 'particles' (waves) " through the vastness of vacuum space all around us, they must be moving at greater than light speeds (so-called superluminal speeds.) I will explain later why information needs to move really fast if we hope to shift our life to a more enjoyable place.

When I delved into the work of physicist Dr. William Tiller (WT), I was delighted to find information that helped shed light on the "now-you-see-it-now-you-don't" phenomenon of limiting unconscious beliefs existing, and then suddenly disappearing due to the influence of exposure to uncut flower frequencies.

In his profoundly significant (and too little known) texts,[1] Dr. Tiller explains how, over several years, in his rigorous laboratory experiments he was able to solidly *disprove* the following assertion: "A fundamental assumption of our present day quantum mechanical (QM) paradigm, and of our earlier classical mechanics (CM) paradigm, [states] that no human quality of consciousness, intention, emotion, mind or spirit can significantly influence a well-designed target experiment in physical reality."

We shall see that WT's theories of information transmission posit the existence of what he calls "deltron substance," which is a coupling agent that essentially transduces complex information from invisible ("supersensible") higher dimensional planes INTO our visible four dimensional plane of existence (characterized by the spatial Cartesian coordinate axes x,y,z and time – so-called "spacetime"). [2]

Dr. Tiller theorizes that "Deltron" substance, activated by intention, contributes to at least a possible explanation of how transformational information can be transmitted from the reaches of distant outer (vacuum) space into the surface of a flower. Once that is understood, then it is a bit easier to envision how that information can be collected from the living flower with the process and apparatus I discovered, and then later transferred to pure water for human consumption. From that point we can examine an exciting current model in neuroscience that could explain how quantized information (i.e., information contained in a living flower) could produce rapid shifts in the emotion/mind complex.

When I was quite young I remember a dinner conversation that took place with my spiritual teacher, Kay, and other members of our small community of intention. She explained that in the afternoon that day she had conducted an in-person session with a very interesting and truly extraordinary man, the pre-eminent scientist, Dr. Bill Tiller from Stanford University. Kay was enormously impressed by the open-mindedness of Dr. Tiller who had contacted her as a resource to gather information about the unseen characteristics of our physical universe.

WT had heard about Kay's extrasensory perception abilities through a mutual friend, and more important, about Kay's deep knowledge of the foundational core

1 Referenced on p. 154.

2 A simple way of understanding the four components of spacetime is the following example: Imagine that you are walking downtown to meet a friend for lunch at 1:pm on a rooftop restaurant. To arrive you will need to walk in two dimensions, left and right along streets (x and y axes); then take an elevator up to the roof (z axis) at a particular time (t) to arrive at 1:pm.

of Theosophy, which is a spiritual movement that was started in the late nineteenth century under the guidance of an "eccentric" clairvoyant named Helena P. Blavotsky, (H.P.B.). H.P.B. was reportedly chosen by illumined spiritual masters from India to be their emissary tasked with introducing into Western societies (Europe and the U.S.), on a grand scale, ancient spiritual teachings of karma, rebirth, and the nature of the unseen worlds.

When meeting with Kay, apparently WT's greatest interest lay in decoding some of the arcane information (relating to the organization of matter and fundamental particles) contained in a massive tome called *The Secret Doctrine*. That work was reportedly dictated clairvoyantly by master teachers to H.P.B. while she was in a hyper-conscious state. Many of the ideas in it served to influence the thinking of numerous luminaries such as Drs. Carl Jung, Rudolf Steiner, and others. I recall that in the following year Kay had contact with Dr. Tiller a few more times.

So it was natural, many years later when I was seeking scientific guidance, for me to reach out to Dr. Tiller, letting him know of my years-long association with Kay and of my previous knowledge of his work with her. When I was finally able to speak with WT in our first phone meeting, his wonderfully resonant voice, kindly and gentle nature, and carefully chosen language of science let me know that we should somehow work together.

An uncut flower essence workshop was organized for me in Scottsdale, Arizona (where WT and his wife live) so that he could attend, witness, and sense in person what might be going on as I treated various participants with the semantic screening process and muscle testing. (Dr. Tiller's long time associate and laboratory manager, Dr. Walter Dibble, was also in attendance.) Due to WT's many years of work exploring the energetics of alternative medicine, he was completely familiar with the advanced muscle testing I was using (applied kinesiology) and other energy medicine procedures.

I tested WT and his wife, Jean, to find flower frequencies that might benefit them, and administered some for evaluation during the workshop. Dr. Tiller agreed to take the flower essences and to report back any shifts he and his wife might note. A month later, WT reported that beneficial shifts occurred for both him and his wife that would likely be related to the flower frequencies. This provided a good rapport for future collaboration.

My job then was to try to understand Dr. Tiller's work (not for the faint-hearted), and to repeat back to him what I thought he had discovered to see if I understood the profound nature of his scientific experiments. That information is presented in the following chapters.

20

Spiritual Intention: Its Relationship to Information Transfer and Consciousness

In previous chapters I have described periods of stillness wherein I hold a single-minded focus on the fullness of the flower I intend to extract. Some awareness of information from or around the flower occurs to me on those occasions that is at a level beyond thinking. I can only describe it as an awareness of intention. As I mentioned previously, there seem to be powerful spiritual intentions streaming from certain flowers I have encountered.

When I read that pre-eminent brain researchers Penrose and Hameroff take the position:

> "Precursors of consciousness have always been in the universe; biology evolved a mechanism to convert consciousness precursors to actual consciousness,"

it occurred to me that intention may be a consciousness precursor that "rides" on information to help convert it to consciousness (and also influence the unconscious/ subconscious mind.)

By making use of Dr. Tiller's insights and intention experiments which are described in forthcoming chapters, a plausible model can be constructed to help explain how highly coherent frequencies (information/"coding" that has been transferred during the extraction process from certain living, uncut flowers to the water that it is contacting) can "overwrite" or supplant what we have held to be true in our unconscious mind so that we develop and live from a different perspective.[1]

In one of my first communications with Dr. Tiller I could see that in few words he was succinctly providing me a huge amount of information. Initially the problem was that I did not understand most of what he wrote. And I don't think you will either! I shall attempt to remedy that as soon as possible.

The following is quoted from his letter to me:

> "Our research into psychoenergetics has shown that there are two unique

[1] In the previously used example of Tulip Poplar frequencies removing poor self-esteem, perhaps the unique characteristics of that flower allow it to "download" information coupled with "Divine intention" that can alter one's personal stored memories and beliefs relating to self-esteem.

> levels of physical reality: our normal electric atom/molecule particle level with a spacetime reference frame (RF), plus a magnetic information wave level functioning at the physical vacuum level (that historically in metaphysics has been referred to as the "etheric"), with a type of reciprocal RF for viewing the phenomena of that domain. In nature, the latter (the magnetic information wave) is actually the precursor or template for the former, but it is not accessible to conventional instrumentation.
>
> Regarding your enhancement of Dr. Bach's flower essence preparation technique, I think you are on the right track, because it is the magnetic information wave essence of the living flower that you want, not so much the electric atom/molecule nature of the dead (cut) flower.
>
> With respect to your question about the physics of information transfer from the surface of the flower you are extracting:
>
> The R-space [meaning 'reciprocal space'] forces of the living flower have long range effects on the magnetic information wave level of the water in which the flower is extracted."

"Oy! What was I getting myself into?" I thought, after reading that short note. For starters, what on earth did "R-space" mean, and what relevance did it have for a theory relating to how mind and spirit can be influenced by flower frequencies?

In order to understand this, I spent a year reading and wrapping my mind around three of Dr. Tiller's complicated texts[2] and works from numerous other scientists.

Another early email from Dr. Tiller (which he intended to be instructive but which initially struck me, rather, as mystically scientific) was as follows:

> "When we condition a space with an Imprinted Intention Host Device (IIHD) to a higher electromagnetic gauge symmetry state (probably SU(2)) than our normal U(1) gauge state, we detect oscillations in all property measurements (air temperature, water temperature, pH, and water electrical conductivity) but with oscillation frequencies in the 10^{-1}, 10^{-2}, 10^{-3}, 10^{-6} hertz [= ultralow cycles per second] range. This is NOT U(1) gauge state behavior."

When I first saw that language it might as well have been Etruscan.

So what is the meaning of a "higher electromagnetic gauge symmetry state" in terms of understanding changes in our subtle energy and the domain of human consciousness? Step by step *it will be revealed!*

In the glossary of his text, *Psychoenergetic Science*, Dr. Tiller described gauge theory

2 *Conscious Acts of Creation: The Emergence of a New Physics* (2001).
Some Science Adventures With Real Magic (2005).
Psychoenergetic Science: A Second Copernican-Scale Revolution (2007).

and electromagnetic gauge symmetry state – very complicated concepts – in a way that almost could make sense to a basically educated reader! (This is not to criticize Dr. Tiller, who seems to function in an intellectual stratosphere accessible only to the extraordinarily well prepared. I merely point out the arduous task I faced in trying to understand his brilliant work, never having studied graduate-level math and physics.)

He wrote: "In general, gauge theories were constructed to relate the properties of the four known fundamental forces of nature (gravity, electromagnetism, the long-range nuclear forces, and the short-range nuclear forces) to the various symmetries of nature. … Electromagnetic (EM) gauge symmetry relates to the inner symmetry condition of a space relative to its electromagnetic nature. At present, the normal EM environment of our world is the U(1) gauge state where Maxwell's four equations, applied simultaneously, quantitatively define the entire range of electric/magnetic phenomena that can occur. The SU(2) state is a higher EM gauge symmetry state wherein both single electric charges (+ and –) coexist with single magnetic charges (N and S), and Maxwell's four equations must now be modified to quantitatively define the range of electric/magnetic phenomena that can develop in a space maintained at this EM gauge symmetry state."

Yikes! What does that mean?

What Dr. Tiller's well constructed scientific experiments revealed (described following) is that intention can change the gauge state in a carefully monitored physical space, raising it from the normal U(1) state to the higher SU(2).

When that occurs in a system it has profound implications because when a space is raised to the higher SU(2) gauge state, it will have a higher thermodynamic free energy per unit volume. What that means is that the space will then have greater coherence (a better state of integration) and decreased entropy (LESS decline of energy and LESS <u>*dis*</u>*organization of matter).*

Whenever one can increase his coherence and decrease his entropy… it is a good thing.

and electromagnetic [illegible] states—very complicated concepts—in a way that almost could make sense to a basically educated reader. (This is not to criticize Dr. Tiller, who seems to function in an intellectual stratosphere accessible only to a [illegible] extraordinarily well prepared. I merely point out the arduous task I faced in trying to understand his brilliant works, never having studied graduate-level math and physics.)

[illegible]

21

The Importance of "Space Conditioning" and Its Relevance in Daily Life

One of the hallmarks of good science is when the researcher sees in his experiment results he never anticipated,results which, when followed and investigated, lead to an exciting discovery. That, we shall see, is what happened to Dr. William Tiller (WT) in his subtle domain experiments.

During the many years of WT's distinguished career (in a branch of physics called "material sciences"), outside of his academic duties at Stanford University, he conducted a large body of research in areas such as anomalous and exceptional energies, psychotronics, "energy medicine" and subtle energy healing involving practices such as qi gong, acupuncture, applied kinesiology and more. In that time it became clear to him that there is an important realm where healing takes place that is not visible in our everyday experience. So he was well suited to investigate that invisible realm.

The influence of intention and directed healing energy from qi gong master practitioners and the like had already been documented many times, but in those experiments the sensitivity level of the findings was very close to the level of ambient background noise, and, as a result, required finely regulated statistics to see the significance. Dr. Tiller felt he had to design a system to measure experimental outcome that would provide a larger magnitude of change so as to be well above ambient noise to provide clearer evidence of influence in the subtle domain where intention operates.

So he helped others to develop some relatively simple electronic circuitry (fit into a small box called an IIED-Intention Imprinted Electical Device) designed to hold human thought intention much like a capacitor stores electrical energy. That intention, he hypothesized, would act like a motive force that could be directed to alter the carefully measured and monitored properties of "target materials" – inanimate and animate substances.

> *As you read the following experimental design to measure the influence of human intention on an inanimate object, the broadcasting IIED,* **remember that this same experimental concept can be used to measure the influence of transformational flower frequencies** – *what I believe is "flower intention." But the flower test system uses the actual uncut flower frequencies directly rather than what is described above, the IIED. And the "target" is the sentient being (human or animal) consuming the flower frequency drops.*

In Dr. Tiller's words: "By using the IIEDs as a transportable host for specific human consciousness, one is able to separate the supposed variable source of this consciousness from the experimental interaction itself between the consciousness-modified surrogate and the specific target experiment. By using two identical devices, one not imprinted to act as a control and the other imprinted to the IIED state, we thought to provide an even more objective measurement of human consciousness influencing fundamental physical processes in both inanimate and animate matter."[1]

WT, along with 3 other highly trained meditators, concentrated very specific intentions into the Intention Imprinted Electrical Devices (IIEDs). These human thought and emotion-imprinted intentions were designed to have specific effects on four target materials when they (the IIEDs) were placed in close proximity to them. The description of those experiments can best be explained by using the following long quote from one of Dr. Tiller's papers (quoted with permission):

"The target materials selected for this study were (1) purified water in equilibrium with air, (2) the liver enzyme, alkaline phosphatase (ALP) and the coenzyme, nicotinamide adenine dinucleotide (NAD), (3) the main cell energy storage molecule, 6 adenosine triphosphate (ATP) and (4) living fruit fly larvae, Drosophilia melanogaster.

From this set of target experiments [influenced by focused human intention for a specific change in each of the above four areas] we first observed:
(1) a shift in pH of purified water, in equilibrium with air, either up (one IIED) or down (another IIED) by **one full pH unit** with no chemical additions [emphasis mine] with a measurement accuracy better than ± 0.01 pH units. This constitutes a total swing of hydrogen ion concentration of 100, with a signal size 100 times our measurement accuracy, a very robust effect indeed (effect sizes ~ 10,000), (2) an increase in the thermodynamic activity of in vitro ALP, NAD, and ATP by a very significant amount (effect sizes ~ 10-25) at high statistical significance (p<0.001) and (3) a reduction of in vivo larval development time to the adult fly state by ~15%-25% at p<0.001.

... In addition to the foregoing remarkable results, **a totally unexpected and critically important phenomenon arose** during repetitive conducting of any of these IIED experiments in a given laboratory space. It was found that by simply continuing to use an IIED in the laboratory space for approximately 3-6 months, the laboratory became "conditioned" in some very fundamental way .... In this "conditioned" space, new physics appeared in the experimental data.

At least three characteristic experimental "signatures" heralded the onset of the space "conditioning" process:

"(1) air and water temperature oscillations, pH-oscillations, electrical conductivity oscillations, etc., with both large amplitudes (~102 - 103 times larger than our measurement accuracy) and strong periodicity in the ~10-100 minute range developed.

[1] First published in VIA, The Journal of New Thinking for New Action , Volume 1 Number 4, 2003, published by Vision-In-Action, www.via-visioninaction.org.

These oscillations were sustained in the locale, even after removal of the IIED from the locale,

(2) with measurement instruments in both an almost unconditioned space and a strongly conditioned space several hundred feet away, when a pH-increasing IIED was turned on in the conditioned space and arranged to produce a well-defined pattern of these pH-oscillations, a highly correlated pattern of pH-oscillations was observed to appear in the unconditioned space.

(3) in an unconditioned space, if one places a disc-shaped magnet under a pH-measurement vessel and continuously monitors the pH for several days before turning it over (so that the opposite pole is pointing upwards) and continues pH-monitoring for several more days, one observes no significant change of pH with magnetic field polarity. However, in a "conditioned" space, when one performs the same experiment, pH DOES change with a shift of magnetic field polarity.

... "If we ask ourselves how one is experimentally able to observe such a DC (direct current) magnetic field polarity result ..., the only reasonable answer seems to be that somehow we have accessed magnetic monopoles in nature [previously never attained experimentally]. Somehow, this space-conditioning process via the use of IIEDs has changed a basic symmetry state in nature [raising it from the U(1) normal gauge state to the thermodynamically more efficient SU(2) state]. A heretofore structural element, that has resisted detection for a century (and billions of dollars have been spent searching for it in normal physical reality), appears to have become experimentally accessible in an IIED-"conditioned" space."

..."At this SU(2) level, the IIED [the intention broadcaster] is able to access magnetic monopole currents in nature to generate and broadcast magneto-electric (ME) waves, even in the electrically "off" state, and these carry the primary intention information to the "control" target causing it to become imprinted. These IIEDs then, in the electrically "on" state, can broadcast a coupled ME/EM signal modulated by the intention imprint information to the target experiment causing it to change in the direction of the intention imprint statement for purely thermodynamic reasons."[2]

Practically what this means is that WT found striking experimental evidence to show that highly focused (coherent) intention in a defined space can reduce the normal

[2] When sacred intention is held on a ceremonial site, or in other areas, they become "conditioned," very probably in the manner described above. One of the great cathedrals, such as Chartres, in France, was built on an ancient sacred site with a long history of spiritual alignment, and I will never forget the very palpable sense of connection with the divine in that place. Even more striking to me is the energy I felt inside the Great Pyramid in Egypt. Very special coherent and attuned energy can be felt as well in the treatment centers of holistic doctors that do outstanding work. Those are all "conditioned" spaces. How remarkable that flower frequencies sprayed into an area (tested in my clinic) will "condition" spaces. More on that later.

energy loss (entropy) and de-coherence (disorganization) that is normally happening.[3] Further experimentation revealed that the mechanism by which this occurs requires participation in the magneto-electric realm, a step above our physical world, where events can transpire *faster than the speed of light!* You will see in forthcoming chapters why that is important if we wish to achieve personal and planetary change as rapidly as possible.

Dr. Walter Dibble, under Dr. Tiller's direction, was kind enough to place a powerful uncut flower extract that I had prepared (called Aseñac) into the controlled monitoring station in their laboratory. This station was created to measure any minute changes in the space of that controlled environment. What he found appears in the following graphs, and it provided clear evidence that the test vial of extract was emitting flower frequencies operating in a higher dimensional domain (R-space where the SU(2) gauge state exists) than our everyday space-time existence (D-space – the domain of the U(1) gauge state). He submitted the following results to me toward the end of 2012:

pH Measurements on Dr. Davis' Uncut Flower Essence Sample: Emergence of Oscillations – Signals from R-space

"A most interesting aspect of the pH measurements of the flower essence, Aseñac, was the new frequency information that was imparted to the system. No oscillations were noticed before this experiment on the control solutions. As soon as this Aseñac experiment was started, pH and air temperature oscillations appeared and became stronger with time. Oscillations are periodic changes in time for the measurement that is being made, in this case, the pH measurement. Similar oscillations were also seen in the air temperature measurement.

All signals such as radio signals involve oscillations, so this measurement is picking up a signal that we believe originates in a domain beyond the physical, such as R-space. There is no physical explanation for such oscillations in both the pH measurement and the simultaneous air temperature measurement.

The 288th harmonic of the 24-hour cycle starts to make an appearance that was not there in previous weeks before the flower essence was added to the water. This harmonic has a period of exactly 5 minutes that is a very high frequency harmonic of the 24-hour cycle. It can be seen in Figure 1 how the 1/300 Hz frequency eventually grew with time to dominate the spectrum for the pH oscillations. This 1/300 Hz signal was not observed at the other measurement stations in the lab."

[3] My clinical experience and patient testimony convince me that the uncut flower frequencies I am developing enhance clarity in people's lives by this mechanism.

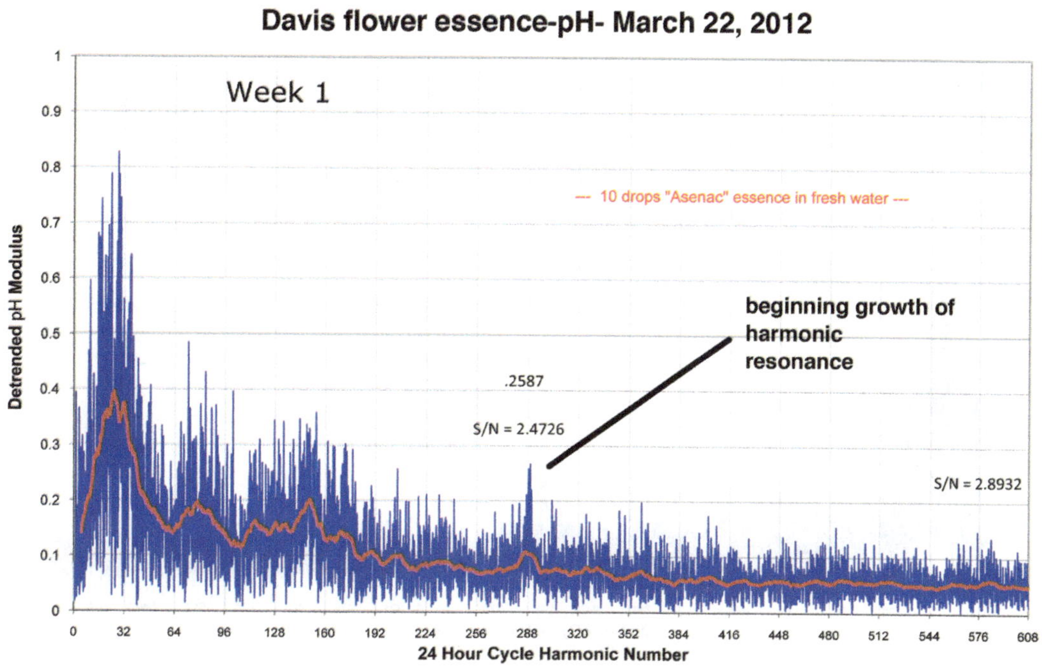
Davis flower essence-pH- March 22, 2012
Week 1
--- 10 drops "Asenac" essence in fresh water ---
beginning growth of harmonic resonance
.2587
S/N = 2.4726
S/N = 2.8932
Detrended pH Modulus
24 Hour Cycle Harmonic Number
0 32 64 96 128 160 192 224 256 288 320 352 384 416 448 480 512 544 576 608
0 0.1 0.2 0.3 0.4 0.5 0.6 0.7 0.8 0.9 1

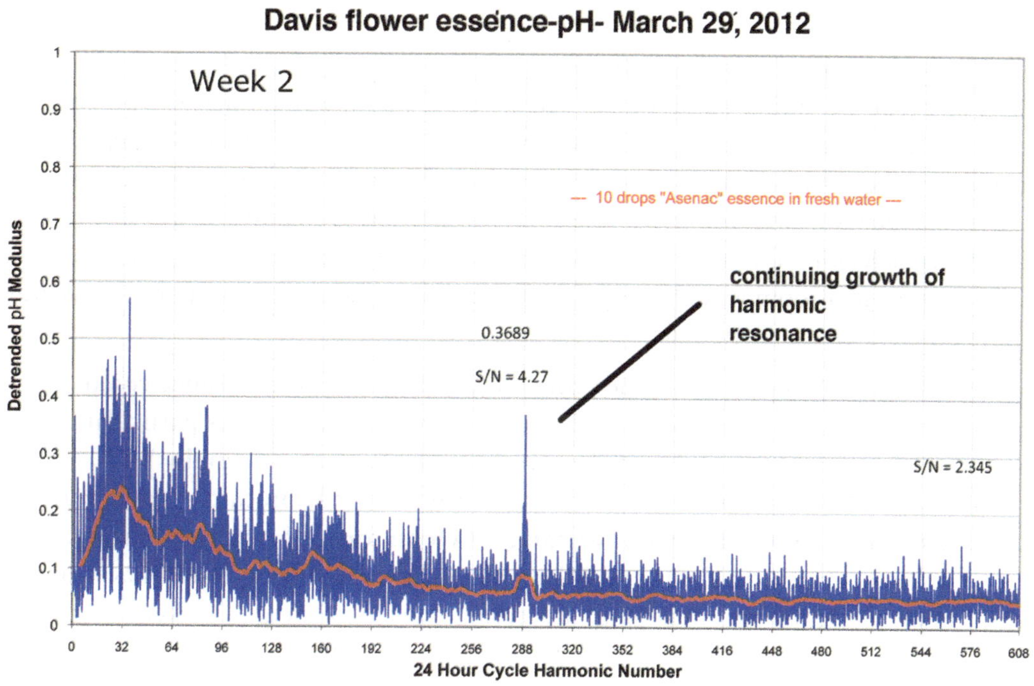
Davis flower essence-pH- March 29, 2012
Week 2
--- 10 drops "Asenac" essence in fresh water ---
continuing growth of harmonic resonance
0.3689
S/N = 4.27
S/N = 2.345
Detrended pH Modulus
24 Hour Cycle Harmonic Number
0 32 64 96 128 160 192 224 256 288 320 352 384 416 448 480 512 544 576 608
0 0.1 0.2 0.3 0.4 0.5 0.6 0.7 0.8 0.9 1

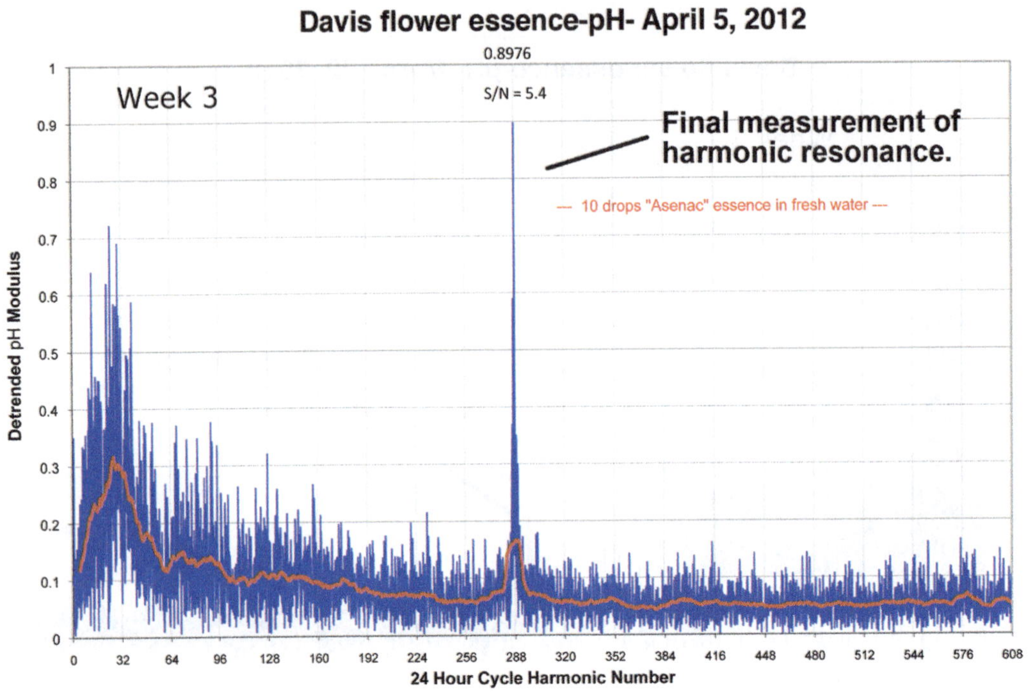

The fact that the "other dimensional" character of my flower extracts showed up did not surprise me because of what I had been seeing clinically for such a long time – nearly instantaneous changes in unconscious mind patterns/beliefs for which there were no explanations in our normal space/time existence. Of course, it was heartening news nevertheless. I did not expect, however, that the mere presence of the uncut flower essence in a room would change the thermodynamic character of that space into a more efficient energetic domain.

It became easier to understand, therefore, how taking the flower essence could powerfully influence those consuming them, and how spraying various particular essences in the air can "elevate" and clear work and living spaces. **I finally had scientific corroboration to lend credibility to my observation that spraying a flower essence can constitute a powerful and clean form of "space clearing."** (Such a process leaves no tell-tale smell that accompanies smudging. And I have found it to be more powerful than smudging[4] in clearing unwanted energies as well.)

4 Smudging is a practice, stemming from antiquity, of burning aromatic herbs such as sage to purify an environment with an effect like incense.

In some instances spraying a mist of the properly selected uncut flower essences[5] seems to be an essential tool to break an individual out of a stuck pattern. That is because the gateway to higher dimensions that affect us is in R-space (just outside the body) associated with a magneto-electric bridge that is part of the acupuncture system.

As soon as I recognized this phenomenon I was able to appreciate why traditional healers in Tibet and Peru take herbal and energetically treated water into their mouth so they can spray it around the candidate receiving healing.

Extraordinary new scientific findings presented in Chapter 24 (that were discovered during analysis of my uncut flower essences by a new technology) corroborated what WT found with respect to the influence of uncut flower essences should they be sprayed into a space.

[5] In commerce, two products are particularly effective for this use: Pure Potential™ and Freedom Flowers Blend™ described on www.FlorAlive.com.

22

Flower Characteristics Relevant to Healing

Once I had read and become familiar with WT's work, I was much more easily able to conceptualize the mechanics of what might be happening for frequencies from a flower to initiate transformation within us. And it inspired me to conceive of possible modes of action that might not have occurred to me otherwise.

Once I had my basic ideas together, I presented them to Dr. Tiller. With his typical courteous reserve, he commented on the possibilities and plausibility of some of my intuitive ideas. I explained to him my flower healing model whereby I saw flowers acting, in a way, like satellite dishes/antennas, receiving signals from physical space and all the dimensions above us that we do not see. When prepared with my uncut flower extraction process (allowing the flower to remain connected to the earth), I explained that I felt flowering plants would draw energy up from the earth as well. As I mentioned that, WT took a pause and said, "I think you have something there, because you know for an antenna to work, it requires a power source to drive it. When the flower is on a plant that is not cut, and rooted to the earth – acting as an antenna – there is your large power source."

Then I continued with my ideas about the semi-crystalline character of the flower petals, full of water, that seemed to me to be able to capture and store the "downloaded" information they receive, and then to transfer it to the extracting water that surrounds them. The surrounding water is collected and diluted (not homeopathically succussed!).[1] This eventually creates the drops that are consumed to shift the pattern of information which humans draw upon to create their reality (our mind "coding").

As part of my background research I found a technical article co-authored by WT from a body of work he conducted relating to the mechanisms by which homeopathic preparations could produce physical effects even though they are diluted so highly that they contain no physical substance.[2]

Therein was stated: "...the core paradigm of materials science [is] that properties of a

[1] Succussion is a particular process whereby a liquid is vigorously shaken in a back and forth motion and abruptly stopped (decelerated) in one of the directions, for the purpose of "energetically activating it."

[2] Rustum Roy, William A. Tiller, Iris Bell, M. Richard Hoover (2005) The Structure of Liquid Water; Novel Insights From Materials Research; Potential Relevance To Homeopathy. In: *Mat Res Innovat. 9-4:93-124.*

phase are determined by structure, not just by composition." The article then describes how the structure of water in which the homeopathic therapeutic substance is stabilized can hold information from the given substance even though, under high dilution, it contains no molecules of the substance (composition) – technically described as being beyond Avogadro's limit (in other words, enormously diluted). It is holding its "information" in the conformation of its structure which is responsible for the therapeutic effects.

The article continues…"Epitaxy is a term which does not appear even in most technical dictionaries, but it is a very well known phenomenon, studied and used in dozens of everyday technologies in materials science. Epitaxy is the transmission of structural information from the surface (hence *epi*) of one material (usually a solid) to another (usually a liquid). [So I thought to myself, 'Aha… from the surface of the flower petals and the amazing architecture of the stamens and stigma TO the water extracting the flower.'] Subtleties of terminology appear in various papers, but it is "information" that is definitely transferred. No matter is transferred, hence concentration above or below Avogadro's limit is totally irrelevant." … "Information and "memory" are transmitted from the … substrate to the liquid phase, which can then completely control the structure of what is formed from it. No chemical transfer whatsoever occurs. …Obviously, the structure of water can be influenced by the structure of solids with which it is in contact."

"O.K. then," I later mused, "there is some science to corroborate my intuitive hunch. Yeah!"

A few weeks later Dr. Tiller submitted to me for my use two masterfully prepared chapters explaining (1) the mathematics and physics of the complex structure of flowers when interpreted as an antenna array, and (2) a summary of the physics behind his "Multidimensional Simulator Model," the latter of which appears in the next chapter. (Another amazing "serendipity?" Dr. Tiller just happened to have an extensive knowledge of antennas.) Those chapters contained such lovely work that I wish I could present it all here, but it is just too complex to understand for the general reader, so I will do my best to excerpt a few of the most relevant and understandable ideas from them.

Antennas in Nature and Industry

William A. Tiller, Ph.D.
Prepared for Brent W. Davis, D.C.

"Many of us grew up seeing various kinds of antennae on homes, factories, office buildings, cars, ships and aircraft. A much smaller number of us realize that antennae abound in the biological kingdom but very few of us know that every living system on this planet contains some kind or other of antenna for sensing and communication. Callahan[3] has provided us with a beautiful description of antenna arrays in moths. He discovered that insects emit a coded infrared signal which contains a unique navigational message; that the trichodea sensilla of the Cabbage Looper and the Corn Earthworm are arranged in a log-periodic sizing so that they would function well as an antenna with wide frequency band capability; he also pointed out that a conical type of antenna was to be found on the Florida Scarab Mite and that thin tapered helical-type dielectric sensilla are found to serve as antennas on many species of wasp. It seems to be a very reasonable assumption that all living organisms utilize antenna arrays of varying degrees of complexity as a major portion of their information gathering and transmitting apparatus. This should certainly apply to flowers.

"... The pattern of radiation from an antenna can be modified to suit the type of service desired. The actual EM [electromagnetic] radiation pattern of the fundamental half-wave dipole (below) is that of a toroid or doughnut-shape with the antenna aligned centrally along the axis of the doughnut.

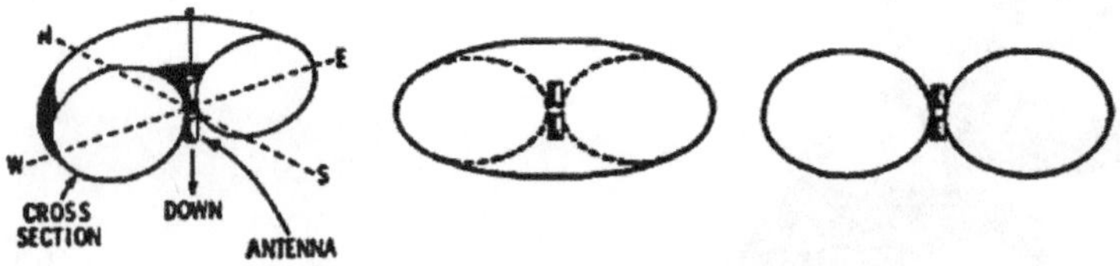

Radiation pattern of half-wave dipole.

"In general, the higher the signal frequency for fixed L [antenna length], the more loops there will be in the antenna pattern. Each loop direction will be a direction of major receptivity or transmissivity of the antenna while the directions between the loops will be null receptivity/transmissivity directions.

"When one sets up a number of identical antennas in a unique geometrical pattern

[3] P.S. Callahan, *Tuning In To Nature*, (The Devi-Adair Company, Old Greenich, Connecticut, 1975).

and controls the relative phase (or timing) of individual members of the array, the actual signal strength at a given point in spacetime of the entire array is given by the superposition of the signals from each of the individual antennas in the array.

"As two relatively simple examples, in Figure 1 we can see the effect of using point sources of equal magnitude leading to a broadside array pattern and an end-fire array pattern from two arrays of almost equal length(3). For the broadside array, the pattern is disk-shaped with a narrow beam width in the plane of the figure, but the beam width is 360o in the plane perpendicular to the page. On the other hand, the pattern of the end-fire array is cigar-shaped both in the plane of the page and in the plane perpendicular to the page.

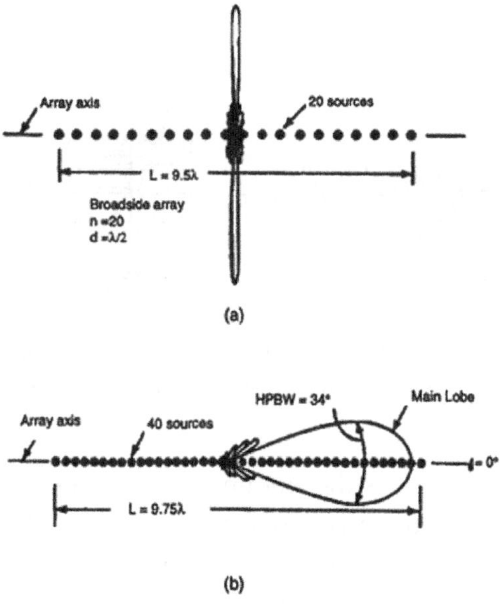

Figure 1. (a) Broadside array field pattern from 20 point sources of equal amplitude and width 1/2 spacing and (b) end-fire array field pattern from 40 point sources of equal amplitude and 1/4 spacing.

"A wide variety of antenna elements, from monopoles and dipoles to spiral and helical, from metallic to dielectric and from stationary to scanning are in use today.[4] In addition, the arrays can be of one-dimensional, two-dimensional or three-dimensional geometry. In Section2 of this book our main area of focus is unique flowers as receiving antennas for both EM energies and higher dimensional energies. These flowers can receive, via their pistil, stamen, and petal array system, higher dimensional information of the EM, ME, emotion domain, mind domain and spirit domain types

4 A. Lytel, *ABC's of Antennas* (Howare W. Sams & Co, Inc., New York, 1971).

[the latter three domains described forthcoming.] The cups and petals of surrounding tissue tend to act as director and reflector elements such as one finds in the very popular Yagi antenna (see Figure 2).

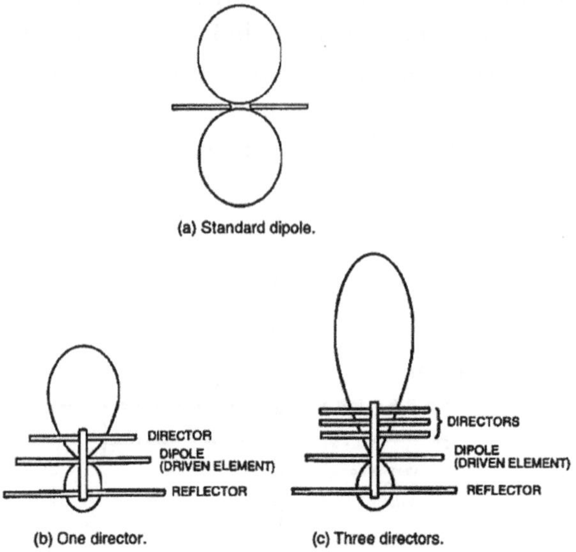

Figure 2. Illustrating the effect of adding reflector and director elements I the antenna pattern, (a) standard dipole, (b) one reflector and one director and (c) one reflector and three directors.

"The gain of an antenna means the amount of increase in signal voltage induced in the driven element of the antenna in question relative to the voltage induced in a reference dipole placed in the same location and with the same resonant frequency. The gain of an ordinary dipole can be increased by the addition of additional elements (called parasitic elements) either in front of or behind the driven dipole element. These parasitic elements are called directors or reflectors depending on their length and position with respect to the driven element. Although they are not connected directly to the driven dipole element, signal energy induced in them is coupled to the dipole through both induction and radiation fields. In general, any antenna having one active element and two or more parasitic elements is known as a Yagi antenna, and is one of the highest gain antennas yet developed in our world."

[Note: the antenna system of the remarkable Passiflora incarnata (on facing page) which I extracted for the first time in the Summer of 2013 because it communicated to me that it was "ready" after four years of having been "conditioned" at the forest edge where it grows. How 'bout that for a complex antenna!]

"It is important to not forget the root system of the plant in touch with the electrolytes of the earth location area and the special electrodynamics active in that particular area. The particular geology of the flower's growth site provides the dominant electrolytes and population of local piezoelectric materials wherein weather conditions create oscillating stresses and strains that, in turn, create oscillating electric fields and electric currents. These, in turn, produce the power source needed to lawfully drive a dipole antenna.

"One must also realize that, at the earth/air interface, a discontinuity in dielectric constant exists but continuity of electric flux lines is required. Thus, a 24-hour diurnal cycle of electric charge transfer develops at this interface as the earth rotates and exposes the flower's locale to the varying intensity of the sun. The more coherent the flower's material medium, the greater will be the number of significant magnitude higher harmonics to the diurnal 24-hour fundamental oscillatory voltage cycle.

"These electro-dynamic oscillatory features are modulated by contributing weather effects to produce some remarkable flowers in remote parts of the earth."[5]

[5] J.D. Kraus and K.R. Carver, *Electomagnetics*, (McGraw-Hill Book Company, New York, 1973).

23

The Multidimensional Simulator Model

What is very interesting to me is that the forty plus years of Dr. Tiller's deep reflection, meditation, and scientific experimentation led him to construct a model – The Multidimensional Simulator – showing how the motive force of intention can travel through space (the vacuum) and influence inanimate and animate matter in the four dimensional spacetime (x,y,z,t) world we see and navigate. That very same model can be used to explain how Higher Intention can travel through the vacuum of space, arrive at the "flower antenna" and install in the extracting water a set of frequencies (information, "coding") that later, when consumed by humans, seem to change the "consciousness address" from which we draw our interpretation of reality.

Dr. Tiller's model arose partly as a result of seeing hard physical data in the experimental outcome that he had not imagined (the phenomenon of space conditioning–among other observations–which necessitates higher gauge state dimensions above our visible space-time with which it is linked.) Even though his "Multidimensional Simulator" model contains theories that cannot overall be tested at this time, it feels right to me, and I think it is the best model that exists to explain the invisible forces I see influencing the material realm.

What is extraordinary about this model is that it bypasses the horribly sticky problem that quantum physicists really haven't been able to answer: when "information" is transmitted through space, does it travel as particles, waves, or both? Furthermore, the particle/wave duality issue concerns primarily the very small quantum level of subatomic particles. But WT's model incorporates the world of the very small (subatomic spaces) AND the world where our body operates (the macroscopic), and posits a very interesting coupling agent called deltron substance that links both worlds together.

The idea that such a coupling agent must exist came as a result of WT further developing the thinking of a Nobel prize recipient in physics, Louis deBroglie, relating to the whole matter of pilot waves coupled with photons of light (seen as particles) to guide them as they travel through space. (It is important to remember that light traveling through space = information traveling through space.)

Relativity theory refers to the speed of light, c, squared ($E=mc^2$) which WT posits exists as two subcomponents: the positive mass particle velocity (which must be less than c) and the information wave velocity (which would have to be greater than c), so that when multiplied together they equal the speed of light squared.

The whole matter of "information" (as a type of light) traveling faster than c thus arises, and WT elegantly developed what he calls "A Biconformal Base-space Approach" to describing physical reality in an expanded model that includes faster than c speed of information transmission. That model defines a domain that is the reciprocal (the inverse: $x^{-1}, y^{-1}, z^{-1}, t^{-1}$) of the normal spacetime (x,y,z,t) reference frame in which we operate.

Our normal space-time reference frame (RF) is named D-space (for Direct space) and the reciprocal RF is named R-space (for Reciprocal space.) Dr. Tiller states, "Since the two aspects cannot directly interact with each other because of relativity theory, it is necessary to invent the presence of an additional substance [a coupler] that is not constrained by relativity theory, because these two aspects clearly interact in the deBroglie particle/pilot wave picture." WT named the coupler "deltron" and felt that it exists as part of "a cosmic activated deltron concentration" linked to emotion. So to this point, the model in nature – without human intervention – consists of two reciprocal 4-spaces interacting to form an 8-dimensional space to which is added a ninth coordinate, deltron substance (δ). WT writes, "When human intervention via human consciousness in the form of the application of human intentionality acts on nature, one must add at least one more coordinate to any meaningful description of nature." That tenth coordinate, I, represents the intensity of human Intention that influences the magnitude of δ.

In old esoteric literature R-space has been labeled as the "etheric" realm (containing the energetic "blueprints" that precede and encode physical manifestation), and WT posits that the parts "that write the waves in this etheric space are the magnetic monopoles. Thus, the electric monopoles operate in direct-space while the magnetic monopoles operate in reciprocal space with a very special type of "mirror" relationship… functioning between them. Via this unique mirror, the magnetic monopoles of R-space generate magnetic dipole images in D-space while the electric monopoles of D-space generate electric dipole images in R-space. This leads to our normal Maxwell equations for electromagnetism functioning in D-space and another set of analogous equations for magnetoelectrism functioning in R-space."

Two features of this model which I find very interesting are:

(1) Objects like planets and stars, which are far away from each other and from earth in D-space, are clustered close together in the very low frequency domain of R-space.

(2) A mathematical connectivity exists between different parts of a defined experimental system even though these parts may be spatially and temporally separated. This forms a solid basis for information entanglement to exist between the various parts of the system.

This is a classical type - as distinct from a quantum mechanical type - of entanglement.[1]

WT proposes that the "9-space domain of emotions is itself imbedded in the domain of mind, a 10-dimensional construct. And all of this is proposed to be imbedded in the domain of spirit (a construct that is thought to be eleven dimensional and higher). The boundary between the 10-dimensional domain of mind and the 11-dimensional domain of spirit is thought to distinguish and separate the relative universe (10-dimensional and below) from the absolute universe (11-dimensional and above.)"

I synthesized WT's entire model into the schematic on the next page.

1 Vision in Action article, p.20.

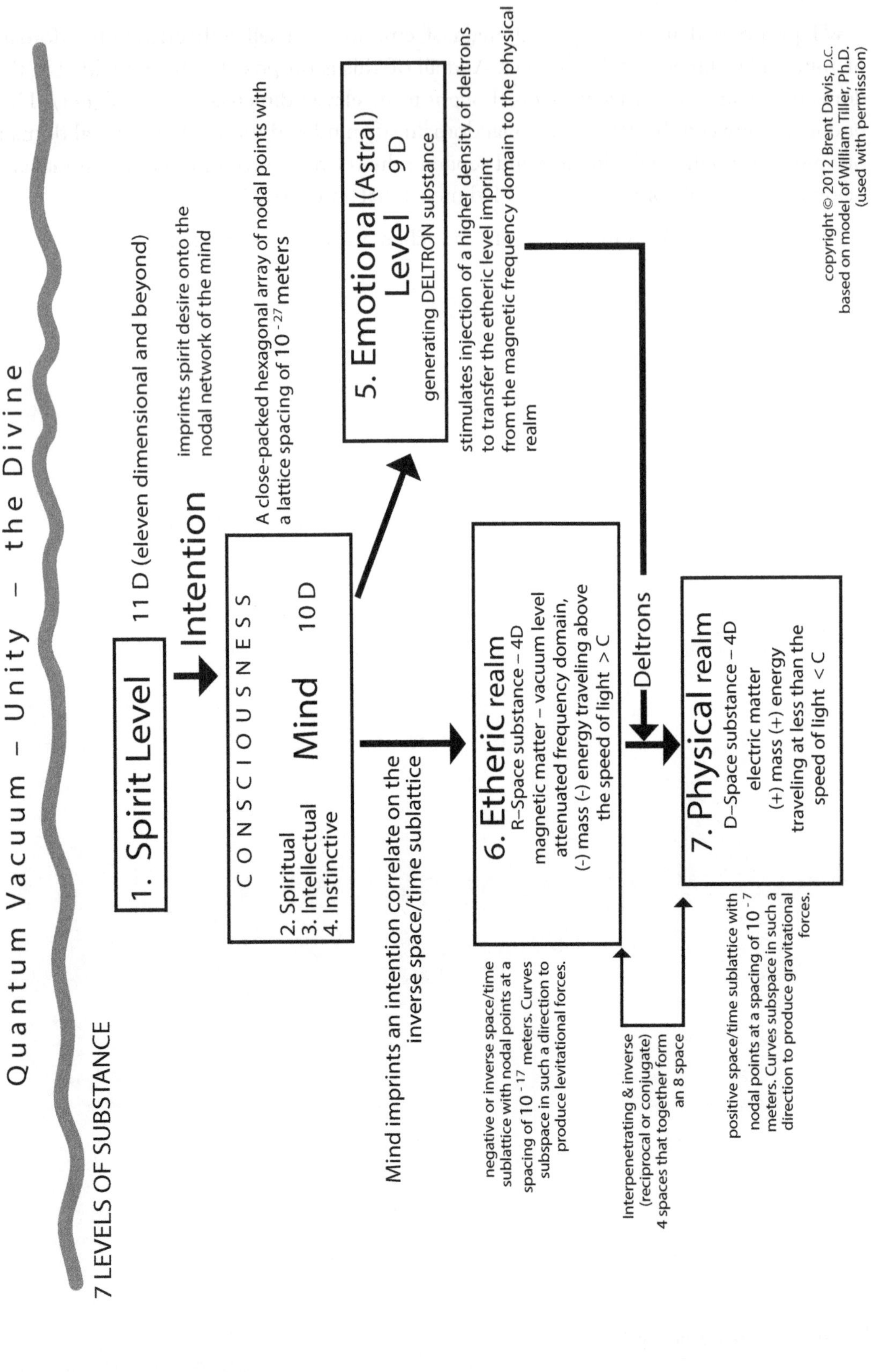
Quantum Vacuum - Unity - the Divine
7 LEVELS OF SUBSTANCE
1. Spirit Level
11 D (eleven dimensional and beyond)
Intention
imprints spirit desire onto the nodal network of the mind
CONSCIOUSNESS
2. Spiritual
3. Intellectual
4. Instinctive
Mind 10 D
A close-packed hexagonal array of nodal points with a lattice spacing of 10^{-27} meters
5. Emotional (Astral) Level 9 D
generating DELTRON substance
stimulates injection of a higher density of deltrons to transfer the etheric level imprint from the magnetic frequency domain to the physical realm
Mind imprints an intention correlate on the inverse space/time sublattice
6. Etheric realm
R–Space substance – 4D
magnetic matter – vacuum level attenuated frequency domain,
(-) mass (-) energy traveling above the speed of light > C
Deltrons
7. Physical realm
D–Space substance – 4D
electric matter
(+) mass (+) energy traveling at less than the speed of light < C
negative or inverse space/time sublattice with nodal points at a spacing of 10^{-17} meters. Curves subspace in such a direction to produce levitational forces.
Interpenetrating & inverse (reciprocal or conjugate) 4 spaces that together form an 8 space
positive space/time sublattice with nodal points at a spacing of 10^{-7} meters. Curves subspace in such a direction to produce gravitational forces.
copyright © 2012 Brent Davis, D.C.
based on model of William Tiller, Ph.D.
(used with permission)

Dr. Tiller describes his Multidimensional Simulator as a teaching machine that places humans in a web-like lattice structure enabling interaction of our mind, body, and soul with the material and immaterial worlds. The simulator consists of consciousness/ energy conversion points that are part of a set of nodal networks, ranging (at the highest level) from a close packed array with very small spacing of 10^{-27} meters all the way down to 10^{-7} meters in the physical realm. (10^{-7} meters is curiously the size range of human DNA.)

Deltron substance (in the emotional realm) interacting with etheric particles traveling faster than light and also with physical particles traveling slower than light brings about energy exchange between them.

The multi-dimensional simulator model cannot be adequately represented on a page because it consists of many planes and curvatures of space in different dimensions that are intermingled with each other. Every nodal point in this model can be seen as a wave interference point in a wave diffraction model. Wave interference points are known to store a great deal of "information."

Dr. Tiller said the following about his model: "The consciousness waves from the mind domain go through the lattice points of the etheric domain because of the reciprocal nature of the two lattices. When the intensity is high enough there is a conversion to a form of energy which is then refracted off the nodal network and through the space-time sublattice. These nodal network points are both converters of consciousness/energy, from the mind to the etheric to the physical, but they also radiate out patterns of energy appropriate for that sublattice."

> *Ancient spiritual traditions and WT's insights lead him to believe that our body/being is constructed in a unique way to interface with the D-space/R-space around us. He posits that the physical/particulate part of our body is fashioned from electric monopole substances, and that the energetic part of our being is fashioned from magnetic monopole, emotional, and mind domain substances. The latter three are all substructures of the physical vacuum, likely enabling us to directly interact with information traveling at greater than light speed – provided the right coupling agent is acting. The previously discussed laboratory finding relating to the uncut flower essence I prepared that was measured in a controlled space showed that the flower frequencies had to be acting outside our normal dimension of space-time, very likely in the magnetic monopole dimension that would then be in direct communion with human "energetic bodies."*

I have alluded previously to the idea that, for the average individual who is not a physicist (or very conversant in math and sciences), there is mind-numbing detail in Dr. Tiller's textbooks. That detail substantiates what I have summarized here. Even in my attempt to make this presentation simple, it is still necessarily complex. That is because we don't normally have a reference frame to orient ourselves to that which is invisible – the vacuum of space – and yet that area is critically important because it contains an astonishingly greater concentration of energy than, for example, the hard material matter of a table or a part of our body. (And the space all around us that appears invisible contains a huge amount of information as well.)

When the vast power in that domain is coupled to reach into our physical world (explained in a model such as that of Dr. Tiller), that is when "magic" occurs, when huge shifts can happen rapidly.

In the Vision In Action article of WT that I quoted previously, he points out that the **vacuum of space** contains an energy density equivalent to approximately 10^{94} grams of mass energy (ten with 94 zeros after it!) – staggeringly large. In practical terms, if we compare the "vacuum energy stored inside a single hydrogen atom (volume $\approx 10^{-22}$ cc) to the total mass energy of all the planets, stars, and space debris in a sphere the size of our universe… the energy stored in the vacuum of this single hydrogen atom is approximately one trillion times greater than that stored in the physical mass of our entire cosmos!"

I believe that specially endowed flowers are connectors that bring an enormous power of spiritual motive force encoded in photon "information packets" from the realm of R-space to help us facilitate change in our D-space physical world.

As I have mentioned previously, it is not possible to clearly define who or what creates the powerful intentions (the deltron substance) that seem to guide information from the magnetic, vacuum realm – at greater than electromagnetic light speed – into the "receiving antennas" of exceptional flowers in D-space to help humans break through their limiting unconscious beliefs that influence our physical reality.

> *Personal experience suggests to me that the flower frequency transformation phenomenon is a co-creative venture with human intention for change being the first stimulus to start increasing the density of deltron substance. Then, quite possibly, "high councils" in the Nature realm coupled with highly evolved "spirit teachers" create the specific information encoding that will be sent to a selected flower, designed to nullify the limiting belief in question, returning it to vacuum space for dissolution.*

The next chapter presents a virtually unknown new scientific technology that was just recently employed to elucidate remarkable characteristics of the five most powerful combination uncut flower essences I have formulated (discussed in Part 3.) Chapter 25 continues exploring the subject of dissolving our undesirable mind conditioning.

24

Bioharmonic Analysis of Five Uncut Flower Essence Combination Formulas

Just as this book was about to be submitted for publication, I received the fascinating information in this chapter from researcher Pier Rubesa (PR). Only weeks before I had submitted to him – for scientific evaluation – samples of five flower essence combinations I created that are performing exceptional feats of mind and spirit transformation.

I was impressed to see that by way of a completely different method PR was able to measure a distinct vibrational pattern outside the glass vial of my flower essence as did Dr. Tiller when he discovered that one of my essences was performing space conditioning. PR's careful analysis demonstrated that the formulas I sent to him for analysis do influence space outside of their containers, and he embraced the possibility that indeed they are performing space conditioning.

Mr. Rubesa is nominally an audio engineer, but it seems to me that he possesses true genius in the area of implementing and analyzing vibrational healing. A friend of mine referred me to his work in 2007. At that time I requested him to run an analysis comparing Combination#1 described in Part 3 to the five-flower rescue formula created by Dr. Bach about eighty years ago (that annually is responsible for over half the sales of all flower essences worldwide). Dr. Bach made his preparation by cutting flowers and immediately immersing them in water for extraction. His original process is being used commercially by nearly all flower essence companies.

PR found that my uncut flower extraction process did produce a clear signature of low frequency vibrations – living information – that was absent in the cut flower traditional essence. Low frequency vibrations are profoundly important in the regulation of living systems.

I was so impressed by his work that I decided to visit PR in his laboratory in Switzerland in 2011. I was accompanied by my friend, Martha, who flew from her residence in Dubai to assist me by serving as a test subject.

So that readers can understand bio-harmonic analysis (performed by the Bioscope), I asked PR to provide me a summary description to include in this chapter. He wrote:

A brief explanation of the term "bioharmonic"

"In my research, I have discovered that living systems emit a subtle vibrational signal that is the result of a "global" organizing force that is inherent in an organism - a plant, an animal, a human being. This signal is related to a cloud of free electrical charges that are part and parcel of all biochemical, physiological and physical interactions combined. In our definition of "life" we need to remember that "life" is not a "thing" but rather it is a "process".

"The term bioharmonic is based on two Greek roots: *bios* meaning "life"; and *harmonia* meaning "to join or to fit together". In science and engineering, the term harmonic is used to describe individual frequency components of a complex signal (i.e. a vibration). Thus in the term bioharmonic, "bio" is related to living things and "harmonic" is related to the joining together (of frequency components). My "unofficial" definition gives us: vibrations that are joined to life and living things - bioharmonics.

"Bioharmonic signals contain information. This can be observed when we capture, record and perform spectral analysis on the signal. The information content that originates from a living system is "carried" on top of the Bioscope reference signal much in the way that "music and voice information" is carried by an electromagnetic radio signal. We "tune" our radio to 107.7 MHz (this is the radio carrier), and we receive a signal containing music and speech information.

"The information contained in the bioharmonic signal can be observed from a variety of perspectives where each is related to a specific quality or parameter of the global vibration. These parameters, or qualities, include the frequency, the amplitude, the phase, the time, the wave shape, and the context (or environment). Our Bioscope reports provide us with the values that are present in the tested samples."

When Martha and I arrived at PR's facility, he ran a base level Bioscope scan of Martha first to look at a read-out of her vibrational status – in essence a real time visualization of the characteristics of her chi field or aura.[1] I then performed a holographic scanning analysis on Martha followed by self-referential statements with applied kinesiology muscle testing to find some of her limiting beliefs. I then administered the corrective uncut flower essence frequencies to remove the limiting beliefs and did my follow-up neuromuscular evaluation to verify the changes. Then a follow-up Bioscope scan was run.

As Mr. Rubesa was observing a significant harmonizing pattern that had been introduced into Martha's field by the essences, he said in the understated manner of a scientist who has

[1] There are many instruments that claim to be accurately showing a visualization of the auric field. The visualizations generated by these instruments are derived values, calculated by complex algorithms, and as such, while interesting, likely do not represent truly valid measurements. Mr. Rubesa's Bioscope obtains direct measurements of vibrational changes in the field energy of living systems based on core technology from the scientifically proven discipline of spectroscopy. They are NOT derived values but are actual direct, real-time values. He has, over many years of effort, taken spectroscopy to a much more refined level.

measured the effect of many different products on the human biofield, "Hmmm. This is VERY interesting."

I knew I wanted to work more with Mr. Rubesa in the future. Wonderfully, he has further refined his analytical methods since that time.

Methods:

An outstanding feature of the Bioscope is its proprietary sensor that is a combination electrode/antenna used to pick up the information carried on frequencies emitted by living systems. The sensor is powered by a computer USB port and uses a very low frequency emission signal, typically between 96 to 250 hertz, that serves as a carrier frequency, that is a low current (milliamp values) modulating electric field with a typical power output that is in the low milliwatt range.

The substance being tested interacts with this carrier signal, and the information of the sample is imprinted onto the carrier signal that is then analyzed. The final graphic display of information in the sample is pure because the carrier signal has been removed from it. Samples can be measured by direct contact (e.g., immersion into the uncut flower essence liquid in a sample vial) OR outside the sample vial container (i.e. not in direct contact with the sample liquid uncut flower essence).

> *Significantly, a fundamental difference was observed between direct contact measurement and non-contact measurement of the samples. It represents a landmark discovery with respect to the potential action of uncut flower essences on humans when they are used as a space-clearing spray rather than being ingested in water. Further, it could have major implications in the whole field of energy medicine and frequency healing.*

Three different analyses were run on samples of each of the uncut flower essence formulas described in Part 3, Combinations 1 thru 5. (The samples were coded, i.e., they did not bear identifying marks of the products as labeled in commerce). The following graphs depict:

(1) Dynamic electric field properties of the samples
(2) Average spectral amplitudes of the samples, and
(3) Average spectral phase of the samples.

These are discussed next in order.

With respect to the following graphs, dynamic electric field properties represent a flow of information over time that is depicted on the X (horizontal) axis. The Y axis (going into the plane of the paper) represents frequency bands measured in Hertz. Here we are looking at bands up to 2500 Hertz (cycles per second). The vertical axis, Z, represents the signal amplitude and is measured in electron volts (between 600 to 800 electron volts).

We see that over time each of the frequency bands shows unique cycles of modulation that represent pulsed information riding on top of individual frequency bands. The different pulse rates on all the different frequency bands represent a HUGE amount of information, which is a distinct identifying signature for each of the five products analyzed.

When PR was explaining the graphs to me he said:

> "Individual frequencies are not that important. The combination of frequencies we see in these graphs, working together form a specific and particular vibration. These products contain frequencies, yes, but vibration is what is important. These products contain unique, specific information and this is demonstrated by the unique energetic signatures (electrical signatures) contained in the products that are displayed here."

I was delighted when I saw the following graphic representations because even though they could not specifically identify the content and action of the information, they did corroborate my thesis that a huge amount of information IS being carried on frequencies emitted by uncut flower essences.

What really surprised PR was the stark difference between the measurement of the uncut flower essences with a probe INSIDE the test vial containing the solution (representative of how the flower energetics could be sensed when ingested) versus the measurement of the flower essences with an electrode/antenna measuring OUTSIDE the uncut flower essence test vial (representative of how the flower energetics could influence an environment when sprayed for space clearing). The dramatic difference between the two types of measurement was consistent with dynamic property, spectral amplitude, and spectral phase measurements.

> *This was heartening to me because it coincided with what I have clinically observed: that the very same essence can affect a patient differently depending on whether it is taken in drops internally or sprayed on or around the body.*

Dynamic Properties

The FECG (Combination#5) direct contact graph below shows an extremely low frequency modulation. PR commented, "The lower the frequency, the more of an impact it has, in certain cases, on living systems. That is because extremely low frequencies are directly related to biological processes. Cell division, for example, is a cyclic process that occurs in the body over many hours."[2]

Sample **FECG** (Combination 5) - Showing the dynamic signal properties in the 1000-2500 Hz range (Y axis) over a period of 15 seconds (X axis)

DIRECT measurement – measurement probe in the sample of the essence. This would be likened to the flower essence's vibrational profile when ingested as drops placed in water.

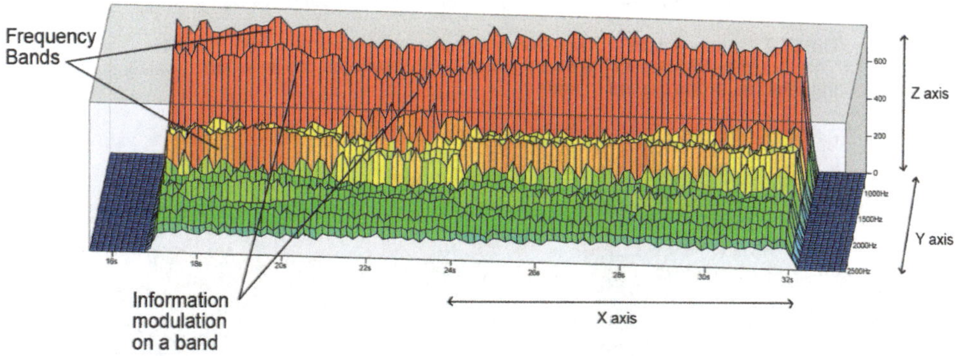

Sample **FECG** (Combination 5) - Showing the dynamic signal properties in the 1000-2500 Hz range (Y axis) over a period of 15 seconds (X axis)

OUTSIDE measurement – measurement electrode/antenna outside the sample of the essence. This would be likened to the flower essence's vibrational profile when sprayed for space clearing.

[2] For ease of reference, each of the coded products that were tested by Mr. Rubesa is correlated with combination formulas listed in Part 3 as follows:
FERV = Combination#1 – called ReviveAll™ in commerce.
FEPU = Combination#2 – called Pure Potential™ in commerce.
FEE2P = Combination#3 – called End2Panic™ in commerce.
FEFFB = Combination#4 – called Freedom Flowers Blend in commerce.
FECG = Combination#5 – called Crowning Glory™ in commerce.

While looking at the graph below of FEFFB-Direct (Combination #4) (measured inside the sample), PR observed, "What we are looking at here is signal coherence. As time goes by we have a strong and organized flow of information inside the system. So if you look at the detail here we see that different frequency bands over time are synchronized. Think about the cylinders in your car. If they are not synchronized, are not organized, as you try to accelerate, your car just will not have the power. Now the same thing happens with individuals. If their field is coherent, their biological processes and the transfer of energy in the body are very efficient. If the system is not coherent then the transfer of information within the system is deficient. And as a result we may experience physical symptoms such as digestive dysfunction, hormonal imbalance, and the like. In essence that is a result of imbalanced transfer of energy."

Sample **FEFFB** (Combination 4) - Showing the dynamic signal properties in the 1000-2500 Hz range (Y axis) over a period of 15 seconds (X axis)

DIRECT measurement – measurement probe in the sample of the essence. This would be likened to the flower essence's vibrational profile when ingested as drops placed in water.

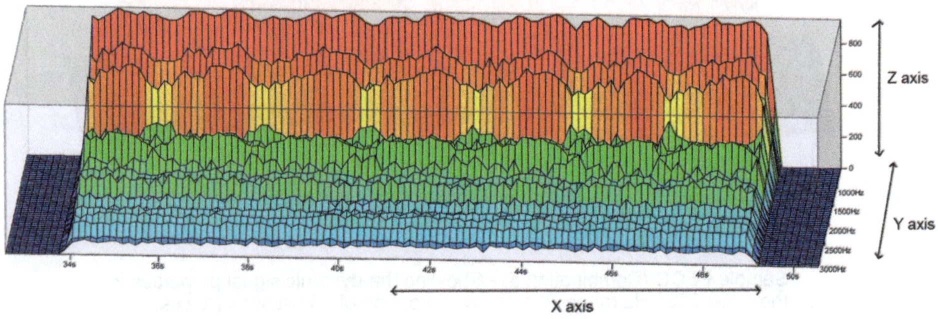

Sample **FEFFB** (Combination 4) - Showing the dynamic signal properties in the 1000-2500 Hz range (Y axis) over a period of 15 seconds (X axis)

OUTSIDE measurement – measurement electrode/antenna outside the sample of the essence. This would be likened to the flower essence's vibrational profile when sprayed for space clearing.

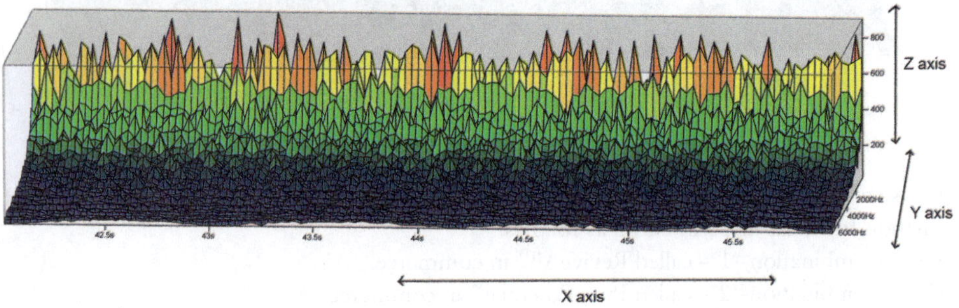

Sample **FEE2P** (Combination 3) - Showing the dynamic signal properties in the 1000-2500 Hz range (Y axis) over a period of 15 seconds (X axis)

DIRECT measurement – measurement probe in the sample of the essence. This would be likened to the flower essence's vibrational profile when ingested as drops placed in water.

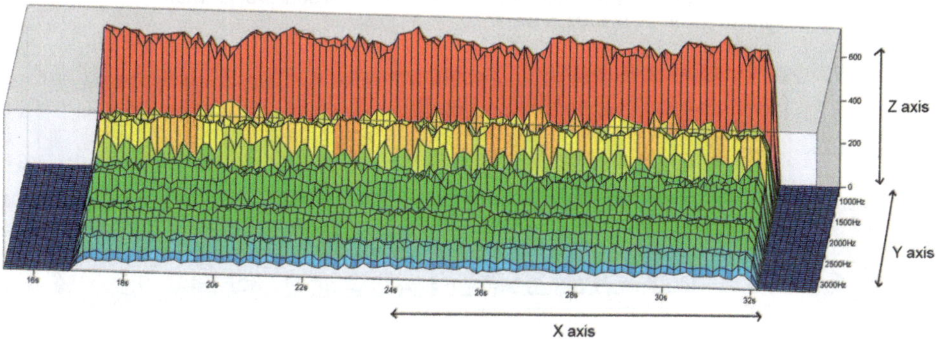

Sample **FEE2P** (Combination 3) - Showing the dynamic signal properties in the 1000-2500 Hz range (Y axis) over a period of 15 seconds (X axis)

OUTSIDE measurement – measurement electrode/antenna outside the sample of the essence. This would be likened to the flower essence's vibrational profile when sprayed for space clearing.

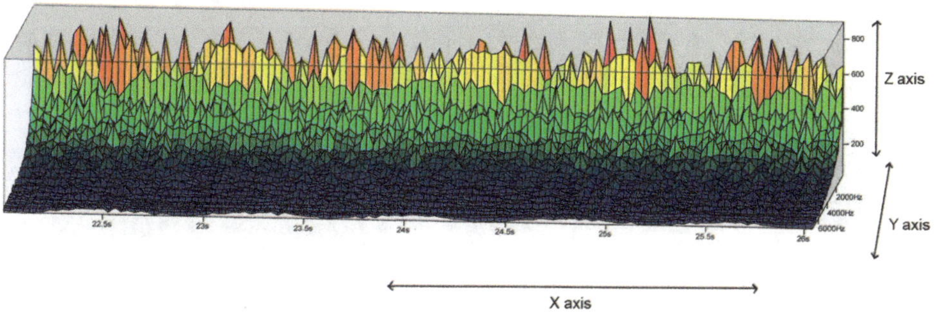

FEPU direct contact

Sample **FEPU** (Combination 2) - Showing the dynamic signal properties in the 1000-2500 Hz range (Y axis) over a period of 15 seconds (X axis)

DIRECT measurement – measurement probe in the sample of the essence. This would be likened to the flower essence's vibrational profile when ingested as drops placed in water.

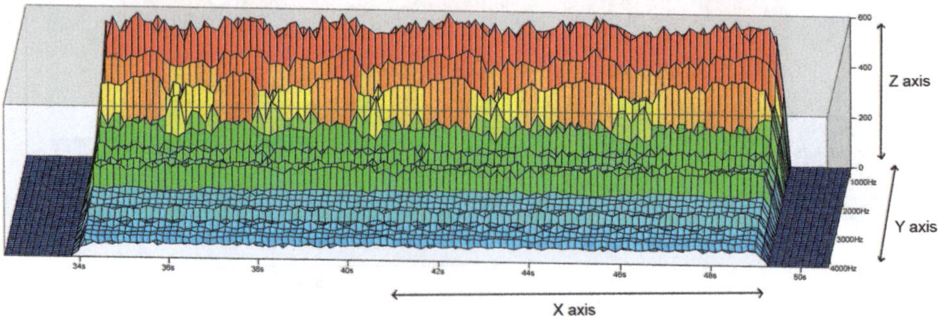

FEPU outside container

Sample **FEPU** (Combination 2) - Showing the dynamic signal properties in the 1000-2500 Hz range (Y axis) over a period of 15 seconds (X axis)

OUTSIDE measurement – measurement electrode/antenna outside the sample of the essence. This would be likened to the flower essence's vibrational profile when sprayed for space clearing.

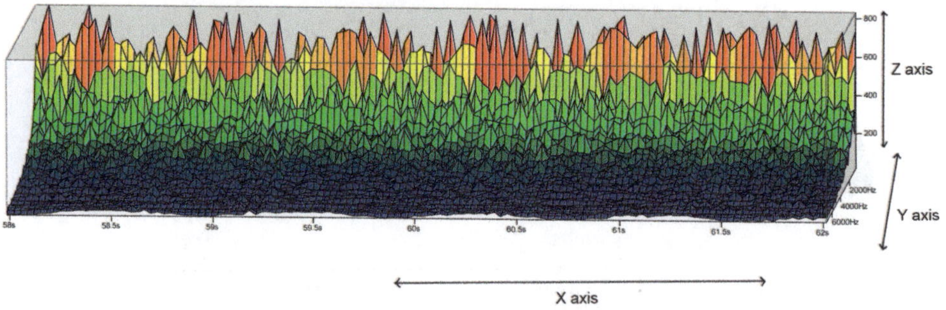

FERV direct contact

Sample **FERV** (Combination 1) - Showing the dynamic signal properties in the 1000-2500 Hz range (Y axis) over a period of 15 seconds (X axis)

DIRECT measurement – measurement probe in the sample of the essence.
This would be likened to the flower essence's vibrational profile when ingested as drops placed in water.

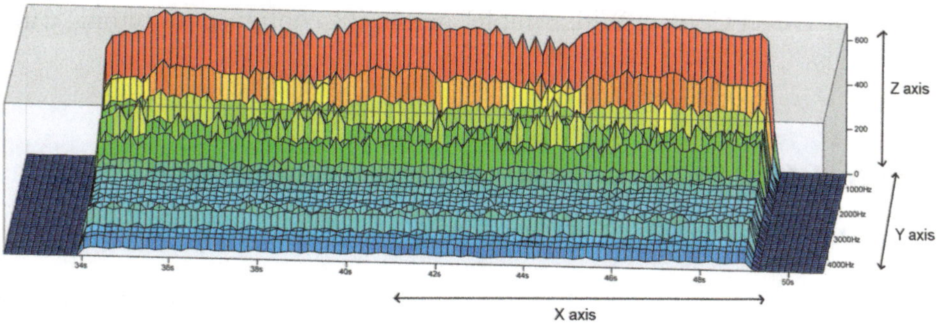

FERV outside container

Sample **FERV** (Combination 1) - Showing the dynamic signal properties in the 1000-2500 Hz range (Y axis) over a period of 15 seconds (X axis)

OUTSIDE measurement – measurement electrode/antenna outside the sample of the essence. This would be likened to the flower essence's vibrational profile when sprayed for space clearing.

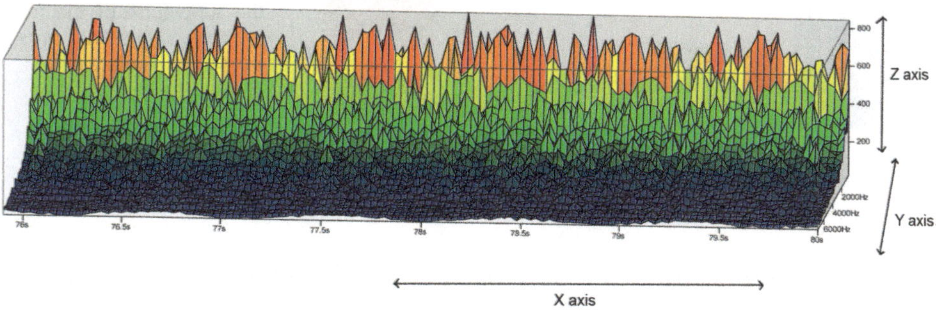

Spectral Amplitude

Spectral amplitude is essentially an absorption spectrum. It is the amount of energy that the sample absorbs or reflects. This type of measurement is basically a measurement of electrical activity of the test samples. While observing the "Spectral Amplitude – Direct Contact With Sample" graph, PR continued his tutorial with me as follows:

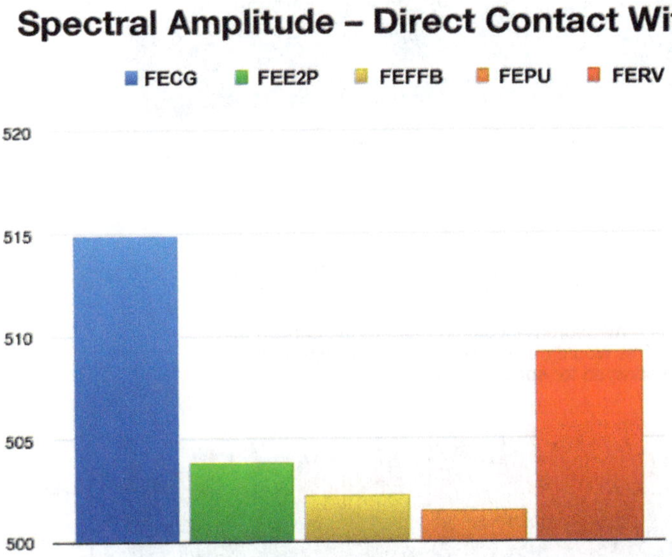

Fig 15. Median Spectral Amplitude Direct Contact The median spectral amplitude is based on the electrical permittivity absorption / reflection characteristics of the samples. Three samples of each product were tested and the first twenty-two (22) frequency components (harmonics) were calculated to obtain the median spectral values, the amplitude of the fundamental excitation frequency was removed from the calculation.

"We see that product FECG (Combination#5) reflects more energy than all the others, and FEPU (Combination#2) reflects less energy than all the others (meaning that it absorbs more.) These flower essence combinations have the ability to affect the electrical balance of a system.

"On an energetic level, one can compare them, in a sense, to stimulants or depressants. If you place FEPU in water it will absorb the electrons from the water, FECG on the other hand will reject the electrons from the water. Due to the fact that FEPU absorbs electrons readily (enters into the body readily) – taking excess electrons out of the body – it would have the characteristic of giving energy to the system (acting as an energizer) because the electrons that are absorbed constitute an energy that has to be placed somewhere, and that energy is immediately returned to the body."

"So we would expect FEPU (Combination#2) to act as an **energetic stimulant when consumed in water.**

"On the other hand, because FECG does not absorb electrons readily it would have the characteristic of forcing more electrons into the body (donating electrons), and that would result in taking energy from the system (acting as a relaxant). The body will work with more difficulty to force the reaction of FECG. This is observed when the measurement electrode is within the sample, directly in contact with it, and this would correlate with the type of reaction we would see when the flower frequency combination is added to water and consumed."

So we would expect FECG (Combination#5) to act as an **energetic relaxant when consumed in water.**

> *When the measurement electrode is placed outside the glass vial containing the flower essence combination it records nearly an inverse effect. This is fascinating because it is showing the interaction of the product (in a closed vial) with the environment. This calls to mind the "space conditioning" phenomenon that Dr. Tiller observed.*

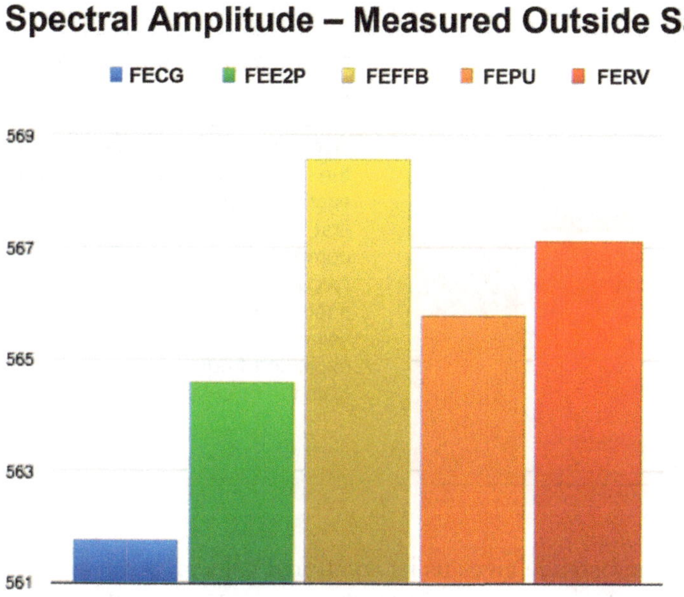

Fig 16. Median Spectral Amplitude Through Recipient The median spectral amplitude is based on the electrical permittivity absorption / reflection characteristics of the samples. Three samples of each product were tested and the first twenty-two (22) frequency components (harmonics) were calculated to obtain the median spectral values, the amplitude of the fundamental excitation frequency was removed from the calculation.

Following the explanation provided in the previous discussion of Spectral Amplitude measured within samples, here as we look above at measurement of samples made on the outside of the test sample vials, we would expect FECG (Combination#5) to act as an **energetic stimulant when sprayed outside and around the body.** On the same basis we would expect FEFFB (Combination#4) to act as an energetic relaxant *when sprayed outside and around the body.*

Spectral Phase

Spectral phase is related to the potential of a system to do work. To understand this, consider the two pins on the electrical jack we plug into the wall. At any one point in time, on one pin the electrical charge is 180 degrees in opposition to the charge on the second pin. Together, they work in a way similar to pistons on a car. As one pushes, the other one pulls. As time goes by, the charge reverses. In the US the reversal time is 60 times per second (60 Hertz), and in Europe it is 50 times per second (50 Hertz).

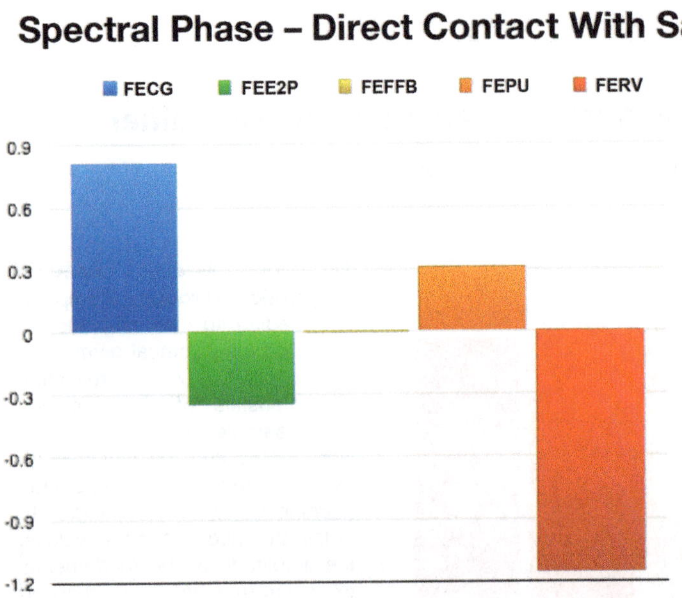

Fig 17. Median Spectral Phase Direct Contact The median spectral phase is based on the electrical spin characteristics of the samples. Three samples of each product were tested and the first twenty-two (22) frequency components (harmonics) were calculated to obtain the median spectral phase values, the phase value of the fundamental excitation frequency was removed from the calculation.

The median spectral phase of a substance gives us its rotational value. Above, for FECG measured within its container, the value of (+) 0.8 on the Y axis tells us that its electrical charge, its electrical spin, is moving CLOCKWISE, whereas FERV (Combination#1) has the strong tendency of its spin moving to the left, that is COUNTER-CLOCKWISE. FEFFB (Combination#4) has a net electrical charge that is neutral when measured in a container. FEPU has a very stable and balancing energy when measured outside its container (graph below).

PR commented, "Spectral phase information is very important from the standpoint of what I have seen scanning thousands of people, because it is likely related to the spin of our chakra system. What we are seeing depicted graphically is the movement of energy in a specific direction.

"This representation shows us movement toward the positive values, clockwise, and movement toward the negative values, counterclockwise WITH AN INDICATION OF THEIR RELATIVE SPEED. FECG is spinning clockwise faster than FEPU."

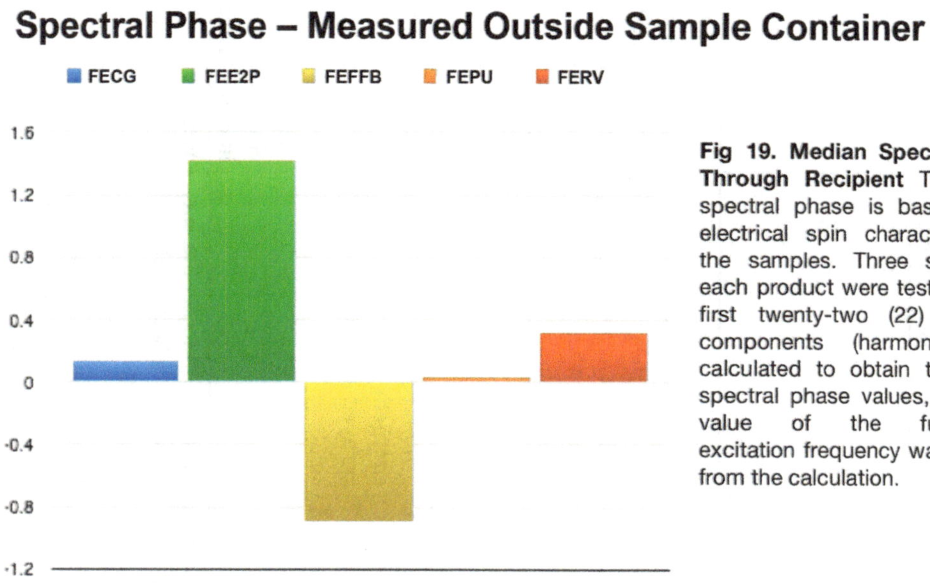

Fig 19. Median Spectral Phase Through Recipient The median spectral phase is based on the electrical spin characteristics of the samples. Three samples of each product were tested and the first twenty-two (22) frequency components (harmonics) were calculated to obtain the median spectral phase values, the phase value of the fundamental excitation frequency was removed from the calculation.

"Looking at FECG, the spin outside the container is considerably slower than the spin of the uncut flower essence inside the container. If you wanted to provide a tranquil setting for someone working, I would ask them to put FEPU on their desk and **spray it** in their space, and for ingesting into the body, I see a potential good use of FEFFB because it is very neutral and would tend to cancel out the extremes of rotational energy in the chakra system whether clockwise or counterclockwise.

"If you wanted to stimulate net movement clockwise or counterclockwise in the chakric system, by **consuming** FECG (clockwise) or FERV (counterclockwise) you would have opposite effects."

Test Sample	Commercial Name	Dynamic Properties Amount of Signal Coherence	Spectral Amplitude Absorption/Reflection Energy Characteristics	Spectral Phase Electrical Potential & Rotational Value
FERV	ReviveAll™	Exhibited the lowest frequency modulation (longest wavelength- strong ability to influence biological systems) of any of the products tested.		Measured within its container its electrical spin is moving counter-clockwise and would tend to move the chakras in that direction.
FEPU	Pure Potential™		Measured inside the sample–absorbs the most energy of the group = would tend to act as an energetic stimulant when taken in water.	Measured OUTSIDE its container its electrical spin is neutral and balancing. **As a spray it would provide a tranquil energy.**
FEE2P	End2Panic™			Measured outside its container (as if sprayed)it spins strongly clockwise.
FEFFB	Freedom Flowers™ Blend	Exhibited the strongest signal coherence=greatest ability to harmonize energy flow within a system.	**Would tend to act as an energetic relaxant when sprayed around the body.**	Measured within its container its electrical spin is neutral. **Consumed internally it would likely balance out extremes of chakric rotational energy in either direction.**
FECG	Crowning Glory™	General Note: All 5 products showed greater signal coherence when measured inside the test sample versus measured outside the sample bottle.	**Would tend to act like an energetic relaxant when consumed in water.** **Would tend to act like an energetic stimulant when sprayed outside the body.**	Measured within its container its electrical spin is moving clockwise and would tend to move the chakras in that direction when consumed.

25

A Quick Way to "Disappear" Our Unwanted Characteristics?

In section 2 thus far, I have focused on the best developed model I have encountered (that of Dr. Tiller) which presents and experimentally tests mechanisms that can help explain how selected flower frequencies might transform us. I wanted to provide the previous details because rigorous science strongly suggests that the sample uncut flower essence I sent for laboratory analysis is operating in a higher gauge state – a realm where information must travel at superluminal (faster than light) speeds. It is a realm where information is much more coherent because of increased thermodynamic free energy. I believe it is that realm with which flowers are intimately entangled (R-space) that draws us into more harmonious alignment with Unity. That is part of what allows flower energetics to coax us into a more balanced life and help us to remove our unconscious mind negative self-talk.

Following the experimental results that have been presented, we can see how, on a fundamental level, flower energetics could "re-write" or reconfigure what we think – above the conscious level – and how we act.

We have seen how selected flowers may install transformational information resident within themselves into extracting water (that we later consume) via their complex antenna array, so that what we access as reality in the form of habituation, stuck in our unconscious/ subconscious mind, can be shifted.

Take heart! For there is another interesting model that can explain a different way flower frequencies might shift our consciousness, and... it is much easier to conceptualize. That's because it came from my very own noggin (intuition) which tends to work from "other dimensional" images that somehow arrive in my brain – in simpler broad brush strokes – rather than in the meticulous detail of brilliant scientists such as William Tiller and Pier Rubesa.

For amusement we might call my following postulate of another floral mind transformation mechanism the: "Down-the-Rabbit-Hole-Into-A-Miniature–Black-Hole-Resorption-Theory!"

What?

Well... as you might imagine, there is a story behind that crazy name. It relates to information that comes from the fields of cosmology and quantum physics. As I was writing this book I searched for what other holistically oriented folks were reading and writing about the quantum mind and the quantum universe. During that time I ran across a book *(Punk Science)* that struck me as particularly interesting because of the background of the author, Dr. Manjir Samanta-Laughton (MSL).

She left the practice of medicine (at an early age, not long after she began), basically due to a series of trials and tribulations that resulted in a shift of consciousness whereby she felt she was able to directly access Source knowledge that revealed some fundamental truths about how our energetic and physical universe is organized. After that, apparently it just no longer made sense for her to practice medicine, as she seemed to be drawn in a different direction.

Then, as often happens, she set about to see what kinds of scientific corroboration might support her theories about the organization of the universe. By amalgamating the thoughts of numerous progressive physicists (including those of Dr. Tiller) with new era cosmology, she came up with specific ideas about how cycles of creation (generation) and destruction (resorption) occur in Nature.

During a peak experience, in an altered state of perception while sitting on an oak tree in the countryside, in her words she "tried to feel the earth's rotation," and was "thrust into an infinity of spinning orbs." She wrote: "In a moment that seemed to transcend space and time, conveying many books of information in just a few seconds, I understood what I now call the Black Hole Principle" (BHP).

In essence the BHP describes "the dynamic balance between the two forces of: creation of particles and creation of light." … "Sometimes light becomes matter and anti-matter and sometimes the balance shifts the other way and two particles cancel out to become light." Remember, light is information.

"First You See It, Then You Don't"

I have previously described the phenomenon of using selected uncut flower frequencies to "disappear" limiting and destructive beliefs we all hold onto that are stuck in the unconscious or subconscious mind. For example, previously mentioned belief in one's inadequacy (poor self-esteem) may materially demonstrate its presence by neuromuscular testing with self-referential statements, and after exposure to frequencies from uncut Tulip Poplar flowers growing on trees in the FlorAlive forest, generally the poor self-esteem indicators vanish nearly instantaneously. (When a retest is done on patients after four weeks of consuming the Tulip Poplar frequencies, in most cases a permanent beneficial strengthening of self-esteem indicators results.)[1] This seems to metaphorically and physically correlate with energy-related features in quantum physics. Background basics will help clarify this.

British physicist, Paul Dirac, felt that information movement in the Quantum Vacuum

[1] See male patient photo p.317.

functions similar to the Bohr atomic model (Fig. 1) which is where he first theorized the existence of anti-matter – the substance that he postulated would have to fill the void of energy left when an electron moves from a lower atomic shell to a higher one.

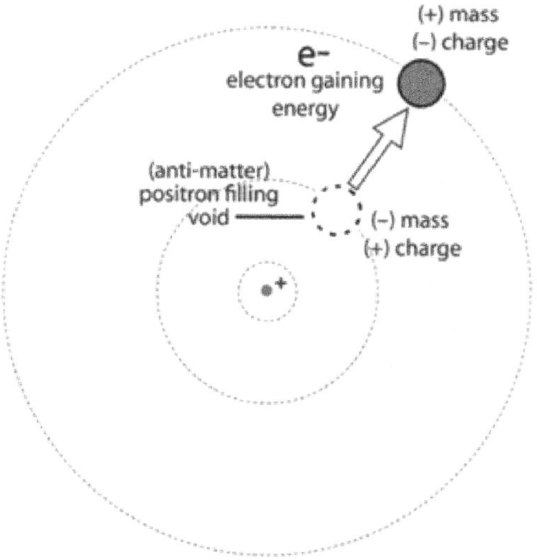

Fig. 1

Figure 2 addresses the "life" of photons as they seem to pop into and out of existence. This information provides important underpinnings in Dr. Tiller's "multidimensional simulator model" as an example of how photons (information) can pop into and out of existence during interactions between anti-matter, matter, and light. Information as photons can leave the vacuum (R-space) and manifest as mass and charge in D-space, and then the reverse can occur.

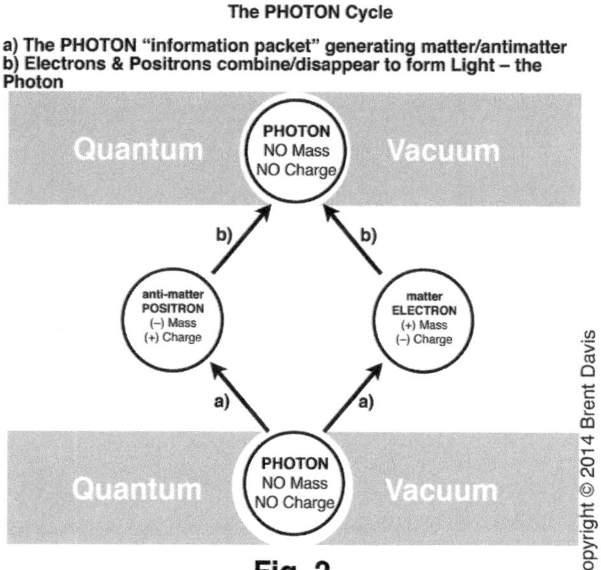

Fig. 2

MSL develops, in her book, a thesis with supporting scientific references that intellectually penetrates the age-old metaphysical model of the cyclic in-breathing and out-breathing of life – how the world is created and "uncreated." The scientific details behind her BHP seem relevant to an unusual experience I had and will now recount. They provide another explanation of how flower frequencies might be "uncreating" the mess of negative self-talk and limiting beliefs that we have stored in our core being which exists largely above the physical domain, in the multidimensional universe – the vacuum of space, or QV (quantum vacuum).

The following peak transcendental experience took place for me just after I finished reading MSL's book. I was in attunement with the flower shown on the facing page, and when I focused my close-up lens on the flower to take its picture, something unwanted from within me was "sucked in" to one of the tubules in the center of the flower (highlighted with the red arrow in the photograph). It felt like something within me disappeared down a "rabbit hole" to be disintegrated in another dimension. And guess what. When I tested that theory clinically on patients in my practice, this flower (which I dubbed "Freedom Flower") eliminates the negativity of some rather extraordinary self-referential statements (listed in Section 3, p.240.) defining beliefs we would never wish to be holding in our mind.

copyright © 2012--2014 Brent Davis

The experience of having a component of myself "sucked into" a tiny opening in the flower (to be disintegrated) made me think of the information that MSL presented relating to miniature black holes – a relatively new theory in cosmology. Before proceeding with that information, however, let us review some basics of black holes in general.

A black hole is classically defined as "a region of spacetime from which gravity prevents anything, including light, from escaping." (Hence it is black because light does not escape). At the center of the black hole is a region called the "singularity" which is subject to infinite gravity and is infinitely dense.

There is a sort of "membrane" barrier between the black hole and the outside world that is called an "event horizon." If something should fall into the event horizon it will be sucked into the black hole's singularity due to infinite gravitational pull, then be resorbed and disintegrated.

There has been a great deal of controversy about the nature of black holes. In 2004 Stephen Hawking presented a theory describing how information could escape from a black hole. MSL cites evidence that light (information) pulsed in the form of gamma rays, X-rays, and sometimes high-energy electrons (which emit light as they decelerate) does escape from black holes.

She then takes a leap of intuition and likens the event horizon to the interface in Dr. Tiller's model of (a) the D-space matter region having light speed <c and (b) the R-space etheric anti-matter realm with light speed >c. She writes:
"The light of infinity reaches the event horizon but splits into antimatter and matter. The positron antimatter occupies the vibration of c2, which is the region that is just faster than ours. This is too fast for us to see or measure, but still exists within space-time. It exists at a faster vibration and has the properties of antigravity and magnetoelectric radiation. It too is found around black holes, and we have found evidence of it."

MSL then continues developing her thesis with mention of the idea that "black holes occur at every level of the universe, from the very large – in the center of galaxies – to the very small – inside atoms and somewhere in between." … "Physicist Nassim Haramein also describes the universe as a holographic black hole fractal with creative black holes at every level."

So… with that background in mind, you can see why I wondered if, perhaps, unwanted "junk" in some part of my being was sucked into a miniature black hole in the Freedom Flower. That, or something similar, may very well have happened and may happen with other flowers as well.

The cyclic "in-breathing (deconstruction) and out-breathing (manifestation) of life" is an ancient teaching that I find to be internally consistent within my experiences. The material action of uncut flower frequencies seems to be operating within that construct.

Nassim Haramein has done a great deal of modeling – with physics and math supporting it – to facilitate a better understanding in modern terms of an ancient unified theory of life. My work with flower essences heightens my awareness daily as to how we may be connected to the Whole, therefore, I particularly enjoy his presentations. After I listened to him speak about the "Resonance Project" he started, I found in one of his online presentations the following statement:

> "The "Schwarzschild Proton" theory describes the nuclei of atoms as mini black holes of infinite density. The space between things, the vacuum, is a fullness rather than an emptiness, and inside the proton is all energy available to all protons in the universe, they being an entanglement of all protons, providing a web of communication across space. This vacuum (zero point) energy connects all things, being ever-present, and defines the material world.
>
> "If everything is connected and is in communication then systems can self-organize. We are participants on the very end of this fractal structure of space looking back at ourselves and receiving feedback from the multiverse, the network of information that we are part of, adding to it from our own perspective. More than being a designed creation, it's a self-organizing system learning about itself, and the information that it gathers coalesces and synergizes to produce the next set of questions in this information feedback network. God is everything interacting with everything, learning about "itself," self organizing and reorganizing, a constantly updating system, making a very complex organism in a short amount of time, that is present in the space-time structure, creating higher and higher levels of complexity and organization.
>
> "There are similar and complementary dynamics occurring on a macrocosmic scale down to subatomic particles, unified by a fundamental physics."

The serendipity in my life that I have described so far could not occur without a connection to the Whole, without a state that in physics is called "entanglement." (There can surely be progressive and regressive entanglement!) So I would like to explore a final mechanism related to that phenomenon.

Could it be perhaps that selected flower frequencies, when they "hit the mark," are removing a tangle of unwanted thoughts and beliefs that seem to be wound around us rather tightly from an historical perspective?

My sense in working with my patients and myself is that some of our entanglement is so extensive that it can be truly difficult to disentangle – to eliminate. **So to me the idea that disentangling flower frequencies are directed through space to help us is VERY heartening.** It is wonderful to think that there can be divinely coded floral information zipping through the quantum vacuum *at greater than light speed* undoing the mess that we (and others) have created over time! If the speed of disentanglement is high enough, it can save us lots of grief (and trips to healers).

26

DisEntanglement

A New Concept for Explaining How Flower Frequencies Seem to Unravel Our Bound Up Past

"Uh Oh. I just keep getting more tangled up!"

Due to "populist physics," there is at least vague familiarity with the meaning in physics of "entanglement." Yet a basic review of some elementary principles will be helpful for many readers. Once we understand entanglement, my concept of dis-entanglement can be more easily appreciated.

Historically, as physics evolved, it was discovered that atoms contain a huge amount of space within relative to the size of its subatomic particles, and when one tries to measure the characteristics of an electron moving in that space at any one point in time, it is challenging. That is because electrons exhibit properties such that they seem to be a wave of probability in a vast sea of subatomic space.

Though it is not an easy concept to embrace, (counter-intuitively) electrons are potentially everywhere within the domain of the atomic orbit at any given time. (That is technically referred to as being in "superposition.") They are a probability wave and can only be accurately pinpointed when they are measured, then an electron can seem to materialize out of a probability wave into actual particle presence. First it is a wave, then it is a particle. As we have seen previously, this is referred to as particle/wave duality. (Dr. Tiller's work sheds entirely new light on this conundrum due to his reciprocal space model.)

Quantum entanglement is a phenomenon whereby particles such as electrons and photons interact, become linked with respect to factors such as position, momentum, spin/polarization, and then upon separation retain a peculiar relationship. When one part of the linked characteristic is measured, it automatically and nearly instantaneously influences the other part, regardless of distance of separation.

The whole phenomenon of entanglement had its origin when Werner Heisenberg (from the perspective of quantum mechanics) wrote his famous "uncertainty" paper of 1927 (that became known as the Heisenberg Uncertainty Principle) dealing with the issue of measuring location within an atom, stating: "The more precisely the position is determined, the less precisely the momentum is known in this instant, and vice versa." He was referring to measuring, at the same instant, the relation between the position and the momentum (mass times velocity) of a subatomic particle, such as an electron. What he proposed was that the more accurately one locates the position of the particle, the less accurately one can determine its momentum. Somehow those characteristics invisibly influence one another, and one cannot know both characteristics accurately at the same time.

The quantum mechanics idea – that linked components of a particle can influence each other instantaneously (or nearly instantaneously) – would require greater than light speed operations, violating the speed limit of light implicit in Einstein's Theory of Relativity. For that reason, Einstein with his colleagues, Boris Podolsky and Nathan Rosen, designed a thought experiment (that became known as the "EPR Paradox") to disprove the implications of Heisenberg's theory, thereby preserving his own theory.[1]

It was many decades until physical experiments were devised and carried out, showing that non-local actions at a distance were a real phenomenon. (Einstein was mistaken!) It is possible using laser light to link a pair of photons (which will have polarization planes orthogonal – at right angles – to each other), separate them at various distances, and then measure the polarization of one of the pair. Without measurement, each of the photons is in a state of superposition with no definable orientation of its plane of

[1] The Wikipedia entry on "Quantum Entanglement" states, "Following the EPR paper, Erwin Schrödinger wrote a letter (in German) to Einstein in which he used the word "Verschränkung" (translated by himself as "entanglement") to describe the correlations between two particles that interact and then separate, as in the EPR experiment."

polarization. As soon as the plane of polarization is measured and determined on one of the linked photons, nearly instantaneously the plane of polarization of the other photon can be accurately predicted. It is postulated that this relationship holds true regardless of a vast distance of separation.

On a quantum level, this collapse of wave function and the influence this has on its paired particle is accepted as valid. (Only photons have been experimentally proven to be entangled.) Science News[2] reports:

> "In 2008 ...Gisin and colleagues measured entangled photons 18 kilometers apart at exactly the same time and calculated that any secret signal between the two would have to travel 10,000 times faster than the speed of light. The long-distance record is held by a team of physicists including Anton Zeilinger of the University of Vienna, who measured entangled photons 144 kilometers apart on two Canary Islands."

This is great news for entangled subatomic particles, but what about entanglement in the larger world that we live in?? That is where the remarkable theories and physical proof of Dr. Tiller stand out. His experiments demonstrated in the macroscopic world that the action of imprinted thought –intention– changes by entanglement, in predictable and intended ways, physical characteristics such as pH and temperature.

When I asked Dr. Tiller why this profound information is not widely known, he mentioned that when he was doing the work (around the turn of the millennium), because it incorporated "paranormal" components (i.e. meditation and projected intention), it would be refused publication in influential journals.

Dis-Entanglement and Uncut Flower Frequencies

My theory of flower frequency dis-entanglement gradually emerged over the years that I have been watching how obstacles are removed, and problematic "knots" in patients' lives seem to unravel, when exposed to the correct flower energetics.

The characteristic that I often sense around a given patient is that he or she is linked in a space-time and reciprocal space-time way such that the physical brain and attendant actions in D-space are entagled with memories and beliefs that are stored in the vacuum in R-space (the akasha). That is cross-culturally consistent with many ancient spiritual insights.

It is clearly suggested from measurements in Dr Tiller's lab that the uncut flower frequencies I sent him for assessment operate in R-space. What I sense and "see" around patients is the operation of that other dimensional influence of flowers

2 November 20, 2010; Vol 178#11(p.22).

(R-space) in a sort of mind map setting. Rev up your visualization and imagination please![3]

Let's use a type of "being map" (depicted on the next page) to represent the entangled states in our past to which we are historically linked (and by which we are often bound up tighter than the bark on a tree!). When we are linked so powerfully to a former state, it often assumes the position of being unalterably real. It is such tightly associated conditioning that often defies our conventional "new age" efforts at removing it.

When I see a new patient, one of the first things I do is assess the influence of the deepest level stressors – those due to our unconscious beliefs and memories. Then I use all means at my disposal to begin unraveling the damage of past hurtful memories.

I have mentioned the great benefits of the manual chiropractic reflex procedure called Bio-Energetic Synchronization Technique. I sense that is very valuable for removing the polarity reversal in the physical brain that occurs with shock and trauma. (From my experience, EMDR – a well known memory clearing technique – does a similar thing but is not as powerful.) To heal trauma from deep in the past, that which is stored in the quantum vacuum, it feels to me like the uncut flower frequencies generally provide more profound clearing and re-patterning as compared to EMDR or BEST.

That is especially the observation of several talented clairvoyant healers who have sat by the side of my patients observing as I administer my flower preparations. There seems to be a consensus seeing and sensing among them that when the right flower frequencies are chosen, they begin disentangling core problems on a deep causal level far into higher dimensions in a manner not seen with hands-on treatments. Then a healing cascade takes place, clearing through the dimensions until it reaches our physical space-time reality: D-space.

It is impossible to represent the complexity of just one person's life in the setting of our multidimensional universe, the totality of everything he/she interacts with and the results of those interactions. So rather than making a futile effort at a more fully accurate representation, I elected in the diagram on the next page to take the simplest approach possible in providing a reference example.

It is a hypothetical representation of three beings interacting in a rather short time frame, and includes none of the multitude of modifying factors and historical characteristics that, in reality, would exist around each of the individuals. A depiction closer to reality would be a tangle of thousands of intersecting lines so multi-dimensionally complex as to be overwhelming.

3 Wikipedia defines a mind map as "a diagram used to visually outline information. A mind map is often created around a single word or text, placed in the center, to which associated ideas, words and concepts are added..."

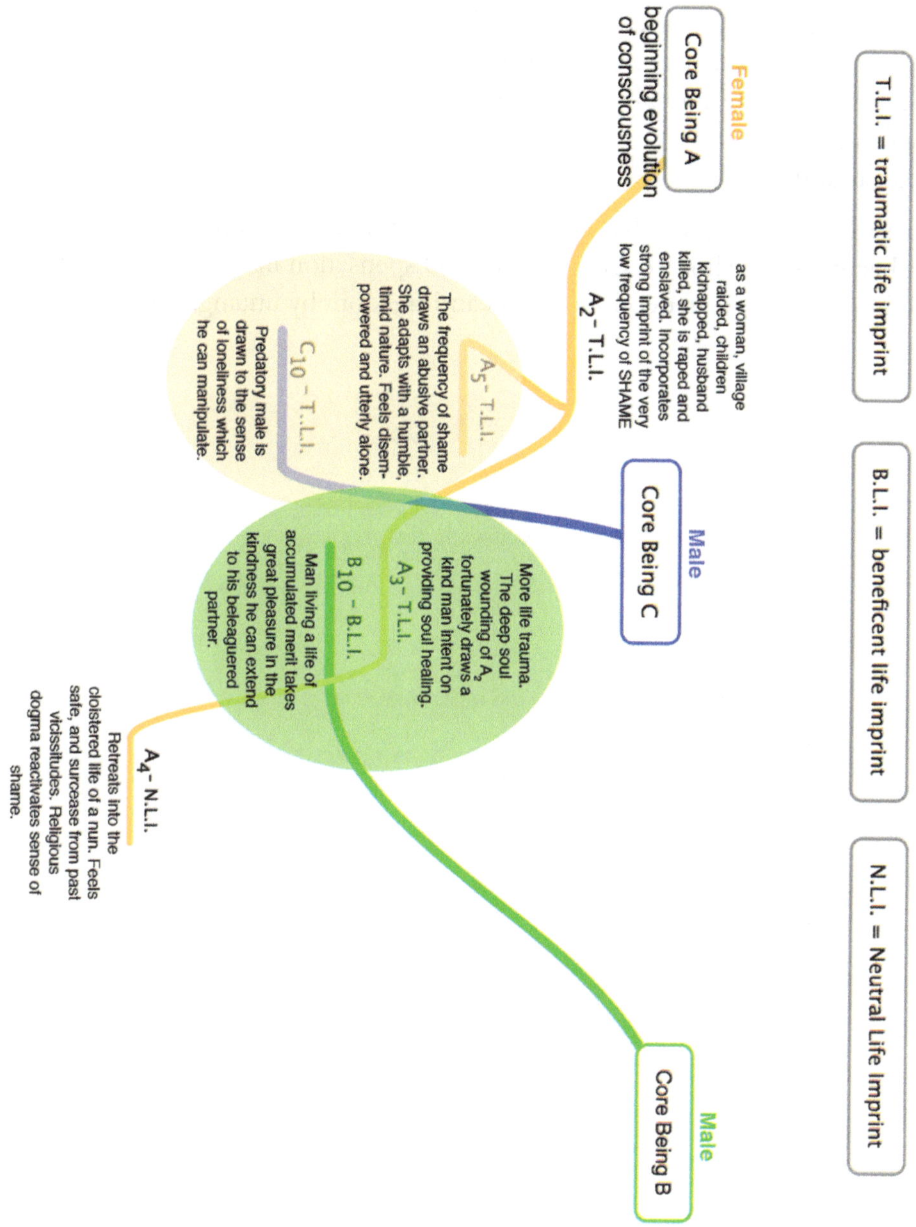
T.L.I. = traumatic life imprint
B.L.I. = beneficent life imprint
N.L.I. = Neutral Life Imprint
Female
Core Being A
beginning evolution of consciousness
as a woman, village raided, children kidnapped, husband killed, she is raped and enslaved. Incorporates strong imprint of the very low frequency of SHAME
A_2 - T.L.I.
Male
Core Being C
Male
Core Being B
A_5 - T.L.I.
The frequency of shame draws an abusive partner. She adapts with a humble, timid nature. Feels disempowered and utterly alone.
C_{10} - T..L.I.
Predatory male is drawn to the sense of loneliness which he can manipulate.
More life trauma. The deep soul wounding of A_2 fortunately draws a kind man intent on providing soul healing.
A_3 - T.L.I.
B_{10} - B.L.I.
Man living a life of accumulated merit takes great pleasure in the kindness he can extend to his beleaguered partner.
A_4 - N.L.I.
Retreats into the cloistered life of a nun. Feels safe, and surcease from past vicissitudes. Religious dogma reactivates sense of shame.

The model in Figure 1 is built around a hypothetical core entanglement with the condition of SHAME, described by Dr. David Hawkins in his popular book, *Power vs. Force*, as the lowest destructive frequency humans experience. That is just one of a score of regressive themes that each of us may have within that must be transmuted or uncreated if we are to evolve in consciousness.

There is a wild flower called False Dandelion (growing in the FlorAlive forest where I have my country residence) that has a profound ability to remove the effects of buried shame within us. Interestingly, on top of shame lies hurt, and then more superficially, rage and anger. When the core energy of shame is diminished, a great deal of additional healing can unfold.

In Part III following, we shall put together all that has been presented up to now so that it becomes clear how to use the Divine Dispensation in special flowers to accelerate humanity's path to greater consciousness and freedom by untangling our "mess from the past."

27

What Happens When Uncut Floral Frequencies "Touch" the Human Being?

How Can They Cause Change?

Cross-culturally, in spiritual traditions of antiquity, there was recognition of the unity of life. The flower frequencies I work with seem to be powerfully tied in to that Unity. Historically our body/mind complex was regarded as being invisibly interconnected with everything in Nature around us, ranging from what was thought to be the beginning of "consciousness" in the mineral kingdom all the way up to super-consciousness of entire star systems. To understand how subtle flower frequencies can influence us, we must consider the interconnected web of life.

Relating to that topic, ancient beliefs in modern language are peripherally explored by sampling the early works of researcher and parasychologist, Dr. Rupert Sheldrake, and physicist, Dr. David Bohm, and then by looking at a more recent broad synthesis of holistic modeling contained in the writings of Dr. Edgar Mitchell, former astronaut and founder of the Institute of Noetic Sciences.

Sheldrake's schema is well defined with precise articulation of components of his model, and that precision is generally not reflected in common present-day usage. In his model, terminology he introduced – "morphic resonance" and "morphic field" – seems to draw considerably from the concept of "morphogenetic field" as it was described in cell biology and embryological development in the early part of the twentieth century. In other words, it was not vitalistic or metaphysical in nature. At that time, "fields" of cells were observed that seemed to influence the development of undifferentiated cells placed adjacent to them. This suggests some sort of action at a distance and that some sort of innate "programming" from a guiding source could be exerting an influence on newly developing cells. When gene theory started to be developed, it marginalized concepts around morphogenetic fields.

At any rate, the common usage of "morphogenetic field" now seems to be more vitalistic in nature than Sheldrake intended. It loosely connotes a zone or a matrix in space (an interconnected web) that can influence matter non-locally and could presumably be linked to some sort of guiding spiritual intelligence.

When I see photos of the face of David Bohm (1917–1992), it affects me similarly to being in the present-time company of Dr. Tiller. One senses a very high level of intelligence, and yet it seems he must have resided in a domain well beyond the ego-dominated realm commonly found in academia. He appears to have been worldly wise and easy to be around. Who knows? I look at a lot of facial photos, and that is just my intuition. What is clear is that his capacity and presence was so enormous that he was able to contribute at the highest level to academic theoretical physics while at the same time being a pioneering "borderline metaphysician."

In a seminar he gave very near the end of his life[1] he spoke about the dilemma of human thought, explaining that it can create more problems than it solves. He gave the following insight which strikes me powerfully because it relates so much to themes within this book:

> "...the general tacit assumption in thought is that it's just telling you the way things are and that it's not doing anything – that 'you' are inside there, deciding what to do with the info. But you don't decide what to do with the info. Thought runs you. Thought, however, gives false info that you are running it, that you are the one who controls thought. Whereas actually, thought is the one which controls each one of us. Thought is creating divisions out of itself and then saying that they are there naturally. This is another major feature of thought: Thought doesn't know it is doing something and then it struggles against what it is doing. It doesn't want to know that it is doing it. And thought struggles against the results, trying to avoid those unpleasant results while keeping on with that way of thinking. That is what I call 'sustained incoherence'."

What an exposé of the destructive component of our unconscious mind – and stated so succinctly! "Sustained incoherence"...Precisely why we benefit from the antidote of massive COHERENCE in selected flower frequencies.

> "Thought doesn't know it is doing something and then it struggles against what it is doing. It doesn't want to know that it is doing it."

I have witnessed this exact phenomenon clinically hundreds and hundreds of times in the process of performing testing of self-referential statements. The statements I use reveal what is generally hidden in the unconscious mind, and the individual being examined is often perplexed because they know they "do not believe that." One of my favorite startling self-referential test phrases (and one that emerged from the first high mountain Peruvian flower I extracted) is: "No matter what action I take, I will be defeated."[2]

Very few people recognize when that unconscious destructive belief is operating, and when it is evident as being true upon testing, the patient frequently looks up at me

[1] 1992. *Thought as a System* (transcript of seminar held in Ojai, California, from 30 November to 2 December 1990), London: Routledge.

[2] Frequencies from a flower named Maquilina (growing around a sacred glacial lake located at 15,000 feet altitude) eliminate this unconscious belief.

startled saying, "I don't believe that!" With a smile my response is, "You don't believe that *consciously*."

Dr. Edgar Mitchell's "Dyadic Model" effectively describes the interconnected web of life using modern language that includes important concepts from physics. It strikes me as the best summary model available. It integrates concepts of holographic information as it exists in the quantum vacuum. It regards every cell of the human body as a quantum device, possessing both local (particle) and nonlocal (wave) aspects. It envisions the "totality of our physical and subjective experience as a multimedia hologram resonant with ourselves and the zero-point field… a quantum hologram."

It posits that "this quantum mechanical resonance is an exchange of energy with the zero-point field such that the "phase change" (interference pattern) of quantum emission carries complete information about the history of the system.… In other words, one may think of the quantum resonance as carrying the information to create a hologram of the entire experience of an individual, including inner experience…In the dyadic model, no experience (information) is ever lost, but carried forward in the quantum hologram that resides in the zero-point field." In addition to resonance, there are three other required components of the model: entanglement; coherence/quantum correlation; and non-locality.

In order to understand what happens to the human body when it comes in contact with the quantum fields associated with uncut flower frequencies, it is helpful to understand the following leading edge information that was compiled for me by the very bright molecular biologist, William Brown, after he had personally experienced the action of uncut flower frequencies I formulated for him.

An Intercellular Matrix Frequency Transduction Model for the Coherent Transmission of Information from Liquid-Crystalline Aqueous Nanostructures.

William Brown[3]

"The Intercellular Matrix is a vast consortium of extracellular and intracellular proteins that form an extensive and continuous network through every tissue of the biological system, linking together every nucleated cell in the body. Anatomically it is comprised of the basal lamina and connective tissue, which together forms an encasing that has traditionally been presented as the dividing border of the tissues of the body. However as functional studies have begun to elucidate, this network is far from being purely structural and compartmentalizing, and instead is an interface that, in association with the immunological cells of the body, defines the function and architecture of the

[3] http://williambrownscienceoflife.com.

biological system.

> *Information encoded in light is transferred from the coherent water-biomolecule complexes within floral cells and is stored in the liquid-crystalline lattice of aqueous [water] nanostructures.*

"At the moment the aqueous nanostructures are introduced into the human biological system, the light is nearly instantaneously transferred to the coherent water-biomolecule complexes within the human tissues. The light is quasi-instantaneously transmitted along the Intercellular Matrix directly to the DNA molecule, where decoding of the information contained within the electromagnetic transmission takes place.

"To understand how the light is transmitted through the Intercellular Matrix to the DNA, it is necessary to understand the molecular architecture of the system.

"One of the primary bio-molecular components of the Intercellular Matrix is Laminin. The connective/vascular tissue is primarily composed of Laminin, and it is the primary matrix protein of the Nuclear membrane. The human DNA molecule is directly attached to the Nuclear membrane, and it is this Nuclear Matrix that is involved in the regulation of the DNA molecule itself. In addition to other matrix-associated molecules, such as proteoglycans, water macromolecules are complexed to the matrix in a specific lattice configuration. (It is important to note that proteoglycans are some of the most electronegative molecules within the biological system, and water is specifically involved in interactions with the quantized electromagnetic field.) Electromagnetic excitations are propagated along the matrix through the extracellular laminins, to the intracellular microtubules to the nuclear laminins where the information is transmitted directly to the DNA.

"Delocalized Pi electrons of the nucleotide residues are excited by the electromagnetic transmission and produce a corresponding electromagnetic signal. The energy involved in this electromagnetic excitation is transmitted via the DNA to a quantum nonlocal field where morphic behavioral patterns are stored in the energetic crystalline template of the field. Note that the crystalline patterns of this field are on the size of 10^{-7} meters, which is the same size as the DNA molecule.

"The information transmitted from the flowers via the aqueous nanostructures and Intercellular Matrix change the Morphic behavioral pattern that is "tuned" into by the DNA molecule. This can result in a nearly instantaneous change in human behavioral patterns and perspectives."

Summary Overview

How uncut flower essences produce personal transformation

For thousands of years the energy (or "essence") of flowers has been used to uplift humans. In recent history, to obtain conventional flower essences, flowers are cut and placed in spring water to absorb their energies. I have pointed out that the action of severing the flower from the mother plant disrupts critical features of "coherence" that influence the degree to which re-patterning information can be collected and conveyed from the flower to the water in which it is floating and which is later diluted and used for treatment.

To obtain a greater degree of transformational ability from flowers, I developed a unique method to extract the totality of a flower's information while preserving the greatest amount of coherence of that information. Second, I developed from the field of applied kinesiology muscle testing (that gave rise to energy psychology) a way to test the action of the transformational flower frequencies real time on living subjects, and to verify the extent to which the change induced by them remains permanent.

Now it is possible by reproducible means to rapidly evaluate an individual to detect specific limiting and self-sabotaging unconscious beliefs. Once those are identified, it is then possible to find flower frequencies carrying pulsed information that will cancel the undesirable beliefs (in a sense "overwriting" them), and at the same time install a new and positive mind and spirit orientation. There is another phenomenon that seems to be occurring due to action of the uncut flower frequencies: dismantling of our transgenerational mess from the past. It is depicted on the following page and is recommended as a visualization process for reinforcement of transformation.

Scientific evidence attesting to the enhanced abilities of uncut flower essences I sent for laboratory evaluation as compared to conventional flower essences is presented in appendices at the end of this book. Please review that information after the FlorAlive Transformation Process on the following pages. Then...on to personal transformation in Section 3!

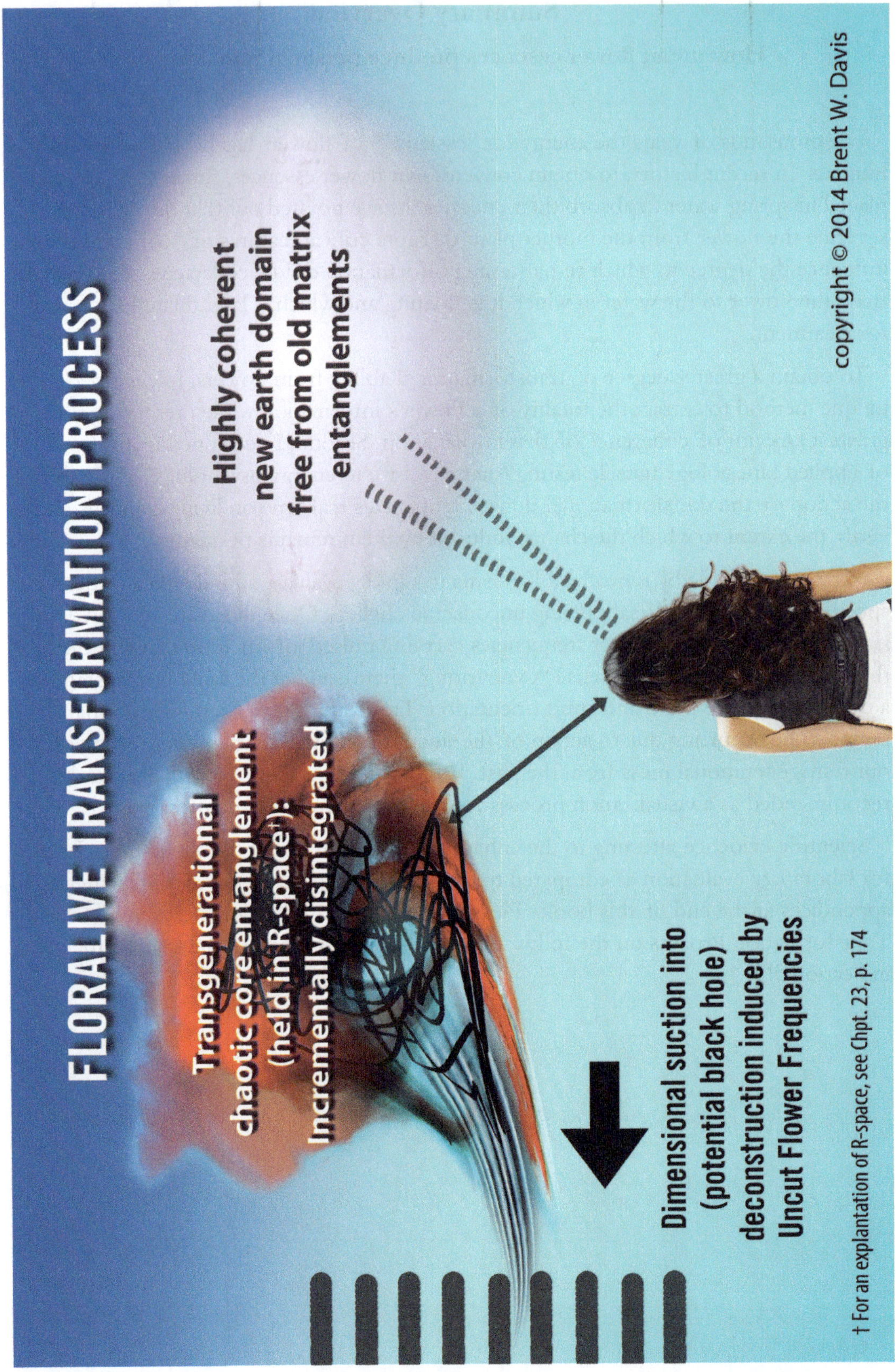
FLORALIVE TRANSFORMATION PROCESS
Transgenerational chaotic core entanglement (held in R-space†): Incrementally disintegrated
Highly coherent new earth domain free from old matrix entanglements
Dimensional suction into (potential black hole) deconstruction induced by Uncut Flower Frequencies
copyright © 2014 Brent W. Davis
† For an explanation of R-space, see Chpt. 23, p. 174

Visualization Process

The depiction of the FlorAlive Transformation Process is true to life, as far as I know. That is, clairvoyants attending my flower essence workshops report that what I show in the schematic is what actually happens multi-dimensionally when a consumer takes the uncut flower essences I have described in this book. (I use this graphic when I teach FlorAlive practitioner workshops.)

In addition to the flower essences' ability to nearly instantaneously "overwrite" limiting beliefs, acting as "liquid software for the mind," they also act as a catalyst to begin a process of deconstructing the consumer's record of stored trans-generational experiences and memories that are tangled and confused.

Individuals that are engaged in personal transformation quite often like to do visualizations. When you take the uncut flower essences described in Part III (and especially the powerful combination essences), I recommend this visualization:

1. Imagine standing in a tranquil space.
2. Above you and to the left (embedded in hyperspace that you cannot normally see) is the stored mass of your past accumulated experiences. On average, there is a lot of tangle and heaviness in this stored record of our being that does not serve us.
3. On the right, you can sense a luminous new domain that has been constructed by benevolent intention and consciousness that is designed to free humanity from suffering. The flowers that I work with are directly linked to this positively coherent space.
4. When you consume the uncut flower essences that I have described, they immediately link you concurrently to both domains.
5. Then, at the same time, the chaotic core entanglement on the left is deconstructed bit-by-bit and sucked from dimensions where it is stored (through a point of entry) to be dissolved (possibly in a black hole.)
6. On the right, the harmonious clear space draws our consciousness upwards for integration into a luminous new reality characterized by the many benevolent and yet powerful forces resident in certain special flowers – the ones that are from "saints among herbs."

FlorAlive Self-Repair/Recovery Model

Premise:
The subconscious holding of memories of emotional trauma and/or abuse causes and maintains our deepest stresses. It is responsible for maladaptations in our personality. The proper uncut flower frequencies can "overwrite" stored memories of trauma, fundamentallty helping to restore balance.

Nearly everyone suffers from emotional or physical trauma or abuse

=

- Recurring violation of one's personal space
- Recurring core invalidation

Leads To:

- "TURNING OFF"
- "CHECKING OUT" of One's body

and eventually what acts like post-traumatic stress syndrome.

Affected individuals close down, for the world is perceived as unsafe. As a result, the afflicted enter into:

- JUDGEMENT to determine what is safe and what is not, and
- CONTROL to manage all of life so that it stays safe.

Those affected lose the ability to receive
– LOVE
– FRIENDSHIP
– FINANCIAL PROSPERITY
and, of course, recovery and real healing.

By Removing Stored Memories of Trauma

You Experience Greater Ease, Joy & Prosperity

PART 3

Self-Help Rapid Reference

- How To Remove Your Deepest Sources of Stress
- How To Liberate Your True Potential

START WHERE YOU ARE

How To Effectively Use This Self-Help Guide

Introduction

As I finish up this book at the beginning of 2014, there is a popular song that is getting quite a lot of airplay. It is produced by a fellow who has a special following among young club dancers. It's got a catchy and fun tune for dancing, and I was surprised to find some profound lines in the song:

Wake Me Up

"Feeling my way through the darkness
Guided by a beating heart,
I can't tell you where the journey will end,
But I know where to start. ...

I wish that I could stay forever this young,
Not afraid to close my eyes,
Life's a game for every one
And love is the prize.

So wake me up when it's all over,
When I'm wiser and I'm older,
All this time I was finding myself
And I didn't know I was lost.

Aloe Blacc, lyrics/vocal
Tim Bergling (known as *Avicii),* producer

"And I didn't know I was lost." A great deal of this book is about the process of discovery – about awakening. There are periods when we don't even know we are lost, so how do we find our next steps?

I made strong efforts in previous sections of this book to explain how, in my practice, I am able to discover in the unconcious mind of my patients hidden characteristics often responsible for keeping them lost. When the right vibrational essences are given to "overwrite" internal "error messages," my patients' mind obstacles are removed, and the next steps in their life open up much more readily. There is often more ease and more joy. They are no longer lost. This is my wish for you. But you must remember, this aid to awakening is an ongoing process. Taking a set of flower frequencies once and stopping is not the way to achieve truly visible results.

So if you have the opportunity to find a friend familiar with muscle testing, or a health professional that will have fun testing you, go for it! Evaluate the remedies that you think might apply in your case (with small test vials you can obtain from the producer [1] for a nominal price) by using self-referential statements (listed following) that apply to each essence.

When you find the ones that work to remove your limiting beliefs or destructive memories, order and use the full bottles that have shown they will work. This is a revolutionary process for employing flower essences, and I hope one that will be widely adopted because it is so much more effective than the questionnaires and interviews used conventionally for flower essence selection.

It eliminates guessing and the question, "I wonder if that essence did anything?" [2]

In many cases, however – where the form of evaluation mentioned above will not be used – I recommend the following:

In the single flower essence list coming up, take special note of Heartmend, for it is needed by so many people. Whenever we have lost a person, relationship, or special animal friend, it can leave a long-lasting energetic "hole" in our heart. When that is repaired, so much in our life can improve and open up to new possibilities.

Right along with Heartmend, pay attention to Flor de la Luna, for it restores our ability to receive love, and that is blocked to a great extent in many good people. Choose some of the other single remedies that may be appropriate, and take them as well.

When you feel that you need to strengthen your direct connection to God-Source, Unity, or however you describe your sense of a Higher organizing principle, consider Flor del Oso (what some Peruvian shamans call "the king of the high places").

Don't forget Tulip Poplar if you would benefit from a boost in your self-esteem!

There is a fascinating way to discover if you might need Blue Water Lily uncut flower essence that can create a profound shift in your life. When you are having self-referential statement screening done on yourself, IF you answer true to your own name (Mary as an example for a woman), "My name is Mary," and your muscle stays strong as it should, and THEN you state something like, "My name is ________," a man's name that is unusual for you, for example, "My name is Fernando," and you test as true to that, there is serious reversal going on within you. Try other men's names, and in this syndrome, they will also test as being your own name. (This same phenomenon applies

1 Available from FlorAlive® by calling 800-274-3727.

2 Along with this book, I have developed conjointly a health professional training seminar that will allow the trainee to rapidly learn a screening technique enabling sophisticated energy matching of the correct flower frequency to the individual client or patient. A description of that program is listed in Appendix 8. Lay people interested in holistic health are certainly able to benefit from this training as well, and with it help their family and friends.

for men using women's test names.) So what is happening? In the many cases I have seen that demonstrate this profound distortion from reality, my sense is that at some time in the individual's stream of development, a shock occurred so large as to "short circuit" normal functioning of reality, and an alternate reality had to be adopted. When the uncut flower frequencies of Blue Water Lily work their magic, the distorted reality leaves and one can achieve more coherent unity. When clairvoyant professionals have watched me administer orally test drops of Blue Water Lily to those who are ready for it (and who fail the screening test described above), they comment that they perceive a huge cascade of higher dimensional shifts taking place in the karmic entanglement of the client/patient, and that there is movement toward unraveling of karmic knots and greater coherence.

Quite often the six flower "initiatory blend" that I created years ago, Combination # 1 is a great place to start, especially if you are eager, ready, and willing to shift. If you have been told you need to shift but are quite resistant to the idea of change, then the best place to start would probably be with Combination #4.

Then... when you are ready for the "Big Guns," look closely at Combinations #2 through #5. Over time, the majority of my patients benefit from all or most of those.

A key concept to embrace deeply is that the most profound source of stress that most people ever experience is very often invisible. So when you discover the stealthy hiding place of stressors and learn to employ the uncut flower essences I have been blessed to discover, you have at your fingertips the most powerful anti-stress tools available – from the standpoint of core cause.

Core Causes of Stress and How To Eliminate Them: Beyond Classical Stress Theory

Classical stress theory derived from a study of the body's physiological response to external agents (stressors) such as exposure to cold and caloric deprivation. *It never examined the greatest stressor of all:* unconscious self-sabotaging thoughts resident within nearly everyone – thoughts that play ceaselessly 24/7 and enervate us at the core.

The main reason that omission occurred was because unconscious mind stressors were not part of Dr. Hans Selye's frame of reference when he conducted his seminal research on response to stressors.[3] His extensive studies were carried out on laboratory animals. Furthermore, interest in the role of the unconscious mind would not come into greater prominence until two things happened. First, there would have to be an emergence of a greater number of transformational thought leaders (teaching us to pay

[3] From 1945 to1977, Dr. Hans Selye had an extraordinary career at Université de Montréal in Canada. He essentially coined the word "stress" which eventually became adopted into languages around the world. He profoundly influenced the entire field of endocrinology.

attention to what we create from our mind realm),which began increasing in the 1980s; and second, the discovery of energy "psychology" would have to emerge out of the chiropractic discipline of applied kinesiology (muscle testing).

At the beginning of this book I wrote a disclaimer that bears repeating:

> "Transformational flower frequencies described in this book are to be used as an adjunct to all practices that support the evolution of consciousness, and are never intended to be used as a substitute for self-reliance and responsibility on the path to greater awakening."

The reason for mentioning this again is to fully address the objection I have occasionally heard from individuals who take pride in their practice of self-growth disciplines. They have made comments along the lines of: "So what? Are you suggesting that all I have to do is just put little drops of uncut flower energy into water, sip that, and all my problems will somehow vanish?"

On the occasions I have heard that, I reply that is not at all what I am suggesting. I then explain that I have discovered a very effective way of speeding the evolution of consciousness and empowerment precisely by having witnessed and clinically examined hundreds of individuals *who have tried*, to the best of their ability, to use mindfulness and all transformational tools available – AND YET still failed to break through some of their most stubborn inner limitations. Upon adding the right vibrational essences, previously stalled transformational efforts begin to yield results.

> *What is remarkable is that when different flower frequencies are used over time–as indicated– it represents a whole new approach to the evolution of consciousness. It is a distinct departure from the main way flower essences are conventionally employed which is for the alleviation of – or rescue from – acute symptoms.*

With the guidelines I present below, we can see prevalent sabotaging unconscious beliefs that are invisibly restraining many good people. We can then maintain what we feel are the best consciousness practices, and additionally take hold of these pure and powerful floral "tools" to turn the tide so that we can more easily achieve our true destiny.

Maslow's Hierarchy of Needs

One of the starkest observations from Maslow's psychosocial model is that no matter how lofty our spiritual and social ideals might be, they are completely irrelevant if we cannot meet basic needs for mere survival.

Please review the "Steps to Self-Actualization" chart on the next page. Table 3.1 on the page after that is a listing of uncut flower essences that help us rapidly transmute the patterns and tendencies that restrain us in our evolution, helping us ascend the Hierarchy of Needs more easily. (Our most intransigent patterns are very likely stored

Steps to Self-Actualization

Abraham Maslow created the "Hierarchy of Needs" model to explain human motivation. His extensive research showed that deficiency needs, in general, must be met before desire will arise to satisfy growth needs and engage self-actualization. Uncut flower essences can strongly accelerate movement up the steps of deficiency needs so that we may live a suffiency-based existence.

ABUNDANCE

DEFICIENCY NEEDS

Self-Actualization

People here tend to be:
a) solution oriented;
b) self-reliant;
c) socially compassionate;
d) accepting of others;
e) appreciative of life;
f) creative and inventive;
g) interested in helping others achieve self-actualization.

Esteem Needs

Due to the fact that many people are carrying the subconscious burden of physical or emotional trauma, they feel diminished, and cannot perform to their true capacity. So it is important for health to be able to achieve, be competent, and gain approval and recognition. Once experienced, undesirable ego issues can be transcended.

Belongingness & Love Needs

The desire for relationships, affection, and family is a strong instinctual drive, and in the absence of our own subconscious barriers, can be fulfilled with greater ease. Several uncut flower frequencies I have discovered support this step in our life.

Safety Needs

The desire for stability, security, law, order, and protection are primitive in our consciousness, and correlate powerfully with our level of trust in Universal Order (or lack of it.) Political agendas in recent history have grievously manipulated our instincts in this area to create a climate of fear and distrust. Many uncut flower frequencies exist to fortify our trust in the Universe, and move beyond worries about safety so that we can take higher evolutionary steps.

Biological & Physiological Needs

The primal need for water, food, and shelter will normally take precedence over the evolutionary needs above.

Humanitarian agencies and spiritual organizations dedicated to helping the disenfranchised, traumatized (PTSD), poor and suffering, would do well to distribute specific UNCUT flower essences to help remove hopelessness, futility, and painful memories of trauma.

as part of our "core memory" in R-space of the quantum vacuum that was described in Part 2. It is my impression, corroborated by the direct viewing of clairvoyants, that by unknowable means select uncut flower harmonics break into that core memory so that it can be re-patterned.)

Table 3.1

Safety Needs	**Combinations #1, 3 & 4** described next all have applications at this first stage of evolution. Generally they are applied most effectively after some of the single essences below have been selected and taken in a blend. **Blue Eyed Grass** – Installs the knowing: "I am free from the effects of emotional abuse/trauma." **Wild Iris** – Abolishes the subconscious belief, "I am disconnected from the source of ALL life." Installs the knowing: "I am free from the threat of all beings." **Herb of the Cross** – Installs the knowing: "I am comfortable being out of control." **Blue Lechenaultia** – Installs the knowing: "All is well in my life" **May Apple** – Installs the knowing: "I am comfortable in all social situations." **Pink Lady Slipper** – Installs the knowing: "I trust in my life." **Madame Fate** – Installs the knowing: "I am free from the influence of negative thoughts and beings." **Green Jade Flower** – Installs the knowing: "It is safe for me to feel." **Yellow Root** – Abolishes the subconscious belief: "I am afraid to feel fully." **Spigelia** – Abolishes the subconscious belief: "I have abandoned my body." **Cat's Claw** – Installs the knowing: "I am free from abusive energies." **Goldenseal** – Abolishes the subconscious belief: "I am an innocent victim." **Herb of the Cross**– Abolishes the subconscious belief: "I am unsafe unless I am in control." **Joe Pye**– Abolishes the subconscious beliefs: "If I step into my power, I will be annihilated." and "I am too sensitive for this world."

Belongingness – Love Needs	**Combinations #2 thru 5** described next all have applications at this stage of evolution. **Flor de la Luna** – Installs the knowing: "I allow myself to receive love." **Wild Iris** – Abolishes the subconscious belief: "I am essentially unlovable." **Heartmend** – Repairs the heart that is broken as a result of loss of love or relationships. **Blue Water Lily** – Abolishes the subconscious beliefs: "I am only lovable when I am disabled," and "I am unworthy of love." **Butterfly Flower** – Installs the knowing: "I have the courage to maintain an open heart." **Door To Change** – Abolishes the subconscious belief: "I can never reverse the consequences of my past negative karma." **White Ginger** – Installs the knowing: "My life is filled with sweetness." **Sacred Lotus** – Installs the knowing: "I can trust my heart."

Esteem Needs	Combination # 5
	Tulip Poplar – Installs the knowing: "My self-esteem is strong and balanced." **False Dandelion** – Abolishes the subconscious belief: "I am filled with shame." **Star Spirit Flower** – Abolishes the subconscious belief: "My mistakes are unforgiveable." **Chagapa** – Abolishes the subconscious belief: "No matter what I do I will never be good enough." **Blue Gentian** – Installs the knowing: "I am kind to myself." **Blue Lechenaultia** – Installs the knowing: "I accept and appreciate who I am." **Button Snakeroot** – Installs the knowing: "I am free from self-doubt." **Zarcilleja** – Abolishes the subconscious belief: "I accept the cumulative suffering of all women as my own." **PurushPurush** – Installs the knowing: "I am comfortable with my feminine beauty" or "I am comfortable with my female essence." **Hydrangea** – Installs the knowing: "I am free from judging myself." **Talla** (the workaholic's flower) – Abolishes the subconscious belief: "My value as a human being is measured by how hard I work." **Culver's Root** – Installs the knowing: "I have released my past failures." **Flor de Oro**– Abolishes the subconscious belief: "I am worthless."

Self-Actualization Needs	Combinations #2 & 5
	Flor del Oso – Installs the knowing: "I am fully receiving input from my highest spiritual resources." **Red & Green Kangaroo Paw** – Installs the knowing: "I have the means and the power to restore paradise on earth." **Button Snakeroot** – Installs the knowing: "I am humble in the knowledge of my power." **Yellow Root** – Abolishes the subconscious belief: "I can't receive anything more because I already have too much to deal with." Installs the knowing: "I allow myself to receive limitless income." **Acrobat Orchid** – Installs the knowing: "Life is a playful game," and abolishes the subconscious belief: "I take myself too seriously." **Blue Lechenaultia** – Installs the knowing: "I know that all is well."

Suffice it to say that drops of vibrational essences from even the most blessed flowers obviously will not eradicate protein/calorie malnutrition in the millions of third-world inhabitants worldwide who suffer that plight, and who do not have the luxury of contemplating evolution of consciousness.

What is remarkable, and also tragic though, is to observe first world inhabitants who have an abundance of food and material resources, living in an unconscious state of psychological starvation. Such individuals live in scarcity consciousness while in the midst of plenty. I have watched that sad condition reversed hundreds of times by employing the following uncut flower essences, and scores of talented health professionals world-wide have reproduced my findings.

Breaking Free From Enslavement

For me, one scene in Quentin Tarantino's 2013 movie "Django" is particularly compelling and relevant to a central theme in this book.

Actor Leonardo Di Caprio chillingly plays the role of Calvin Candy, an unbearably arrogant proprietor of the infamous Southern plantation, "Candyland." Mr. Candy takes pleasure in his reputation for the brutal treatment of slaves, some of whom he has conditioned to kill each other for mere sport. Lecturing his guests at the dinner table, he emphasizes his view that blacks are miscreants, destined to suffer and languish because of a pathetic inborn trait of submissiveness. With the following quote, he disdainfully questions how that could be:

> "I spent my whole life here in Candyland surrounded by black faces, seeing them every day – day in and day out. I only had one question: 'Why don't they kill us?' Three times per week Ben [the head of the household slaves] would shave my daddy with a straight razor. If I was Ben, I would have cut my daddy's throat – but he never did. Why not?'"

This disturbing movie scene highlights the dilemma of the earth's most disenfranchised inhabitants (though resorting to murder or violence to escape from domination is certainly not a solution). What is it that keeps people feeling that they are powerless to change their lot in life? For the most part, they seem not to be able to summon the strength to break the chains that bind them, ensuring a bleak existence.

I took a look on the internet to see what others might have written about the phenomenon of mind enslavement. I found the following articulate statement on a blogpost from an interesting site called New Civilization Network (http://www.newciv.org):

> "You are governed, your mind is molded, your tastes formed, your ideas suggested, largely by people you have never met or heard of before. This is the logical result of the way in which society functions today. Vast numbers of human beings must co-operate in this controlled manner if they are to live together in peace and prosperity. The real issue or concern is whether or not you are aware of the fact that your freedom has been substituted by mind enslavement. The conscious and intelligent manipulation of the organized habits and opinions of the masses is an important element in society. Those who manipulate this unseen mechanism of society constitute an invisible government that is the true ruling power."

In addition to the "unseen mechanism of society" mentioned above, there surely seem to be convoluted "programs," inherited beliefs, and memories in peoples' unconscious mind that maintain complacency and prevent the evolution of consciousness. That upsetting notion is born out again and again clinically when I screen, on my patients and on myself, self-referential statements (that prove to be beliefs) which are limiting and self-sabotaging. It is a marvel to me how I have somehow run across rare flowers having a vibrational character that can dismantle and remove terribly disempowering beliefs from the subconscious mind.

I have been further amazed when I have retrospectively analyzed *the sequence* in which I have been guided to discover flowers that clearly possess actualizing powers as well and enhance positive manifestation. Analyzing the characteristics of the flowers in the five most powerful combinations that I have discovered to date brings home this point. The combination essences below are listed in the order in which they were developed by the Guidance assisting me.

LIBERATION and EMPOWERMENT!

Uncut Flower Essence Combinations

I created my first combination essence around the turn of the new millennium. I felt there was a need to develop a flower essence combination more relevant for overcoming obstacles that must be confronted in modern times (as compared to Dr. Bach's five-flower rescue formula created early in the twentieth century to help people recover from shock and trauma).

Recall from previous explanations that when my unusually prepared vibrational essences work their magic, destructive and limiting test phrase statements will be rendered untrue and nullified, and liberating and empowering beliefs will be installed within us as a new reality. "Coding" collected directly from Divine Source with absolutely minimal human interference[4] appears to be achieving something unique and truly beneficial for these times.

The first formula I created is comprised of the following six flowers listed with their associated test phrases. It is based on the beginning implementation of a model that developed on its own in the context of my clinical practice, where I saw that fundamental concepts from trauma work in holistic psychology had been taken into consideration by my guiding "heavenly steering committee," and apparently transmitted to me. The model is simple yet profound. (See the schematic on the next page.)

- First, remove and transcend subconscious memories of emotional and/or physical abuse or trauma;
- Second, restore the ability to receive (especially, to receive love) which has been shut down as a result of emotional injury,
- Third, initiate the beginning of empowerment of our High Mind – that direct connection with Divine Source. This leads to our maximum potential.

[4] Insights that gave rise to an advance in flower essence preparation is described in Chapter 5.

FlorAlive Stages of Repair

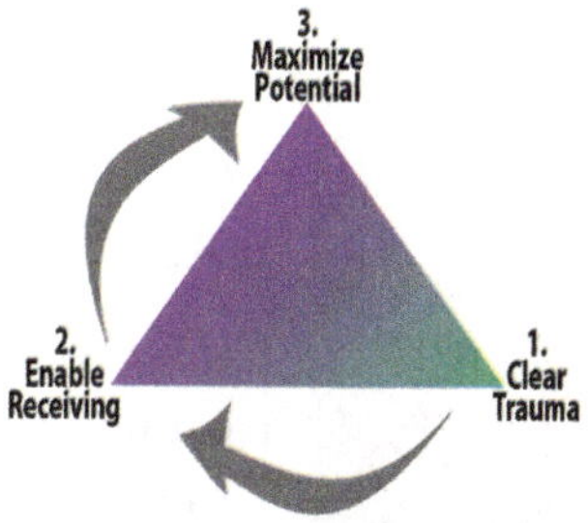

Combination #1

A combination of frequencies from UNCUT flowers of: Blue Eyed Grass (Sisyrinchium angustifolium), Wild Iris (Iris cristata), Tulip Poplar (Liriodendron tulipifera), Maquilina (Bomarea species), May Apple (Podophyllum peltatum), Pink Ladyslipper Orchid (Cypripedium acaule)[5]

Potential Uses:

This assembly of vibrational essences from living, uncut flowers can:
1. Help reduce emotional pain and trauma from this life or trans-generationally;
2. Effect mental and emotional uplifting;
3. Diminish body/mind response at a core level to a broad range of stressors and limiting beliefs.

It is still chilling for me to look at the depth of meaning in some of these phrases following and to ask, "What would naturally be the consequence of believing these test phrases to be true?"

A type of mind enslavement would naturally be one of the effects.

A huge number of individuals in the world believe at the level of their unconscious reality that the following inhibiting phrases are true, and that the empowering phrases are not. It explains some of why we see such great depths of hopelessness, feelings of personal disempowerment, and despair.

It is critical to remember that many people are not aware (or find it hard to believe) that they hold these unconscious beliefs. When disabling unconscious beliefs are revealed in clinical screening, I frequently hear, "Oh, I don't believe that!"Yet, when evaluated with properly administered muscle testing and self-referential statements (as described previously), characteristics often reveal themselves that people are hesitant to accept because they could be interpreted as frailties or failure in any number of ways. I explain to those I work with that self-sabotaging beliefs are not frailties, but are simply part of the human condition on earth at this time, *and are up for change now.*

[5] This multi-flower uncut flower essence combination is sold under the trade name ReviveAll™.

	**Maquilina -** *(Bomarea species)* (Border of a Sacred Lake in the High Andes Mountains): (removes belief): "Regardless of my efforts, I cannot influence the outcome." (removes belief): "No matter what action I take, I will be defeated."
	**Wild Iris -** *(Iris cristata)* (FlorAlive forest): (removes belief): "I am disconnected from the Source of ALL life." (removes belief): "I am essentially unlovable."
	**Blue Eyed Grass -** *(Sisyrinchium angustifoluim)* (FlorAlive forest edge): (affirms belief): "I am free from the effects of emotional trauma/abuse."

	**Tulip Poplar -** *(Liriodendron tulipifera)* (FlorAlive forest): (affirms belief): "My self-esteem is strong and balanced."
	**May Apple -** *(Podophyllum peltatum)* (FlorAlive forest): (removes belief): "I lose my power when others don't listen to me."
	**Pink Lady Slipper -** *(Cypripedium acaule)* (The Wilds of Northern Canada): (affirms belief): "I trust in life." "I trust in my life."

When I was in college, I happened to study the ethnology and herbal traditions of people in the Balkan states. I remember reading a curious account that always stayed in my mind. A famous gypsy herbalist from that region was describing how critical it was for his success to collect certain herbs from special sites. He was speaking about the therapeutic ability of a particular herb that happened to be common, growing plentifully right near his encampment. He mentioned that to obtain the desired effects from that herb, there was no point in collecting it locally. He had to travel several days' journey to a spot underneath an old stone bridge. He would collect and use only the herb from that area.

When I began fieldwork in the High Andes mountains years later, a knowledgeable shaman there iterated a similar observation. He told me that some of the flowers I was interested in would only express their powerful transformational abilities IF they were collected in specific areas. Keeping that in mind, I had the ability to prove that observation to myself. The Maquilina flower grows over a range of several hundred miles. I collected its frequencies from flowers growing in many different locations, but only one site (at the edge of a glacial lake at 15,000 feet elevation) yielded flowers with the profound transformational ability mentioned above. I found that phenomenon to be true for another flower I treasure from the Andes, Flor de la Luna, and for many other flowers worldwide as well.

Combination #2

A combination of frequencies from UNCUT flowers of: Flor del Oso (*Puya* species), Flor de la Luna (*Wernervia nubigena*), Totora, Heartmend (*Dianthus armeria*) supported by an individually matched complementary base of rare global shamanic flower essences.[6]

Potential Uses:

(1) To act as an energy shield, deflecting destructive fields away from us for dissolution into Source;

(2) To help us clear and upgrade our unconscious mind so that we can more easily overcome life obstacles and diminish stress;

(3) To remove particular self-sabotaging beliefs listed below;

(4) To add light and a sense of ease into our being;

(5) To help us prepare for a more enlightened age on earth.

[6] This multi-flower uncut flower essence combination is sold under the trade name Pure Potential™.

Flor del Oso

Flor de la Luna

Heartmend™

Totora

The development of this floral energy combination took me 19 years to complete, spanning three trips to Peru, until I was able to finally collect flower frequencies from a remote and energetically protected part of the High Andes.

The story of the evolution of this remarkable assembly of flowers begins in 1992. At that time I was able to arrange a meeting with Peru's most preeminent botanist, who at the time was working in Lima at a university called Pontificia Universidad Católica de Perú. I had hopes of creating a friendship (and perhaps even an alliance in spirit) with a man whom I presumed would be a fount of herbal knowledge, since Peru is one of the botanically richest countries in the world. I was saddened to encounter what I soon discovered, and my original lofty intentions rapidly evaporated. What I found that was so disappointing was that this professor's prominence did not derive at all from congeniality, but rather from the fact that he simply intended to dominate – to rise in his field as a result of producing a flood of publications. He succeeded. In academia that is sad to see but is not uncommon.

I was uncomfortable in this meeting from the start because of the way the professor's staff cowered in his presence. It occurred to me then that I had no status that would appeal to his ambitions, so it seemed unlikely he would help me. Due to the professor's facial structure and to the harsh emotional climate I was perceiving, I quietly thought to myself, "I wonder if I am in the company of a man whose ancestry came from the destructive group of Spanish aristocrats, convinced of their supremacy, that were installed around the world at the height of Spain's colonial domination. Such persons constitute a coterie in the upper echelons of society from Mexico through Latin America, Spain, and the Philippines where one can still observe a regrettable quality of entitlement in some individuals of "noble blood line." As a result of those feelings, I didn't expect to develop a rapport with him despite our mutual interest in plants.

I normally ask questions of academics in a way to see if they have any appreciation of the sacred use of medicinal plants in antiquity, and if they have some sort of reverence for plants themselves. After a few failed attempts at that strategy, I felt I could not succeed, so we mechanically went through questions I had about the location of certain plants, population densities, and that type of dry information.

When our uneasy session was over, I thanked the professor for his time, and as I was about to stand and head out the door, I noticed a rather odd expression on his face. It was as if something or someone was rattling around in his brain, dislodging information stored years back in his unconscious. He then said something to me that was totally unexpected: "Oh… I just thought of something that I should tell you, for I think you will find it interesting. When I was a young botanist, just after I got my Ph.D., I did extensive fieldwork all over Peru. I found one location that is truly curious, and I think you should know about it." (We will call the region he described "El Místico," located deep in a remote mountain range.) He continued, "In folklore it is said that there is a sacred lake high in the mountains of El Místico where the forces of nature become visible and the spirits of healing show themselves to those of honest intent. Native people from surrounding countries make pilgrimages to receive healing from the herbs that grow in this region, and it requires of them great effort. I think you will want to go there. Yes… (with a pensive pause) you should visit that place."

Then we were done. I was amazed. Where had that come from? I thanked him for sharing that insight and left. I never forgot what he said.

In 2002 I had the prompting to make an exploratory visit to El Místico, and I called upon my great Peruvian helper, Jorge, to make the necessary arrangements to get to that destination. Travel in remote areas of Peru can be slow and arduous, and it was in this instance.

What I soon found out was that a diverse collection of *curanderos* (healers) and shamans inhabited the village where I was headed – the entry point into the mystical mountain valleys beyond. "*Maestros*" that were bent on accumulating personal power by the exercise of earth magic dealing with manipulation and control were on one side of the spectrum of shamans, and those intending to be servants of Higher Will, operating with the intention of liberating and empowering their students, clients, and those with whom they interacted were on the other side of an apparent motivational divide.

My physical stamina in that era was not fully intact, so I was more prone to be affected by unkindly energy, and I soon felt the wrath of foreign bacteria at work in my gut. One cannot explore at all when confined to the bathroom! I had to rest two days in the only lodging available in the small town – a youth hostel – a few miles from El Místico.

The majority of the uncut flower frequencies in Combination 2 come from this extraordinary location, which since ancient times, in shamanic tradition, has been held in sacred trust and protected. Individuals simply cannot gain entry to this area unless they are "allowed in." Due to storms, unexplained "energetic barriers," and other blocking phenomena, it takes perseverance to enter this "Shangri-la."

On the trip in 2002 I did manage to get to the village guarding the entrance to the mystical valleys, and in a feeble state rode from there on horseback with a kindly shaman who could see how much I had hoped to encounter at least a few of the great flowers from this region. We went perhaps only a mile, just long enough for him to show me the astonishing flower, Flor del Oso, and a few others. Then, out of nowhere, an ice storm hit us, and without protective gear we had to return to the village.

I finally succeeded in deep exploration of this area in 2011, when I organized a full scale expedition with porters, pack animals, two mountaineering guides, plenty of waterproof /cold-proof clothing, and a cook, for two weeks of highly focused trekking and flower essence preparation. I was not about to be turned away on that trip! The details of that amazing and unforgettable adventure will be a chapter in a forthcoming book.

I refer to the flower frequencies from this region as a "Divine dispensation," for they possess a miraculously broad capability of removing many energetic obstacles from one's life.

There are far more flowers in this particular combination formula than I normally combine, but in this case there is remarkable synergy between them. As a result of the vibrational essence frequencies from many flowers, there are a lot of possible test phrases, so I will list several of the important ones here. Remember, for any given individual, not all test phrases will apply.

Due to obstacles that were challenging my team and me as we packed in to our first encampment (I was thrown from my horse into quicksand, for example), my heavenly "Steering Committee" led me to discover an enormously powerful flower within minutes after awaking at our first destination, which we reached at dark the previous day. I immediately prepared it and dispensed some of it to everyone. From that point forward, we were quite invincible against enormous odds. The following primary test phrase derives from that one flower.

After I returned to the U.S. and sent Combination #2 to the most advanced clairvoyant seer I know for her to characterize it, she reported with respect to the first protective flower I prepared (mentioned above):

> "I have never seen anything like this. It will energetically reflect back to the sender one thousand-fold any malevolent energy and distortion from harmony. Any perpetrator of ill intent toward one who has taken of this essence will, by virtue of this flower's power, be held to a much higher degree of accountability for destructive actions, and will not be able to persist."

Her comments would be very hard to believe if I did not have the ability to measure and observe patient response to this remarkable collection of flowers. This combination works particularly well as a "space clearing" spray, described later in this section.

Primary Test Phrase:

– "I am free from the influence of negative forces and fields directed at me." (Affirms this belief that is absent initially.)

Additional Test Phrases:

1. "If I feel happy, I must feel guilty." (Removes this belief that is present initially.)
2. "If I desire something, I won't get it." (Removes this belief that is present initially.)
3. "I am free to be me." (Affirms this belief that is absent initially.)
4. "If I question authority, I will be destroyed." (Removes this belief that is present initially.)
5. "It is impossible for me to forgive myself for my past failures." (Removes this belief that is present initially.)
6. "Being completely vulnerable in my relationships is too risky." (Removes this belief that is present initially.)
7. "I easily find joy in my life." (Affirms this belief that is absent initially.)
8. "I allow myself to receive love." (Affirms this belief that is absent initially.)
9. "I am free from the effects of emotional trauma/abuse." (Affirms this belief that is absent initially.)
10. "I cannot release my past completely." (Removes this belief that is present initially.)
11. "I am fully receiving input from my highest spiritual resources." (Affirms this belief that is absent initially.)
12. "I cannot be happy until things change." (Removes this belief that is present initially.)
13. "I cannot desire what I have." (Removes this belief that is present initially.)
14. "My life is ease and joy." (Affirms this belief that is absent initially.)
15. "I am certain I can enjoy delightful sexual intimacy." (Affirms this belief that is absent initially.)
16. "I am patient with myself." (Affirms this belief that is absent initially.)
17. "I cannot have my sexual desires fulfilled."(Removes this belief that is present initially.)
18. "I am free from the need to employ the negative aspects of myself." (Affirms this belief that is absent initially.)

19. "The loss of (person's name/relationship or a pet animal's name) leaves a hole in my heart." (Removes this belief that is present initially.)
20. "I can accommodate joy in my life." (Affirms this belief that is absent initially.)
21. "My spiritual mission is clear to me now." (Affirms this belief that is absent initially.)
22. (For men missing female companionship) "I am fully receiving all necessary female polarity." (Affirms this belief that is absent initially.)

Born Out of Suffering...

Combinations #3 & #4

Sometimes in a man's life he feels impelled to take action, even though he fully knows the risks and is aware he might fail. In history, some of the most compelling examples of that are men risking their life in battle to save the lives of others. In many of those cases the heroes died.

Though I shall not receive the accolade of hero, I had to "die" for the successful development of combination essences 3 and 4 – not in battle but in the interests of "love." And I must trust that my figurative death will benefit many, for I would never recommend that anyone repeat my mistakes relating to an effort at partnering. Or... was my year-long struggle with a magnificent woman (who was a mismatch with me in fundamental ways that could not be overcome) really a mistake after all?

We must have encountered each other at a vibrationally similar point. We each really wanted a change in our life. We wanted to create a family. I never imagined myself with a woman who had Anna's credentials. She was a Fulbright scholar. In Spain, she had her M.D., a master's degree in public health, and she was a Gestalt therapist. She had been a vegetarian since age 19. She was an accomplished macrobiotic cook. It didn't hurt either that she bore some striking similarities to the beautiful Spanish actress Paz Vega. Though I had to really question myself, I am certain I was not enamored with her just for her beauty and intelligence. Above all, she possesses a genuine nobility of spirit, deep soul wisdom, and kindness. So what happened?

Perhaps "the great intelligence in the sky" brought us together in order that enough mutual respect could be generated so that we might withstand the enormous discomfort of our emotional pain bodies colliding continuously, even though we both made heroic efforts to avoid that. Anna brilliantly understood my flower essence work, so much so that we were able to turn to that to find extraordinary capabilities in flowers that I had prepared from different parts of the world, but had not had the opportunity to characterize.

It was through our tragic misalignment that we were compelled to explore the deepest recesses of the unconscious to try to find and dismantle what was obstructing our ability to get along. We succeeded in characterizing an amazing group of flower frequencies. From recent clinical trials and multi-center corroboration, I can take heart in knowing that something wonderful was born of our association (though not the family we had hoped for)![7]

To be kind to myself, if I should reflect on my personal failure in that relationship, I remember with a smile what a great astrologer told me, who had analyzed our mutual charts. In a pronounced French accent she uttered the huge understatement: "Braant, you must remember zat Sagittarius (Anna) and Virgo (Brent) are NUT celestial friends!"

Combination #3

A combination of frequencies from uncut flowers of: California desert Creosote Bush (*Larrea tridentata*), Colorado Rockies' Green Helbore (*Vera trumviride*), and *Gentiana* species, supported by an individually matched complementary base of rare global shamanic flower essences.[8]

Potential Uses:

(1) To halt emotional disconnects that may result in unfounded panic
(2) To produce greater mind/spirit coherence

California desert Creosote Bush
(Larrea tridentata)

Colorado Rockies' Green Helbore
(Veratrum viride)

[7] I was so fascinated with the profound areas in Anna's soul that I failed to take note of practical considerations that would have stopped the relationship before it started. She is so deeply wedded to the urban European life style characterized by walking (and not driving) everywhere; the camaraderie of friends that dine out often in intimate cafes; close knit association with her siblings and parents, that to be away from that in a foreign country where she could not work because she didn't have a visa (and where she felt alone and isolated in the "hinterlands" of wild Tennessee), all created friction that was too large to bear. Furthermore, I learned by the amazing Imago process that arose from psychotherapy, that what each of us required emotionally to be fulfilled (due to our karmic and inherited traits) was unfortunately what the other could not supply.

[8] This multi-flower uncut flower essence combination is sold under the trade name End2Panic™.

Gentiana species

The newborn infant has eight primitive reflexes that are an essential part of the developing nervous system designed to protect it and support wellbeing in the first months of very vulnerable existence. A well-known example is the Moro reflex (or startle reflex), because it generally occurs when a baby is startled by a loud sound or movement, which serves to draw attention. When startling occurs, the baby throws back his/her head, extends the arms and legs, cries, then pulls the arms and legs back in. These reflexes should disappear from the infant at about 18 months. If these reflexes do not disappear at the appropriate time (i.e., they are retained into adulthood), it is referred to as "retained primitive reflexes."

When primitive reflexes are retained, it can cause enormous undesirable consequences manifesting as learning disabilities, hyperactivity disorders, social ineptitude, and the tendency to panic unnecessarily in the course of normal events that should not elicit such a dramatic reaction.

The following flowers seem to have emerged to mitigate the hyper-vigilant nervous system that is seen commonly in chronically stressed patients, and to remove the unconscious psychological damage from primitive reflexes retained into adulthood.

Primary Test Phrases:

- "Life is a series of panic reactions." (tests true initially – blend eliminates this belief.)
- "I can focus on what is important to me." (failure on this phrase initially – blend affirms this belief.)
- "I cannot recall and reclaim essential parts of my soul that have been scattered throughout the universe." (tests true initially – blend eliminates this belief.)

Additional Test Phrases:

1. "When one of my ideas is questioned, I feel attacked (assaulted)." (blend eliminates this belief.)

2. "If I am confronted with two or more simultaneous tasks, my nervous system will fail." (blend eliminates this belief.)
3. "If I rest and relax (feel vulnerable), life won't support what I need." (blend eliminates this belief.)
4. "If my message is not heard and understood I will perish (will be killed)." (blend eliminates this belief.)
5. "If I allow myself to receive love it will kill me." (tests true initially – blend eliminates this belief.)
6. "If I am not always alert, I will be taken advantage of/abused." (blend eliminates this belief.)
7. "I cannot intuit the negative from the positive." (blend eliminates this belief.)
8. "No matter what I do I can never choose wisely enough." (blend eliminates this belief.)
9. "If I fail I won't be loved/ I don't allow myself to fail/Failure is not an option." (blend eliminates these beliefs.)
10. "I am at peace with myself whether anyone else accepts me or not." (blend affirms this belief.)
11. "I deserve a different mother (father) and a different childhood." (blend eliminates this belief.)
12. "I belong." (blend affirms this belief.)
13. "I allow myself to receive the love of my life." (blend affirms this belief.)
14. "All that is rightfully mine finds me easily now." (blend affirms this belief.)
15. "It is no use trying to initiate what I need to do." (blend eliminates this belief.)

Combination #4

A combination of flower frequencies from UNCUT flowers of: Wild Fivespot (*Nemophila maculata*) (U.S. FlorAlive forest center), Ko' Oko' Olau (*Bidens campylotheca*) (Hawaiian Pali), and Madame Fate (*Hippobroma longifolia*) (Jamaica mountains), supported by an individually matched complementary base of rare global shamanic flower essences.[9]

Potential Uses:

(1) To protect against negative psychic energy & break unwanted attachments;
(2) For powerful soul retrieval;
(3) To link to and empower our Light resources.

[9] This multi-flower uncut flower essence combination is sold under the trade name Freedom Flowers™ Blend.

Wild Fivespot (*Nemophila maculata*)

Ko' Oko' Olau *(Bidens campylotheca)*

Madame Fate (*Hippobroma longifolia*)

As you read the language of the test phrases below (especially 4, 5 and 6), contemplate the absolute and chilling meaning of some of the statements that represent unconscious beliefs. If one aligns with them, they leave no room for escape or remediation; we become "frozen" in spiritual space. Thank heavens they can be reversed!

I hope this blend will become widely adopted, especially by a class of therapists that dedicate themselves to what is called "soul retrieval."

It is also very beneficial to use as a room spray for "space clearing." When it is sprayed in a space, it can remove heavy psychic "muck" left as a result of people undergoing the type of emotional purging that commonly takes place in psychology and energy healing practices. (It is much faster than smudging by burning sage, leaves no odor, and acts profoundly in ways that sage does not.)

Test Phrases:

1. "I am trapped in the activity of my mind." (blend eliminates this belief.)
2. "I am confronted with insurmountable obstacles." (blend eliminates this belief.)
3. "I am free from the influence of negative thoughts and beings." (blend affirms this belief.)

*4. "I am powerless to reclaim my kidnapped soul identity." (blend eliminates this belief.)

*5. "My soul, held in the captivity of a stasis state, is not accessible to me." (blend eliminates this devastating belief, acting as soul retrieval.)

*6. "I am convicted throughout eternity for my crimes." (blend eliminates this damning & paralyzing belief.)

7. "I am free from all unhealthy attachments." (blend affirms this belief.)
8. "I am free from ancestral curses." (blend affirms this belief.)
9. "I am free from destructive genetic manipulation." (blend affirms this belief.)
10. "I do not have the light resources to overcome the challenges I face." (blend eliminates this belief.)
11. "My reality is joy and gratitude." (blend encodes this belief.)

Combination #5

Turning Confidence Into Certainty

Time will tell if a remarkable discovery I made in 2013, relating to this combination of flower essences, could possibly be true. I was working with one of my patients, attempting to find a flower frequency blend that would break through his persistent pattern of self-sabotage, when I discovered the following. This combination of flowers enables our unconscious mind to move from CONFIDENCE to CERTAINTY.

My patient tested true (with normal muscle strength) to this belief: "I am **confident** that I will successfully market and make a profit with my Internet business." Just by changing one critical word in the test phrase to, "I am **certain** that I will successfully market and make a profit with my internet business," his test muscle collapsed in weakness – signaling that that belief was not true for him. When I gave him drops of this combination blend, he strengthened – now certain at the unconscious level that he would succeed. What a wonderful power of support! I have since seen numerous patients who, with the help of these flower frequencies, show they can turn confidence into certainty. I am astonished.

> *The difference between confidence and certainty is the key to the whole transformational thought and self-help movements. Out of all the attendees at a self-help/motivational seminar, only those few who emerge with certainty that they will accomplish an objective will, in fact, accomplish it. The rest of the attendees – the majority – will simply feel more confident that they might achieve the objective. Generally they do not.*

A combination of flower frequencies from UNCUT flowers of: wild Passion Flower (*Passiflorain carnata*) (U.S. FlorAlive forest center),and Honeysuckle (*Lonicera japonica*) (U.S. FlorAlive forest center), supported by an individually matched complementary base of rare global shamanic flower essences.[10]

Potential Uses:

(1) To clear confusion from the mind and fortify heart-centered awareness;
(2) To integrate Higher Mind energies to produce mental focus;
(3) To enable financial freedom;
(4) To enable greater energetic possibility for genetic repair.

When the patient or client is ready for this essence, after administering a lingual test dose, the negative test phrases below will be abolished, or the positive test phrases that failed in testing will be fortified in belief.

Passion Flower (*Passiflora incarnata*)

Honeysuckle (*Lonicera japonica*)

Test Phrases:

1. "I cannot create coherence out of the chaos in my personal life." (blend abolishes this unconscious belief.)
2. "All of my life experience is in perfect harmony, perfect order, and perfect alignment with Divine light." (blend affirms this belief.)
3. "I do not trust that the Universe will provide for my financial freedom." (blend abolishes this unconscious belief.)
4. "I am able now to fully repair genetic damage to my DNA & RNA." (blend affirms this belief.)
5. "I cannot overcome my inherited family stressors." (blend abolishes this unconscious belief.)
6. "I cannot change the memory of stressful living." (blend abolishes this unconscious belief.)
7. "I am not strong enough to resist the negativity of the external world." (blend abolishes this unconscious belief.)

[10] This multi-flower uncut flower essence combination is sold under the trade name Crowning Glory™.

8. "It is impossible for me to correct defects in my genetic programming." (blend abolishes this unconscious belief.)
9. "I am fearless in love."
10. "It is safe for me to be completely vulnerable with my partner."

A note to practitioners: Construct test phrases for your patients/clients that will evaluate their belief as to whether they are **certain** VERSUS **confident** with respect to a particular outcome they desire. Then administer Combination#5, retest, and see if "confidence" nearly instantaneously changes into "certainty."

FlorAlive Stages of Repair

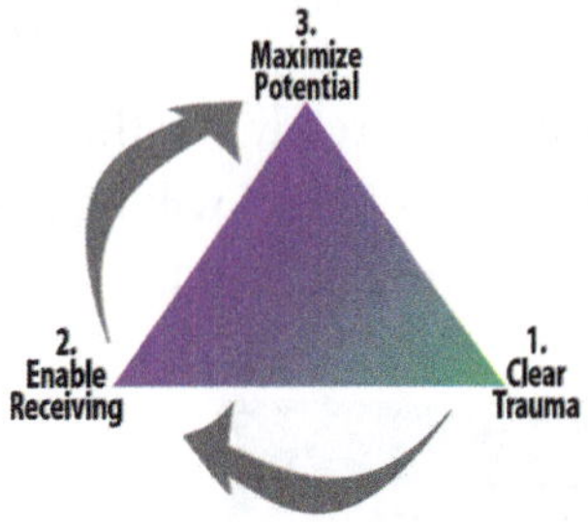

Single Uncut Flower Essences

Uncut flower essences I have developed since the turn of the millennium follow with their accompanying test phrases.[11] The flowers are not listed alphabetically, rather they are listed in more or less the order that I discovered them. It turns out that for screening and transformation purposes, it is best to screen the flowers in the order listed below. When the first six strongly indicated flowers show up, stop at the point of the sixth flower, make a combination blend of the "positive flowers" you have found and consume it. Have your phrases re-tested in 4 weeks, and then carry on with the next blend for more transformation.

[11] Sheets of test phrases from 49 flowers are produced in color for use in patient screening by health professionals and are available by contacting floralive.com.

Maquilina (Bomarea species)
– To overcome futility and hopelessness.

Test Phrases:

- "Regardless of my efforts, I cannot influence the outcome."
- "No matter what action I take, I will be defeated."

Wild Iris (Iris cristata)

– Feeling alone, isolated. Connection to Source. Safety.

Test Phrases:

- "I am disconnected from the Source of ALL life."
- "I am essentially unlovable."
- "I am safe in the midst of all beings."
- "I am free from the threat of any beings."

Tulip Poplar (Liriodendron tulipifera)
– Self esteem (astonishingly effective here.)

Test Phrases:

- "My self-esteem is strong and balanced."
- "I appreciate myself."
- "I am down on myself."

	**Blue Eyed Grass** (Sisyrinchium angustifoluim) – To erase the feelings of hurt, rage and anger at being physically abused or emotionally controlled. **Test Phrases:** • "I am free from the effects (hurt) of emotional trauma/abuse." • "I am suffering the after-effects of emotional/physical abuse." • "I am patient with myself."
	**May Apple** (Podophyllum peltatum) – Feeling inadequate; socially inept; shy. **Test Phrases:** • "I lose my power when others: a. don't listen to me. b. invalidate me." • "I am too shy to show my capabilities and my talents." • "I am (fear being) alone."
	**Pink Lady Slipper** (Cypripedium acaule) – Trust **Test Phrases:** • "I trust in life." • "I trust in my life." • "I am free from life's threats."

	**Star Spirit Flower** (Stellaria pubera) – The motivator. To overcome procrastination. To forgive oneself. **Test Phrases:** • "I am free from [filled with] procrastination." • "My mistakes are unforgivable." • "I am overwhelmed by too much work that lies ahead of me." • "The cellular functions of my body are heavy and obstructed."
	**Heartmend** (Dianthus armeria) – Helps repair the loss of love. Produces profound healing when needed **Test Phrase:** • "The loss of __________ leaves a hole in my heart."
	**Madame Fate** (Hippobroma longifolia) – A shield against attack from negative energies. In ancient Africa, used to prevent spirit possession. **Test Phrases:** • "I am free from the influence of negative thoughts and beings." • "I am filled with self-confidence."

	**White Ginger** (Hedychium coronarium) – To help one awaken to the sweetness in life that may be overlooked or unappreciated. **Test phrases:** • "My life is filled with sweetness." • "I miss sweetness in my life."
	**Dogwood Flowe**r (Cornus florida) – Forgiveness **Test Phrases:** • "I am filled with forgiveness." • "My life is filled with forgiveness." • "I have forgiven ______________."
	**Chagapa** (Gentianeta species) – Being good enough. Freedom from belief in the fate of suffering. **Test Phrases:** • "No matter what I do, I will never be good enough." • "It is my destiny to suffer at the hands of fate."

Blood Root Flower (Sanguinaria candensis)
– Allowance.

Test phrases:

- :I am in harmonious allowance of all things in my life."
- "I am filled with allowance."

Flor de la Luna (Wernervia nubigena)
– Receiving

Test Phrases:

- "I allow myself to receive."
- "I allow myself to receive love."
- "Receiving love puts me at risk (–or– increases my vulnerability.)"

Spigelia (Spigelia marilandica)
– "Checking Out" of the physical body. Energizing the second chakra and reseating in the physical body.

Test Phrases:

- "I have abandoned my body."
- "I allow full activation of my sexual center."
- (Provisional) "I have the power necessary for self-transformation."

 	**Cat's Claw Flower** (Uncaria tomentosa) – To help protect against the invasive/abusive energies of others. To knit together the fabric of the psyche after emotional abuse/trauma. **Test phrases:** • "I am vulnerable to the invasive energies of ____ ." • "I am suffering from the invasive energies of ____ ." • "I am free from the abusive energies of ____ ."
 	**Hydrangea** (Hydrangea arborescens) – Non-judgment. **Test Phrases:** • "I am free from judgment." • "I am free from judging myself." • "All too often, I make judgments about others."
 	**Goldenseal** (Hydrastis canadensis) – Overcoming victimization. **Test Phrases:** • "I am an innocent victim." • "I am a victim."

Talla (Lupinus species)
– The workaholic's essence.

Test Phrases:

- "My value as a human being is determined [measured] by how hard I work."
- "(Provisional) I feel betrayal of my loyalty."

Herb of the Cross (Euphorbia rigida)
– Desiring to be in control

Test Phrases:

- "I am comfortable being out of control."
- "I am unsafe unless I am in control."
- "My sexual identity is confused."

Manzo Root (Anemopsis californica)
– Integration; Harmonization.

Test Phrases:

- "All the dimensions of my being are harmoniously integrated."
- "I am fully grounded."

Zarcilleja (Brachioto naudini)
– Hormonal relief. The woman's helper.

Test Phrases:

- "I accept the cumulative suffering of all women as my own."
- "I am free from my genetic links to cumulative female suffering."

Purush Purush (Passiflora species)
– Tranquil beauty. For women to be comfortable with their feminine essence.

Test Phrases:

- "I am comfortable with my feminine beauty."
- "I am comfortable with my female essence."

Flor del Oso (Puya species)
– Translates as "flower of the bear." A great herbal presence with unfathomable power. The Andean Indians call it "The King of the High Places."

Test Phrases:

- "I am fully receiving input from my highest spiritual resources."
- "I am in full contact with my highest spiritual resources."

(Possesses the ability to vibrationally undo some of the damage caused by the entities that have created suffering and inhumanity on earth. An example is the damage from artificially created weaponized bacteria. In that light, the following test phrase can be created with the appropriate word to fill in the blank.)

"I know I can eliminate the modernly constructed ______________ I am experiencing."

	**Blue Water Lily** (Nymphaea caerulea) – Issues of being lovable; clearing higher brain structures. To clear MASSIVE REVERSAL. **Test Phrases:** • "I am only lovable when I am disabled." • "I do not deserve (am unworthy of) love." • "My higher brain centers are free from obstruction." • "It is safe for me to open my heart."
	**Viola Father** (Viola species) – Missing the father. **Test Phrases:** • "I miss the cellular frequency of the loving father/the wise father/the mentoring father."
	**Viola Mother** (Viola species) – Missing the mother. **Test Phrases:** • "I miss the cellular frequency of the loving mother/the wise mother/the mentoring mother."

False Dandelion (Tyrrhopappus carolinianus) – Venting of rage and anger.

Test Phrases:

- "I am filled with shame."
- "I cannot release the hurt that is trapped inside me."
- "I cannot release the rage that is trapped inside me."
- "Anger controls me."

Button Snakeroot (Eryngium yuccifolium) – Personal power.

Test Phrases:

- "I am humble in the knowledge of my power."
- "I am confident in the use of my power."
- "I am free from self-doubt."
- "I am constantly being the power that is me."
- "I have fully reclaimed my personal power."

Green Jade Flower (Strongyloden macrobotrys) – The flower directly communicated to Dr. Davis the odd second phrase.

Test Phrases:

- "It is unsafe for me to feel."
- "My links to my natal star system are clear."
- "All my chakras are free from obstruction."

Culver's Root Flower
(Veronicastrum virginicum)
– Release.

Test Phrases:

- "I can release (have released) my past failures."
- (Provisional) "I have released past romantic attachments."

Huishko (Estenomeso species)
– Self-perpetuating illness.

Test Phrase:

- "I am destined to perpetuate my own suffering and illness."

Maroon Bethroot (Trillium cuneatum)
– Women's liberator. Breaks the attractor field that draws troubled men to women. It sometimes is applicable for men who draw to themselves troubled partners. Secondarily, overcoming condemnation and guilt.

Test Phrase:

- "I am destined to draw troubled (unavailable) men (relationships) into my life."
- (Male) "I am destined to be a troubled man."
- "I am condemned and can never be purified" (provisional).
- "I am guilty" (provisional).

<table>
<tr>
<td>
</td>
<td>Butterfly Flower (Asclepias tuberosa)
– The flower communicated to Dr. Davis the unusual message that it wanted to be known as "Dragon's Heart."

Test Phrase:
• "I have the courage to maintain an open heart."</td>
</tr>
<tr>
<td>
</td>
<td>Yellow Root (Xanthorhiza simplicissima)
– Acceptance, fearlessness, RECEIVING.

Test Phrases:
• "I accept Source energy."
• "I allow myself to receive unlimited amounts of money."
• "I am afraid to feel fully."
• "I am angry at Creator."
• "I can't receive anything more because I already have too much to deal with."</td>
</tr>
<tr>
<td>
</td>
<td>Joe Pye Flower (Eupatorium fistulosum)
– Hypersensitivity, RECEIVING.

Test Phrases:
• "I am too sensitive for this world."
• "I allow myself to receive unlimited amounts of energy and attention."
• "If I step into my power, I will be annihilated."</td>
</tr>
</table>

	**Flor de Oro** (Castilllejia fassifolia) – Self-devaluation. **Test Phrases:** • "I can never overcome the infinite worthlessness (devaluation) of my being." • "I am worthless."
	**Claytonia** (Claytonia virginica) – Forgiveness and Source connection. **Test Phrases:** • "I cannot forgive the injuries others have done to me." • (Provisional) "I feel fully I will self-destruct."
	**Red Agrimony** (Agrimonia species) – Abolishes deep internal tension and stiffness. **Test Phrases:** • "I cannot overcome my excessive internal tension." • "I am free from internal conflict."

<table>
<tr>
<td>
</td>
<td>Ko Oko O Lau (Bidens campylotheca)
– Transmutation of hopelessness from the past. Unconscious futility. Self-nurturing.
Test Phrases:
• “I am convicted throughout eternity for my crimes.”
• “I absorb and utilize all the nurturing energy available to me.”
• “I am confronted with insurmountable obstacles.”
• “I know I will joyfully overcome all obstacles placed in my path.”</td>
</tr>
<tr>
<td>
</td>
<td>Blue Gentian (Gentiana species) (High Andes–Peru)
– For those prone to disregard their personal needs.
Test Phrase:
• “I am kind to myself.”</td>
</tr>
</table>

Jack-In-The-Pulpit (Arisaema triphyllum)
– Helps us to remove self-defeating patterns that escape our conscious awareness.

Test Phrases:

- "I cannot speak to or address that which challenges my comfort zone."
- "I cannot find my true love who is hidden from me."

Acrobat Orchid (Caladenia species)
– Creates a lighthearted life.

Test Phrases:

- "Life is a playful game."

	**Sacred Lotus** (Nelumbo nucifera) – Strengthens connection to the heart. **Test Phrases:** • "I can (cannot) trust my heart." • "My mind is fully integrated with my heart."
	**Blue Pentangle** (P. caeruleu) – Self-worth and immunity to stressors. **Test Phrases:** • "I am incompetent." • "I feel incompetent." • "I cannot break my pattern of indecision."
	**Blue Lechenaultia** (Lechenaultia biloba) – Knowing all is well. Self-appreciation. **Test Phrases:** • "I know deeply (cellularly) that all is well in my life." • "I accept and appreciate who I am." • "I accept diminishment."

R&G Kangaroo Paw (Anigozanthos manglesii)
– Empowerment. Nervous system balancer.

Test Phrases:

- "I have the means and the power to restore Paradise on earth."
- (Provisional) "My brain-mediated hormonal controls are balanced."

Door To Change (Houstonia pucilla)
– Resolution of karma. Hopelessness.

Test Phrases:

- "I can never reverse the consequences of my past negative karma." –or–
- "I know I am able to revise my past negative karma."

Healing Heart (Dicentra spectabilis)
– Promotes deep healing of heart energy.

Test Phrases:

- "My heart will always be broken." (This phrase can also be reversed with HeartMend™)
- "I am fully connected to the heart of Mother Earth."

Dancing Goddess (Petrophile linearis)
– To attract the partner we desire (works for men and women.)

Test Phrases:

- "I fear abandonment."
- "I am being the goddess energy that draws the ideal partner into my life."
- "I am broadcasting the frequencies that draw the ideal goddess energy I desire into my life."
- "I am allowing the full expression of my feminine essence."
- "I am afraid of committing to completion."
- "I am not equal to the woman I desire to be."

Practical Applications of Flower Frequencies in Commerce and Daily Life

The major issues that have hindered the adoption of flower frequencies in commerce and daily life are:

1. Inability to prove that highly dilute energies from flowers actually do anything, that is inability to meaningfully measure pre-administration and post-administration effects of flower frequencies on living subjects. (Due to the fact that flower frequencies presumably accomplish much of their work in the subtle domain of R-space that is not accessible to mainstream scientific measurement [see page 176-177], we cannot depend on conventional laboratory and analytical science to substantiate the value proposition of

developing products from the energy of flowers.)

2. Absence of familiarity that would enable matching the capability of special flower frequencies to the potential of many possible products in selected target markets.

3. Absence of awareness that the appeal of flowers (illustrated by the millions of bouquets gifted annually) naturally lends itself to the creation of many more products than aerosolized room deodorizers, laundry detergents, and the like – the major way we see flowers represented in commercial products.

> *With respect to number two above, in order to understand the market where products can be sold containing what we might call "validated" uncut flower frequencies – those that have shown positive effects clinically (and socially) – we must graduate out of the notion that the domain of flower essences is solely for the fringe elements of society.*

If we look at the matter of where selected flower frequencies can add great value to our life, there is a much larger area than one might initially imagine. To understand this area, we should briefly examine a group referred to as the "LOHAS – Lifestyles Of Health And Sustainability " segment of our population.

History of LOHAS

Sociologist Paul Ray conducted research in the 1990s that yielded a rather startling finding at the time. He found that nearly one fourth of the U.S. adult population held a world view that highly valued health, sustainability, and social justice, and significantly influenced how they lived their lives. He referred to these individuals as "cultural creatives."

A marketing group called Conscious Media was interested in defining the segment of the population described by Ray and psychologist Sherry Ruth Anderson in their book, *Cultural Creatives: How Fifty Million People Are Changing the World.* In 1999, Conscious Media coined the term LOHAS (Lifestyles of Health and Sustainability) to define that demographic. They founded the LOHAS Journal to help advance an understanding of what appeared to be a rapidly developing global trend of consumer choice based on more conscious buying decisions.

In their important book, Ray and Anderson presented a questionnaire that enabled the reader to identify if he or she was a "cultural creative." One can adopt that moniker by recognizing within oneself ten or more of the sixteen attributes they list, including characteristics such as:

1. Caring for and love of nature and an interest in its natural balance and preservation
2. Major interest in psychological and spiritual development

3. Willingness to pay a higher price for goods if it would support improving the environment
4. Recognition of the importance of developing and maintaining relationships
5. Possessing an optimism for the future and wanting to be involved in creating a new and better way of life
6. Appreciating different or exotic people, places and things
7. Desiring to see a change in the way big business generates profits and a cessation of exploiting the environment and poorer countries
8. Belief that spirituality is an important aspect of life
9. Ascribing importance to the support and wellbeing of all women and children

Worldwatch Institute reported that in 2006 approximately 30% of the U.S. consumer market consisted of the LOHAS market segment, worth an estimated 300 billion dollars. The Natural Marketing Institute (NMI) reported that in 2007 the LOHAS demographic consisted of 40 million Americans. (Ray and Anderson's book, published in 2000, estimated a possible 80 to 90 million cultural creatives in the European Union.)

Adding that all up, I would suggest that in developed countries there are probably at least 100 million people who would be delighted to adopt into their lifestyle products containing transformational uncut flower frequencies that I have been blessed to discover –IF they only knew they existed.

Let's explore why that is the case, matching number for number the LOHAS list above with the characteristics of uncut flower essences I have had the good fortune to discover.

1. The process of preparing highly concentrated uncut flower essences is the ultimate green business (for the concentrate is vastly diluted for final distribution, similar to homeopathic products). A huge amount of product can be prepared from rare natural resources with no damage to the environment and virtually no footprint. Here is just one example:

   In my early field work in Hawaii during the late 1980s (assisted by botanists and naturalists extraordinaire Ken Nagata and Wayne Takeuchi), I was determined to rediscover and bring back into usage the most revered of all Hawaiian herbs – Ko' Oko' Olau (*Bidens campylotheca*) – which had essentially been lost from use due to a deterioration of indigenous herbal knowledge and practice followed by a decline in plant populations.[12] If that herb had been collected from the wild for the commercial herbal marketplace, it would have been rendered extinct very quickly because it only grows in one small area in the world.

I knew how useful it was because I had collected small quantities for my own clinical use.[13] I took great pains to re-seed the wild population when I ventured to Hawaii from West Los Angeles each year to take a break from my practice as part of my own health retreat. High on a beautiful Pali, overlooking the ocean, the tiny wild population of Ko'Oko' Olau slowly started increasing, but I knew it could never sustain commercial exploitation. So when I discovered the uncut flower extraction process, I was thrilled with the possibility of producing an extract of the living flower right where it grows so that I could collect its profound healing ability. I did just that and celebrated with the plant what I felt was a victory. The herb would be able to bring its huge blessing to many, but would not be harmed in the process. Years later, the flower gave to me its astonishing test phrase. It can "overwrite" and remove the chilling and devastating belief that resides in the human unconscious: "I am convicted throughout eternity for my crimes." This flower's transformational power is part of Combination #4.

2. This topic on the cultural creatives' list is a central theme in *The Floral Hand of God.*

3. There is a wonderful opportunity to create products in the premium pricing category that are readily accepted because of their huge value. At the same time part of the earnings can be redistributed directly to indigenous peoples so they

[12] Sadly, what is being used by Hawaiian healers as a substitute for the real herb is the non-indigenous species commonly called Beggars Tick (Bidens pilosa), originating from South America. I finally took measures, that have now succeeded, to start organic production of the true Ko' Oko' Olau in Hawaii so that it can be used in an important herbal product produced by my herb company.

[13] I was so impressed with specific physiological effects I observed in the real Ko' Oko' Olau that I asked Professor Hildebert Wagner, director of the pre-eminent Institute For Pharmaceutical Biology at the University of Munich, to technically characterize it. I explained to him that in my applied kinesiology clinical practice I had observed strong anti-inflammatory effects from the herb, and wondered if he would please verify if that was so. He assigned his brilliant graduate student Rudolf Bauer to investigate the herb, and that study resulted in two publications:
– Bauer, Rudolf; Redl, Karl; Davis, Brent (1992) Four Polyactylene Glucosides From Bidenscampylotheca. *Phytochemistry*, Vol.31, No. 6, pp. 2035-2037
– K. Redl, W. Breu, B. Davis, R. Bauer (1994) Anti-Inflammatory Active Polyacetylenes from Bidenscampylotheca. *Planta Med.* 60, 1-98, p.58-62.
In the Planta Medica article it was reported that a previously unknown chemical discovered in this herb "exhibited a significant inhibitory effect on prostoglandin biosynthesis. … Compared to indomethacin, which is one of the strongest inhibitors of prostoglandin synthesis, this is a remarkable effect." As part of the discovery agreement, I had the right to patent any valuable findings from the study, and license those findings to drug companies for potential use. When I was contacted by the Institute with an offer to proceed to patenting and licensing, I had to decline because I could not in good conscience be involved even peripherally in the pharmaceutical industry's control of medicine and what felt to me like the co-opting of true healing.

can safeguard and improve their ecosystems and be enabled to achieve a more comfortable standard of living.

My "heavenly steering committee" directed me recently to the Philippines – a part of the world where there is abundant opportunity to implement this profit sharing model. I was shown in my mind's eye a very rare and beautiful orchid that will likely have an enormous value, and I am getting closer to discovering it. As a result of this awareness I researched the status of orchids in the Philippines and found that it is similar to many other tropical areas: not good at all!

In a conversation with directors of a large Philippine orchid conservatory, I found out how they obtain wild orchid stock for laboratory propagation. They have to go to the habitat where the orchid grows and try to negotiate a purchase from black market orchid poachers that sell to vendors in local town markets OR sell to international brokers that supply rare orchids illegally. I was not surprised but was saddened to hear this account.

I soon had the opportunity of speaking with the head of the Natural Resources Department on one of the major islands where I will be doing orchid research. I explained that I was able to extract energy from flowers that have especially transformational properties without cutting or harming them in any way. I indicated that if I found such an orchid in his precinct, and could find a way to place the flower essence product in the commercial marketplace where substantial sales could be developed, there would be a way to implement what is called "access benefit sharing" – a way for third world countries that produce valuable natural resources to actually be paid a fair income for the products growing in their region rather than being exploited. He welcomed the opportunity and gave me his blessing.

In the particular case of uncut flower essences, rare orchids would not have to be harvested to obtain the commercial product. I explained that this type of project might appeal to philanthropists that love orchids (there are lots of them!). Such a project would require special commitment and funding. I felt that once a great healing property was shown to arise from a rare orchid, a project would have a chance of being funded to grow that orchid in the wild, paying the indigenous peoples to increase the wild orchid population, watching over their potential harvest rather than illegally poaching. Then a special mark could be created by the government in concert with a private agency denoting that a very special (and beautiful) orchid was preserved in its habitat and could be safely sold in the marketplace. I would like to see that happen.

4. I do not know of any natural products that have a greater capacity to improve relationships than what I have outlined in this section.

5. A truly unusual and outstanding feature of the essences I have described is their remarkable ability to clear from the unconscious mind inhibiting beliefs, and hence make way for a brighter future.

6. If my crazy "Indiana Jones" type adventures that result in practical outcomes don't satisfy an interest in "exotic people, places, and things," then I don't know what would. (See Chapters 8, 9, and 11.)

7. In my number 3 discussion above, just one of many possible models is outlined which, if implemented could fulfill an ardent desire in the minds of many cultural creatives.

8. A profound effect of consuming and utilizing frequencies from uncut flower essences is the enrichment of our spiritual life.

9. My "Steering Committee" showed me the future vision of a non-profit organization started by women to administer programs that teach mothers and fathers how to clear the limiting beliefs in their young children and in their families. This is possible when people take the training I am offering to become registered and certified uncut flower essence practitioners. It will give me deep satisfaction to see this vision materially manifest.

From LOHAS to Participation in Mainstream

In the course of speaking with marketing consultants exploring ways that the wonderful transformational effects of uncut flower essences could be more widely disseminated, I heard comments several times that made me pause. At first, I was put off by what I heard. If I were to summarize all of the comments, it might go something like this:

> "Well Doc, it's really great that you have an interest in science, and like to know how things work. But what I do is sales. I have to be honest with you. I don't care about how they work. And you know what? Average people don't care about how things work either. They care about the benefits that they receive from the products or *think* that they will receive."

"Wow. They couldn't all be wrong," I thought to myself. Eventually I realized that what they were telling me was probably spot-on for the non-LOHAS community.

Most of the readers of this book are likely members of the LOHAS community. So you do care rather deeply about how products are created and about the motivation behind them. But share with me for just a moment the glee I will feel when someone in mainstream catches on!

Imagine:

• World-class tennis players, golfers, and other professional athletes when they find out that there is a quick way to test for unconscious sabotaging beliefs that are reducing their competitive edge (reducing their income), and that by taking the appropriate harmless drops of flower "energy," those beliefs can be removed and verified by simple testing. Of course, the obvious way this will catch on is by outcome. Through trial it will be possible to create some blockbuster off-the-shelf products for increasing focus and performance in professional athletes.

• Salesmen, saleswomen, and sales teams when they reduce their personal rough edges by consuming appropriate flower essences so as to produce greater cohesiveness and effectiveness in the corporate environment.

• The joy of people who would do anything to help their precious animals that are chronically ill to feel better. (I have seen remarkable benefits of the uncut flower essences mentioned in this book when applied to domestic animals. Testimonials from pet owners can be seen at FlorAlive.com.)

• The common practice of using space-clearing sprays (that leave no odor) to:

– improve the work environment in the offices of health professionals who deal with the "heaviness' of emotional trials and physical illness;

– enhance the romantic atmosphere of private residences and commercial spaces;

– clear disturbed energy from a place after an argument, or prepare a space for greater tranquility when there is a possibility of a contentious encounter.

These are just a few of many possibilities!

ESSENTIAL Instructions for Taking Uncut Flower Essences

Background:

It is "information and memory" that are transferred from the surface of a living flower to the water surrounding it in the uncut flower extraction process.[1] Then that water is highly diluted, to be taken in drops, so that the "information" (benevolent energy somehow coded into the flower) can more easily influence our stored unconscious memory in R-space (reciprocal space). R-space is the magneto-electric realm in the space outside our body that influences our subtle, non-material bodies AND our emotions. (Refer to page 174.)

Therefore, uncut flower essences contain NO material substance and are absolutely harmless to our physical body – that area that is the focus of pharmacology and which, in the mainstream, defines the domain where there can be so-called "adverse reactions." Physically, flower essences cannot cause adverse reactions. That does NOT mean that they have no effect.

Their effect comes from a phenomenon that is known in homeopathy which is the stimulation of our non-material "vital essence," and that is linked to how we feel. The way we take flower essences can influence the way we feel, and the next schematic is created to illustrate that.

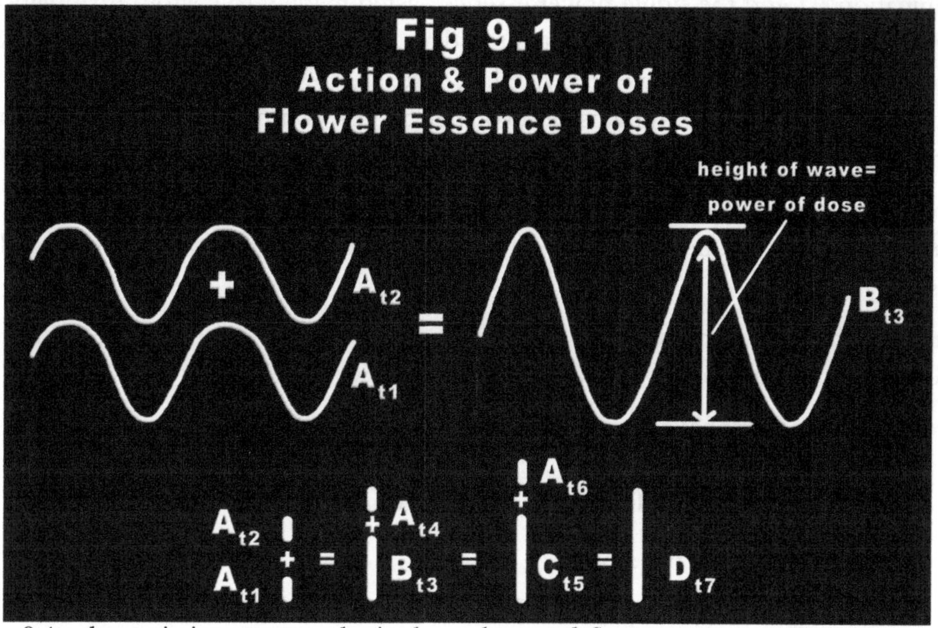

The 9.1 schematic is meant to depict how drops of flower essence will exert an influence upon us over time with repeated dosing. In the upper part of the schematic we see that A_{t1} (let us say that is a dose of three drops in a swallow of four ounces of

[1] Conventional cut flower essences have minute amounts of sap from the cut stem of the flower that leaches into the water, so they have some dissolved chemical substance in them.

water), when repeated at a little bit later time interval (A_{t2}), will additively become a larger wave form of energy in the next time interval, $B_{t3.}$ How big the wave grows (its amplitude) will influence how strongly it impacts our being.

Looking at the lower part of the schematic we see that the example dose of three drops shows a power level depicted by the height of the small line next to A_{t1}. At a second time interval A_{t2} (let us say 30 minutes later) another three drop dose is taken. The effect of A_{t1} + A_{t2} adds up to an increased wave-form amplitude at the next interval of time, B_{t3}. B_{t3} as an energy wave has grown in size and power over the original A_{t1}. Let us say that 30 minutes later another three drop dose A_{t4} is taken. That will add up to the energy amplitude of C_{t5}, and so on. When we arrive at D_{t7} we have a much larger force of influence on our body than the single dose of A_{t1} that was taken some time before. **The effects of energy-based dosing are additive.**

The important point is this: it is not so much how many drops of the flower essence you take AT ONE TIME that determines its power level and influence. Rather, it is how often you repeat the doses.

The newer flower essence combinations I have described in Part 3, Combinations #s 2-5, are very potent, and seem to act differently than Combination #1. Combinations #s 2-5 should NOT be taken as often therefore. Very commonly Combination #1 and the single flower essences listed made into custom formulations can be sipped 30 times throughout an entire day. That builds a very large additive wave form, yet quite often can be well tolerated. There is a huge variability in the emotional structure and resilience of humans, and you MUST use common sense in determining what is right for you.

You must decide…how much do you want to change, how quickly, and what can you reasonably tolerate in terms of receiving strong stimulus for transformation. How "sensitive" are you??

Now, for the sake of humor, let's take a look at how much—or how little— common sense product manufacturers in our country believe we have:

- Gas caps on personal recreational vehicles such as ATVs, Jet Skis, and the like bear this sticker:

  Never use a lit match or open flame to check fuel level.

- A major sleeping aid pill advises

  Warning: May Cause Drowsiness

Oh well, back to the topic at hand.

The vast majority of LOHAS (Lifestyles Of Health And Sustainability) folks do very well with uncut flower essences and naturally understand how to employ them. Individuals in that category over the years have reported to me that they have had fun experimenting with how much shifting they can take! Many people want to achieve the fastest shifting in the least amount of time, while at the same time avoiding the discomfort of too much shifting too rapidly.

Combination#1 (and single essences made into combinations blended into one bottle) can be prepared by placing one drop of essence per ounce of drinking water (16 or 24 ounce bottle), and can be sipped up to 30 times per day. This produces a powerful movement toward shifting our undesirable unconscious mind obstacles. You sip the amount of times per day that you can comfortably incorporate.

Hypersensitive individuals may tolerate only three sips per day with one or two drops placed in the water they are drinking. In cases that are "dimensionally unstable" sometimes no drops taken internally can be tolerated. In those cases fine results are achieved by rubbing the diluted essences externally on the skin OR by spraying the essences around the body. (In chapter 24 I have presented what would appear to be the first-ever scientific documentation that demonstrates a rationale for a spraying type of application.)

The following special circumstances require particular attention:

- If you are feeling emotionally unstable and/or vulnerable, I do not suggest taking any flower essences unless you have someone to monitor you closely and check in as to how you are doing. Under those conditions try a few doses (three drops in a four ounce swallow of water spaced three times throughout your waking hours) to see how you tolerate it. If you feel either extremely elated or the opposite, "bummed out," you may be taking too much or may be taking a flower essence that is not matched to you vibrationally. In either event, stop and re-evaluate.
- If you have been prescribed anti-depressants or other mind altering drugs do not take any flower essences unless you have the assistance of a licensed holistic health professional to closely monitor you.

Appendix 1

Let The New World Begin

Adventures in Conscious Living and Conscious Business

Upon observing the varied, deep, and beneficial changes that some of my patients have reported after consuming the uncut flower extracts I have developed (and upon hearing my colleagues report the same experience), it occurred to me that the huge store of different flower frequencies that I have collected should be widely disseminated and used around the world.[1]

In order for that to occur, it seemed at the very least I would have to do some networking. Shortly after I realized that, I came across and joined an organization called CEOspace whose mission is to maintain a training and meeting place for entrepreneurs.

There are many great ideas that are shared at the CEOspace forums that take place several times per year. When I attended the first forum in 2008, I noticed a bulletin board next to the registration area that caught my attention and made me smile. It was called the "Adopt A Dream" board, and it was covered with index cards (printed by the organization).

The 4x5 cards are filled out by attendees who have extra ideas or inventions (in addition to their principal pursuits) which they would like to see developed, but do not have time to do on their own. There is a space on the card for the visionary's name and contact information, the description of his invention or project, and the way he would like to be compensated for his participation. Following is my version of "Adopt A Dream," interspersed with anecdotes, a bit of social commentary, and actual "downloads" of waking dreams of encounters that I actually see taking place.

[1] I have to restrain myself from launching into the creation of more new essences. Since my "steering committee" would like to see many, many more essences available to the world, and there are numerous special places I have yet to visit that will yield wonderful transformational flower energies, it would be so easy just to keep adding new flower frequency extracts to the huge inventory that already exists. Yet, from over one hundred flower frequency extracts that I have prepared, only forty-nine single flower frequencies and nine combination formulas are commercially available. Common sense dictates that they must be well utilized before more are added.

"Creation of Jobs"
A World Conundrum of Early Twenty First Century

Our political leaders from all parties can never save us from the economic and social decline that is gripping much of the world because they are operating (and are generally active participants) in a meticulously crafted artificial technocracy designed to massively polarize wealth. Civilization as we know it will be destroyed before special interests (of old-world consciousness) stop perverting the beauty of spiritually inspired democratic governance.

Our true hope lies not in the "creation of jobs" but in the job of liberating creativity. How do we do that? By developing methods to break from social, economic, and thought conformity in ways that are socially constructive. And how do we do that? By removing all limiting and self-sabotaging beliefs from the subconscious mind of everyone possible. You will see in Section 3 ahead that even at this nascent stage, I have identified a sufficient number of flower frequencies, which, if fully utilized could massively transform society by removing creative restraints.

Even without reference to the central question of spiritual motivation, what is the value of one liberated being in the form of Steve Jobs throughout his creative years at Apple – or another in the form of Mark Zuckerberg, the well-known founder of Facebook? Yes, those two are examples of unusual geniuses in technology who, on their own, were naturally free from certain limiting beliefs. But how many more geniuses would emerge if the tyranny of our subconscious shackles were to be broken at large?

If my "floral society-transformation" musings seem outlandish, I do not believe they are. We have seen in Section 2 how they can be explored in light of quantum physics and how they can be scientifically investigated.

> When I walk in solitude in the forest surrounding my house in the country, I often have waking dreams in which I meet and converse with individuals who are in positions of progressive social influence and economic authority. Other times, I see and meet (in the "dream" state) individuals who are not well known or influential, and I witness characteristics or unfolding in their lives in ways that relate to themes in this book. The images I see feel materially very real. Let me offer a few examples.

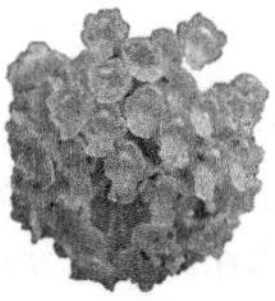

Exceptional-Integrity.com

Michael is an enigmatic man with both his head and his heart in the future and the past. He strongly feels both of those time-space continuums. He is dedicated to understanding and fully occupying the present, and yet it is a great challenge for him.

He believes that if he could encounter or create a "community of the heart" in the present, then beautiful and noble traditions from the past could unite with a luminous future's promise of an enlightened civilization.

Michael has studied the teachings of our best transformational thought leaders. He could recite chapter and verse the importance of living in the now, and logically it makes sense. He is quite aware that whenever he is not fully seated in his body, in the present moment, he is actually jeopardizing his power of manifestation.

Yet, he has been haunted by the refrain of an inner voice questioning, "If I am in a blissful state of allowance and acceptance, then what would motivate me to use my particular gifts to help materialize the paradise that Earth can be? The recognition of what is out of balance has a great deal to do with making the restoration of balance possible." At the soul level, Michael feels that the darkness, willful manipulation, and destruction so evident in the transitional state of our present-day Earth should be eradicated as soon as possible.

Then one day Michael perceives a resolution of the apparent conflict between the passivity of the self-satisfied individual versus the unrest of the spiritual activist. He remembers a lecture he had heard, when he was in his twenties, from a revered Tibetan teacher. The theme of that discourse was the importance of recognizing the emission from one's being of the frequency of "unsatisfactoriness" (the best English language equivalent of a Tibetan concept).

The master explained that in a state of awareness we will recognize harmful or unpleasant energies, often in advance of their physical manifestation. If we simply observe them, do not engage or identify with them, and fortify the core of our own Light, then generally all is well. If we do otherwise, we run the risk of making a judgment that instills within us the resonance of "unsatisfactoriness," which is a core component of the unhealthy ego, and cancels positive manifestation. Michael recognizes, with the recollection of this teaching, that if he succeeded in rooting out from himself the frequencies of "unsatisfactoriness," he would more easily succeed with his vision of transformation.

Michael knows that it would likely be fruitless if he were to search outside of himself too much for what he felt would be the "magic" solution of encountering right community and right feminine partnership. So he decides, at least for a while, to follow a two-fold path: the continuation of his own internal transformation coupled with a review of new era and progressively organized intentional communities.

What soon becomes evident as Michael examines "alternative consciousness communities" in different parts of the world is that quite often they are centered around a charismatic figure, supporting his or her vision. Michael's own mission is so strong that he could not abdicate it in favor of supporting someone's else's life work – even if theirs were a noble one. And Michael finds several communities that were inspired by high ideals and beautiful activities. Neither does Michael want to become some central figure around which a community organizes. So how would he ever encounter the special people and the personal partner with whom he wants to move through life, he wonders?

Unexpectedly, when Michael is on a trip to Los Angeles to attend a workshop, and is driving through town, he hears an advertisement that spurrs a revolutionary concept. If it could be developed, he thinks, it would solve so many of the problems of light-workers who were searching for "alliances" but had failed to find an appreciable number of individuals with whom to carry out their life work.

The advertisement on his car radio was for a member company of the California Psychic Network. It described the rigorous screening their psychics undergo before being hired, that they only hire one or two individuals for every one hundred that apply, and so on. Michael has no interest in calling a psychic in this company, but the advertisement triggers in him a cascade of ideas.

He realizes that a council of psychics with especially high integrity could render a great service in a novel way. "Yes!" he thinks to himself as he contemplates how the new service he envisions would function, "I can see all the pieces necessary to put this together: the help of my teacher, who is the clearest and most powerful sensitive I have ever met and who has the necessary "sight" to help select just the right psychics to serve as a board of directors (charged with the duty of choosing pure and clearly motivated applicant psychics); the layout and structure of the website; and the programmers necessary to construct it. It will need only management and funding."

In an amazing way, the new web site that would be created, Exceptional-Integrity.com, would serve as a sort of modern day mystery school like Delphi in ancient times.[2]

In the most practical way, it would deliver to the subscriber an "assessment score" based on a carefully crafted questionnaire and the collaborative viewing of a specially

[2] Herbert William Parke, The Delphic Oracle, v.1, p.3. "The foundation of Delphi and its oracle took place before the times of recorded history. The Pythia, commonly known as the Oracle of Delphi, was the priestess at the Temple of Apollo at Delphi, located on the slopes of Mount Parnassus, beneath the Castanial Springs. The Pythia was widely credited for her prophecies inspired by Apollo. The Delphic oracle was established in the 8th century BC, although it may have been present in some form in Late Mycenaean times, from 1,400 BC and was abandoned, and there is evidence that Apollo took over the shrine from an earlier dedication to Gaia."

chosen review board of clairvoyants. Here is how Michael sees it operating.

Exceptional-Integrity.com is a worldwide subscription site where each applicant's profile is kept for selective viewing. Each applicant is rated on a score of one to four with four being the highest level of integrity. For the lowest level approval score that permits registry on the site at a level of one, core characteristics are evaluated such as: truthfulness, spiritual valor, emotional stability, freedom from religious dogma, patience, kindness, the ability to receive love, the ability to give love, freedom from judgment, honorable sexual conduct, propensity to anger, freedom from fixed ideas, the spirit of youthfulness, humor, artistic sensitivity, perseverance, discipline, and more.

Each attribute is evaluated on a scale of one to ten by the psychics who are remotely viewing and assessing the applicant, and collectively when those scores are combined, they determine the overall integrity rating. With each progressive step upward from level two to three to four, more stringent questions must be answered by the applicant and evaluated by a committee of six seers. (Characteristics such as the applicant's association with angelic forces and evolved spirit guides might be an important part of the rating at level two and above.) Probably level three and surely level four ratings are determined by the most advanced seers, and for level four, the head seer, with a status similar to the ancient oracle of Delphi, has a heavily weighted influence for final approval of that level.

What is quite wonderful about this commercial site is that it is a powerful spiritual tool. When the applicant receives back his rating, once he has been evaluated, he knows that individuals that do not have a personal agenda have truthfully assessed him.

When the applicant chooses the "evolutionary path membership," he will receive uncut flower essence formulas that will initiate movement toward the light, and will receive automatic notification at three months and six months to submit his current digital photo for energetic assessment and an indication of evolutionary progress. That level of membership includes one-on-one counseling. As he evolves, his rating can climb.

The fee structure of the site offers many levels of participation. Non-members of Exceptional-Integrity.com, wishing to know if a particular individual is a level one (rated) member, can access the site a certain number of times for free. This lowest tier of access shows only whether the member in question is at least a level one rating, but gives no details. Should a non-member wish more details, he has to join, and has many choices of fees for services. If a member should desire to have a non-member gain access to see his rating, he can generate a one-time code that will allow the non-member to see the part of his files that he designates.

Michael is thrilled when he envisions the following example scenario:

Let us say a single, spiritually motivated entrepreneur (William) wants to introduce his product to Asian markets, starting with Japan. He knows no one in Japan, and is aware that under normal circumstances, by virtue of cultural norms, it would be virtually impossible to do business without the support of a Japanese partner with whom he had established trust. Exceptional-Integrity.com could solve this dilemma, and much more.

William has an integrity rating of two, and feels that with his business ideas, anyone registered on Exceptional-Integrity.com in Japan will likely respond to his letter of introduction. He finds there are thirty-five Exceptional-Integrity.com members listed in Tokyo, and begins correspondence with them. Several are delighted to make his acquaintance, as the barrier of the question of trust is a non-issue.

William finds that he can travel to Japan and immediately have a close connection of trust with four highly relevant business contacts. Additionally, William just happens to notice that of the seven women listed on Exceptional-Integrity.com in Tokyo, three of them are single. Each of them is delighted to hear from him, as there are no issues around trust. Without wasted time of the conventional dating scene, Michael knows, before he even gets to Tokyo, that he could have an in-depth meeting of heart and mind with at least one woman there.

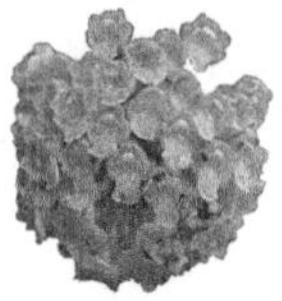

Wireless Transmissions and Flower Frequencies

Charlie Simms is VP-Marketing and Sales Operations at Verizon Wireless. He had worked his way up the corporate ladder, and previously held the position of Area Sales and Operations Manager at AT&T Advertising.

Charlie was a basic, Mid-Western kind of guy, but was known for his openness to new ideas. Even so, it was a real stretch for him to seriously consider a simple proposal put forward by Andrea Wilson, one of the twelve regional sales managers assembled for quarterly project coordination in the conference room of the Verizon building where Charlie had his office.

Due to Charlie's previous job, he was quite familiar with AT&T's marketing strategies, and there were some real challenges to be solved, centering around the question of how Verizon could acquire some of AT&T's market share of the all important iPhone.

Andrea listened to comments from, and conflict between, several of the regional sales managers, and really didn't feel like contributing anything. Commentary had been going on all around Andrea, and after everyone had voiced their ideas, objections, and frustrations, all eyes turned toward her. She was in the regional market that had the largest iPhone potential, and was expected to have some important insights as to how certain challenges could be met. Before she said anything, she asked for permission to speak honestly. Permission was granted. What Andrea had to say really surprised just about everyone.

She began by recounting the personal journey she had been on over the last year. Everyone had known Andrea for that length of time, so some of the details were known to them – many were not. She described the challenges of being a single mom while attempting to maintain high level performance in her very stressful job. She pointed out that regardless of the level of her intelligence and her problem solving capabilities, a year ago she felt she was failing in her ability to provide the kind of parenting her daughter needed and that she would also fail in achieving her business objectives. She wondered why she did not have the kind of loving bond with her child that she desired. So she sought help from a doctor who practiced integrative holistic care, which Andrea also described as mind-body healing.

She brilliantly summarized how performance, attitudes, creativity and many other features in our life are influenced by our stored subconscious memories and beliefs. She recounted that when her doctor examined her by newly developed methods of reflex analysis (assessing changes in muscle strength), he was able to locate self-sabotaging beliefs hidden in her unconscious mind. Then she described how she was amazed when the unwanted beliefs were diminished and eventually eradicated by consuming quantum frequencies collected from uncut flowers. All she had to do for this amazing "intervention" was to place drops of the frequencies in her drinking water! After consuming the flower frequency drops, she was was able to more easily and joyfully accomplish all her duties, obligations, and commitments.

She gave even more personal details. The doc found, during his initial exam, that at the unconscious mind level Andrea:

- was losing energy from her heart because of a cycling memory of the shocking news she received by phone that her husband had died;[3]
- was not able to receive love;[4]
- had poor self-esteem despite her enormous capabilities and good looks;[5] and finally,
- felt her mistakes were "unforgiveable."[6]

The doc ordered a custom blend of four flower frequencies for Andrea, each containing energetic countermeasures to remove the destructive beliefs from her unconscious mind. At about three weeks after starting the drops, Andrea started noticing that her daughter was more emotionally expressive and loving toward her.

When the bottle of drops was gone at four weeks and Andrea went for a follow-up assessment, the doc found that upon retesting she demonstrated the ability to receive

3 P.247, Heartmend for resolution.

4 P.249, Flor de la Luna for resolution.

5 P.245, Tulip Poplar for resolution.

6 P.247, Star Spirit Flower for resolution.

love – the flower administered to facilitate that shift had worked! He explained that once Andrea was able to receive love, that transformation naturally called out to her daughter to give of love.

The lifting of all the unhealthy unconscious beliefs that were discovered in her last year of treatment had truly changed her life: relieving unnecessary burdens, improving relations with her daughter, and all together contributing to her improved and outstanding performance at work.

With disarming sincerity and genuine loving intention Andrea outlined a new way to succeed in business. She suggested that if Will would try taking frequencies from a remarkable flower she had encountered, he might experience less need to be in control[7] at their meetings (at which point everyone laughed); she pointed out to Sarah that there was a flower whose frequencies instilled a sense of self-love,[8] and that would be accompanied by true empowerment.

Ms. Wilson diplomatically suggested transformational uncut flower essences (which she had been studying over the last year of her care) for each of the sales managers. She wrote down the names of the flowers for each attendee, and when she checked in a few weeks later, most of the sales managers had ordered and were taking their flower drops.

Andrea anticipated that greater harmony and cohesiveness would ensue in her team members, and that would be THE feature that would sharpen everyone's competitive edge. Regardless of the outcome, she felt a significant event had occurred in just one conference room among many in all of Verizon's offices.

To achieve a clear business objective, everyone had agreed to try a new and rapid process to remove internal mind obstacles that would result in the liberation of creativity. And without even knowing it, all the participants would be infused with a pure spiritual light. Surely there would be no harm in that!

L.A. Socialite Hatches Plan
To Rapidly Elevate Human Consciousness

Tinsley Kensington was lounging under an umbrella on the large deck of her house on Amalfi Drive, in the posh neighborhood above the Riviera Country Club in West Los Angeles. (The estate of Steven Spielberg adjoins her land.) She was staring at a spectacular view of the Pacific Ocean, looking across a large canyon bordering on Will Roger's State Park and beyond. On clear days the Catalina Islands are visible about 26 miles offshore.

She was perplexed. Here she was sitting in one of the most beautiful and privileged

7 P.251, Herb of the Cross.

8 P.260, Blue Lechenaultia.

settings in the world, and why wasn't she happier? What on earth was she to do next? The idea of attending another political fundraiser, Junior League ball, or red carpet Hollywood event was repellent.

"Hello mother," called Phoebe, "I'm home!"

"Oh wonderful!" Tinsley said to herself, "my sweet girl is back with us for a few days." Phoebe had just arrived in L.A. on her Thanksgiving break from Boston College. She shouted down to her mom as she ascended the sweeping stairway toward her room, "I'll be down in a sec. Just have to change my clothes."

Tinsley simply adored Phoebe who seemed to be equal parts daughter, sister, and girlfriend. Phoebe was far wiser than her years, and her mom actually relied on that quite a bit. Phoebe was appreciative of her father because she saw that he always had made welfare of the family a priority, and of course she had benefitted from his financial generosity and security. But she departed tremendously from her dad's political and social points of view. She was closer to her mom in that arena.

Tinsley smiled radiantly as Phoebe – now in comfortable jeans and t-shirt –passed through the screen door onto the deck. "Come sit here with me, and tell me what you've been up to," Tinsley said to Phoebe, who plopped down on the weatherproof outdoor lounger where her mom was ensconced. They exchanged the normal small talk for a while.

Then Phoebe carried on,"Well… let's see, there is something a bit more serious… Do you remember last month when I sent you an email telling you that I was finishing up my counseling with Tom Wilcox… you know, my therapist?"

"Umm…Yes"

"Well, he just released me from care, and we had a really interesting conversation at that point."

"Tell me about it."

"He explained to me that we had taken a wonderful first step on my path to self-discovery. He said that his purpose and scope of therapy was to help me identify the source of my conflicted feelings with respect to Dad, and other men that may enter my life, and, well, you know…"

"Yes, go on."

"Then he said that talking about the source of my problems is often an essential step, for the simple reason that it allows me to at least know why I am experiencing upset. But then he said -and at first it seemed kind of weird - that as important as talking is, the act of talking may not have changed my unconscious beliefs. And if those don't change, it's unlikely that I'll make different and healthier choices in the future. I mean, it makes sense, but I just hadn't ever thought of that.

He recommended that in my case, especially, he wanted me to see a holistic doctor that does what he called "unconscious mind re-patterning" using a new protocol.[9]

"Apparently this guy took training to allow him to match flower frequencies (that you take in drops) to "overwrite" and remove the frequencies of hidden sabotaging thoughts that keep holding everyone back. He used the analogy of installing clean software over a defective program. Tom made it clear that my intention to shift has to be in place for this whole thing to work, and he feels we have accomplished that.

"Anyway, I made an appointment to see this doctor after I return from break, and I would like you to check out his web site and some others, and tell me what you think."

"Oh, of course I will, sweetheart, this sounds… interesting."

"Mom," Phoebe said, "you seem kind of distracted. Your energy is off. Are you O.K.? … What's going on?"

Tinsley managed a meager smile, "So you noticed?"

Then a conversation erupted which Phoebe had not expected. She was astonished. Her mom seemed to be having some sore of spiritual awakening. Wide-ranging topics were discussed the whole rest of the afternoon. Essentially they dealt with nothing less than a deeper look at the meaning of existence.

Tinsley was a strikingly beautiful and intelligent forty-four-year-old woman wondering what to do with the rest of her life. What kind of advice could Phoebe give? All she could do was listen. Eventually her mother arrived at the most difficult topic, her relationship with Phoebe's dad, Phillip.

Phillip was the same man he had always been: bright, personable, handsome and fit, intensely focused. He hadn't done anything wrong… really. Or had he, Tinsley kept questioning herself. You see, Tinsley's conundrum and ambivalence centered around wealth and the question of how her and her husband's net worth could now be over two hundred million dollars, when in 2008 they had a "mere" thirty or so million in total holdings.

As the vast majority of people were suffering hardship and some severe financial stresses, especially since 2008, her wealth was increasing by leaps and bounds. And as Phillip had enthusiastically described to Tinsley, he was just finishing up his "worst-case-scenario" business plan which, in anticipation of EU and US financial collapse, would allow him and several of his buddies to acquire key pieces of corporations for pennies on the dollar and reassemble them into a global business giant worth billions.

Phillip had the knack of persistently being in the right place at the right time. Could he be faulted if he "leveraged" information he obtained freely, for example: in the midst of a close-knit round of golf when a pumped up CEO "let slip" that his company's top secret merger was finalized and would be announced tomorrow. Wouldn't he be stupid

9 The FlorAlive holographic scanning process.

if he didn't call his broker during lunch with a significant buy order to earn a couple of million dollars overnight?

Phillip was known as a "deal closer." He started his training in neuro-linguistic programming in college and continued thereafter studying advanced "negotiation" tactics from mentors unknown, until he acquired what, in Tinsley's current consciousness, was a dubious distinction. Phillip was able to use what would honestly be called a type of mind control. He could skillfully manage desperate business owners and executives about to be severely exploited so they would end up feeling good about corporate "restructuring" whereby their company (including employees' pensions) would, in the end, be destroyed. He just had a gift. Compensation for his "gift" was a fee or stock options that could go as high as ten percent of the valuation of the new company formed.

Phoebe had had misgivings about her family's wealth since her junior year in high school, and she was astonished that her mother had now arrived at a higher level of motivational awareness. As Tinsley spoke, Phoebe was calculating what she could say to her that would be encouraging.

"Mom," she began, "I have an idea. You have some pretty substantial business savvy of your own. Why don't you look for an entirely different form of business opportunity?"

"What are you suggesting?" Tinsley replied.

"A couple of things come to mind. For example, if a shift toward higher consciousness does occur in 2012 and thereafter, then even if there is economic upheaval, and a lot of the old social order collapses, new companies will arise that provide needed services in a sustainable and ethical way. Start working on identifying what those will be."

"You know," she replied, "that's a really good idea."

During the remainder of Phoebe's stay she didn't discuss any heavy topics again with her mom. She hung out with her L.A. friends, enjoyed Thanksgiving dinner and the family get-together, and returned to school after a few days.

About four weeks later, Tinsley got an email from Phoebe with the subject line,

"Hoping For Amazing Transformation!" and, of course, that got her attention. Phoebe described her first visit with Dr. Thomas Wilson and what had transpired. "Basically," Phoebe wrote, "he found on me what he finds on a high percentage of new patients. That is, in spite of my counseling and my knowing the source of my problems and confusion, I nevertheless still have lots of negative self-talk going on, and this attracts negative experiences to me.

On the unconscious level, he found that I did not believe 'love is good.' Can you imagine that?! And get this. I had a really big subconscious belief causing me to broadcast the frequency, 'I am destined to attract troubled men into my life.' Jeeze! He gave me flower frequencies to cancel that belief, and also to allow some love in. His retest on me shows that the drops I am putting in water are working, so we'll see as time passes what happens. I must say, I feel lots 'lighter' ." Then she continued on with more banal news.

In about a month, Phoebe reported further progress with Dr. Wilson, and this time Tinsley was truly delighted with what she heard. "Doc retested me and confirmed that I have created and am expressing the pathways that allow me to receive love. The little "Flower of the Moon"– Flor de la Luna – did its job! Perhaps that explains why this wonderful guy showed up in my life just about two weeks ago. He is so different from previous boyfriends. Definitely NOT a troubled man. (He is probably more evolved than I am.)"

Phoebe's report inspired Tinsley to investigate the whole discovery of the new approach to accelerating consciousness by using uncut flower frequencies, and she really studied the FlorAlive.com web site. I was later to find out how deeply it interested her.

Acting on Phoebe's recommendation when she had visited over Thanksgiving, Tinsley accepted an invitation from socialite and web media entrepreneur, Arianna Huffington. Scores of Hollywood and L.A. society heavyweights had been invited to an event taking place in her home at the beginning of the new year. (A similar event had taken place in 2007.)

Dr. Peter Diamandis (Xprize founder)[10] was going to be speaking at that gathering about his experiences in fostering a new type of entrepreneurship to encourage discoveries and technologies for the betterment of humanity. Perhaps, Tinsley thought, she would meet the kind of people and learn about the types of business that would be worth supporting, as old molds are being broken, and a new era of consciousness might well have the chance to finally emerge.

Elegantly attired in a subdued dinner dress, Tinsley went to the Huffington event alone. She did not want to attract attention and intended to circulate in the background listening and carefully observing the attendees for signs of "consciousness." She sensed and observed, as always, that wealthy people tend to be rather mainstream when they invest time or money in a philanthropy project. They like the tried and true – things that are bankable and institutional. (Although curiously she mused, "They can drop a fortune on a personal whim without even thinking about it!")

[10] The X PRIZE Foundation (a non-profit organization created in 1995) has the mission to bring about "radical breakthroughs for the benefit of humanity" through incentivized competition. It fosters high-profile competitions that motivate individuals, companies and organizations across all disciplines to develop innovative ideas and technologies that help solve the grand challenges that restrict humanity's progress. In 1996, entrepreneur Peter Diamandis offered a $10 million prize to the first privately financed team that could build and fly a three-passenger vehicle 100 kilometers into space twice within two weeks. The $10 million purse was awarded on October 4, 2004 to Mojave Aerospace Ventures. (Source:Wikipedia).

Like many of the other attendees, Tinsley couldn't help but be impressed by Dr. Diamandis. She discovered that his academic background is truly impressive: MIT degrees in molecular genetics and aerospace engineering, followed by an M.D. from Harvard Medical School. But more than that, she could tell that he believed in what he was saying, and he was a compelling speaker.

She took special note when he was describing his incentive cash prize awards only given to teams when they had completed and proven their prototype or discovery : "What we try to do is really reach down into the souls of people and say, 'You have the ability to solve the problems… it doesn't take the government, it doesn't take a large corporation. In fact, most brilliant solutions to problems come from the mind of an individual …We believe there is a new model. It's putting out a clear set of rules and a large cash challenge and saying, 'We don't care where you are, where you're from, where you've gone to school, whatever you've done before – you solve this problem, you win.' " [11]

Tinsley had done enough study of mind/body healing and holistic behavioral therapies to have learned about specialized brain imaging and multi-lead electroencephalogram readings that can be used to non-invasively monitor rapid changes in brain activity that correlate with changes in mood and emotion.

She learned that it is possible to demonstrate with live images where blood circulation or electrical activity in the brain is centered, and after an intervention procedure (like the administration of uncut flower essences) to re-measure to see if the center of brain activity has moved to a different brain area of expression – say from a rage center to an area of tranquility. She couldn't help but think about how exciting it would be to create a large cash prize for anyone who could show that they had developed a natural set of harmless frequencies (NOT pharmaceuticals with side-effects) that shift brain activity from disruptive to more positive areas.

She met a few people at Huffington's gathering who really impressed her and took down their contact information for the future.

When she returned home she read a little bit more about Dr. Diamandis and ran across the following that he had written in his blog:

"So you're trying to fight cancer, solve poverty, educate children...solve the grand challenges of our day. How would you like to make sure that your philanthropic donation was actually used to solve your chosen challenge? Not to fund attempts at a solution, not to fund ideas, but to fund THE solution that would be known in history books as a pivotal moment when an intractable problem was conquered."

What, she wondered, could be a greater achievement than to be able to administer – at will – safe flower frequencies that can immediately shift the brain's negative self-talk to a more positive expression (and that additionally constitutes a massively "green"

[11] Quote recorded by journalist Robb Mandelbaum.

business because the product is made with essentially zero footprint)?

She thought of personally contacting Dr. Diamandis but then realized that his background was so mainstream that he would probably not recognize the enormous potential of the project she was contemplating. His large cash incentive prizes had all dealt with highly technical areas such as aerospace, genomics, and the like. How sad, she thought, that the enormous pure power of healing and transformational frequencies within flowers would likely be overlooked by him.

Tinsley's thoughts continued to progress until she arrived at the following idea which felt truly inspired:. She thought to herself, "I will find someone who is holistically oriented, and who has a private research foundation that, at the present time, does not have funded projects. Then I'm going to put a little of my own money into that foundation so they can do the non-profit paperwork and see to it that a flower essence pilot study is carried out. If it is successful, then I will speak to some of the charitable donors I met at Arianna's (and maybe Arianna herself) to see if we can get some real interest in this amazing possibility."

I was astonished and delighted when Mrs. Kensington shared her enthusiastic idea with me. I mentioned to her that a professionally conducted small pilot study (overseen by a reputable research Ph.D. in neuroscience) could likely be conducted for under one hundred thousand dollars. Her response: "That just might be doable… Let's see how it can happen!"

Enlightenment in Carver Park

Jamal Williams was a jewel in the rough, a prodigiously brilliant fourteen-year-old living near Carver Park – one of the worst projects in Chicago, close to the corner E. 133rd St. and South Greenwood Ave. In spite of the fact that he didn't have a dad, that his beleaguered single mom was worn out from her work and seldom had quality time with him, and that his surroundings seemed hopeless, he maintained a dynamically positive attitude. He knew that his life would be charmed and that his circumstances would change. Or rather, he was certain that on his own he would be able to change his circumstances.

Jamal had an insatiable desire to learn about why people become impoverished, why they stay poor and disenfranchised, and how rare individuals break free from the bleak existence that he saw around himself every day.

On his thirteen birthday (he chose thirteen as his lucky number) he decided to bolster his odds for success by "consuming" every book he could find written by self-help and motivational teachers. His first book was the classic written by Dale Carnegie, *How To Win Friends And Influence People*. Then he "galloped" through an historical list of personal development resources: Napoleon Hill's *Think and Grow Rich*; Zig Ziglar's training material; Jim Rohn's teachings; "peak performance coach" Anthony Robbins' *Awaken The Giant Within* and other of his books; ending with the books of Wayne

Dyer. All of this was completed by his fourteenth birthday.

As he analyzed the works of all these dynamic individuals, he realized that he shared a profoundly important characteristic with them. All had to have possessed an indefatigable belief, deep down, that success would be a natural consequence of their life. How is it that people are born with that knowing, he wondered? How much of that internal confidence can be taught? Can it be transfused from a book into a human being? That was the burning question that additionally motivated Jamal's reading marathon of self-help books. He wanted to know what he could do to help his dear friends Da-Shawn and Lemarr, for they did not share Jamal's inspired outlook on life. They were a couple of years older than he was. They lived in the same difficult circumstances that he did, but they were damaged and immobilized by it.

Even though they were not natively brilliant as he was, Jamal saw promise in each of them. To watch Lemarr on a basketball court produced a state of wonderment because it was hard to imagine how a human body could be constructed with such a perfect form – free from any distortion – presumably capable of all physical movements requiring superb coordination. But on some days, Lemarr would begin to play and then suddenly walk off the court with a pale and hollow demeanor. Jamal discovered that those days occurred for Lemarr when his mother had been physically beaten or verbally abused the night before by yet another loser "boyfriend."

With the exception of Da-Shawn's over-weight condition, Jamal could not help but envision a great life for him. He was patient, enormously kind, highly perceptive, and he really knew how to listen. Jamal always saw Da-Shawn as head of a human resources department. Da-Shawn had a father, Jimmy, but he might well have been better off without him. Jimmy was the kindly sort of alcoholic – self-effacing and overall rather pathetic. Jamal reckoned that the father's poor self-esteem was a core cause of Da-Shawn's terrible self image and his obesity.

From his self-help repertoire Jamal selected books and training material specific to Da-Shawn and Lemarr. He reminded and cajoled each of them to persevere in their reading and study of the material, attempting as often as possible to quiz them. They did not respond to his support and all the best motivational literature presented to them. They persisted in their self-destructive ways. Jamal was very disappointed but not really surprised.

As a result of his failure to shift the lives of Lemarr and Da-Shawn, Jamal resorted to what I imagine is one of his great strengths: creatively reframing a challenge to arrive at the possibility of a new solution.

He analyzed the motivational literature that he had studied and realized that it covered the time period from the early nineteen hundreds to about nineteen eighty-five. He decided to research what had been developed in the areas of personal transformation from the mid eighties to the present. And that is how, in a very unusual way, I became acquainted with him.

Jamal discovered that the next step of development in the personal transformation movement taking place in the late eighties was the remarkable (and unfortunately little known) discipline with the misnomer of "energy psychology." It wasn't really psychology at all. Rather it was the brilliant insight of chiropractic physician, George Goodheart, that normal muscle strength could be manually evaluated in a way that could measure "turning on" of muscles (facilitation) or weakening (inhibition) depending on what the test subject (patient) verbally stated. In other words, an examining health professional could, with the patient's permission, query his mind to find out at the subconscious level what is actually believed.

Also profound, Jamal thought, was the possibility to practice a transformational exercise (or read a book) and measure afterwards if a person's original/habitual unhealthy beliefs changed as a result of the exercise or reading information in a book. This really got Jamal excited.[12]

More internet research resulted in Jamal discovering a chronology in this new mind/body area of natural healing, beginning in the late eighties, including: TFT (thought field therapy), Neuro Emotional Therapy, Psych-K, and at the turn of the millennium, FlorAlive uncut flower frequency therapy. The FlorAlive.com website really intrigued Jamal with its dozens of consumer testimonial videos attesting to major life changes by simply consuming drops of flower frequencies in drinking water. This interest prompted Jamal to call my company, speak with one of my assistants, and with his charming and persuasive manner, to arrange a phone meeting with me to hear his presentation of an "important research project" he had devised.

My assistant told me about Jamal's fervor, that he was just fourteen years old, and that I should really hear him out. I am glad I did. I was amazed by his keen insights and maturity.

He succinctly presented a case study of Lemarr, Lemarr's mother (Brianna), and Da-Shawn. He surmised that to strengthen and balance Lemarr would first require the healing of Lemarr's mother and the cessation of her damaging relationships with men. He similarly had analyzed Da-Shawn's situation. He had studied the characteristics of each of the 49 different FlorAlive flower essences and assembled "custom blends" for each person. I was astonished and impressed with Jamal's comprehension of mind and spirit transformation through quantum flower frequencies. So when he let me know that he had no money to pay for the three custom blends he was requesting, I was already inclined to help him out in his very unusual situation. But he didn't let me get that far. Up front he addressed the matter of doing an exchange with me, and I was nearly speechless and certainly amused initially. But the more Jamal spoke, the more I recognized he was completely serious and very likely filled with integrity.

He had reasoned that Brianna must have suffered substantial emotional or physical

12 P.3, Measuring Our Invisible Mind Activity.

abuse as a child, and having studied the FlorAlive healing model, he knew that had to be addressed first thing (with the FlorAlive flower frequency extract of Blue Eyed Grass). He imagined that her self-esteem was very poor, and that she needed to have that bolstered by the energy of Tulip Poplar flower. He knew that her heart had been broken many times and wanted to have Heartmend in her formula. He wanted her to finally be able to receive love (from the flower frequencies of Flor de la Luna "Flower of the Moon"), which he assumed she had rarely if ever experienced, and certainly not least, he was sure she would need the special FlorAlive preparation of Maroon Beth Root flower to enable her to shift so that she would no longer attract troubled men.

Jamal said to me, "Dr. Davis, if Maroon Bethroot works and frees Lemarr's mom from the mess she's in, it's really going to benefit your company. Because… if it works, I'm going to tell a lot of people, and… Lemar abruptly stopped speaking. After a few moments, he resumed speaking in a very measured tone. "You know who I am going to tell about this? … Oprah Winfrey! She's right here in Chicago. If it works, I'm going to let her know. She'll love it." To which I replied, "Yes, Oprah would love this, and that would be great to let her know."

I wished Jamal well with his desire to turn around people's lives, and told him I would be interested to hear of any progress. He replied, "Oh, you'll hear from me, Dr. Davis, don't worry." I passed him back to the order desk where they recorded his order and took his mailing address. About a month later, one of the order desk staff mentioned that Jamal was on the phone asking for a refill of each of the custom blends, and I gave them a thumbs up for one more free round of the combinations he originally ordered. What I didn't know was that he had obtained my email address so that he could send me the documentation of the changes he was witnessing, and I got that communication from him several weeks later.

I wasn't amazed at what Jamal observed and described, because I had seen similar scenarios myself. But I was truly impressed by the way he documented the changes he had observed in Lamarr, Brianna, and Da-Shawn. He said what he witnessed relating to Brianna was "unbelievable." Immediately after she began taking her flower frequency drops (containing Maroon Bethroot), the emotionally abusive relationship Brianna was in "exploded and evaporated." Astonishingly, the other "loser guys" that were always vying for her attention simply were not coming around. "It was like she was wearing some sort of 'idiot' repellant," he wrote.

Then, true to his word, he related how he had been attempting to contact Oprah Winfrey through her staff at Harpo Studios. He was disappointed to find out that her Angel Network Foundation had ceased operations, because he thought that organization would have been able to test projects that could document if flower frequencies could alleviate suffering among inner city residents. He promised he would not give up on contacting Oprah, and that he would let me know of any progress. I thanked him for his efforts and smiled at his perseverance. I didn't imagine I would hear anything more about it.

So you can imagine my surprise when I got a call about six weeks later from a staff assistant to Dana Brooks, the executive producer of Oprah's Lifeclass which airs on the cable channel OWN – Oprah Winfrey Network. She explained the very unusual circumstances of how she ran into a young man named Jamal![13]

She was so captivated by him that she decided to listen to his pitch, and when he was through he had nearly convinced her to suggest a trial of FlorAlive to her boss. She then took the time to call two of the doctors giving testimonials on the FlorAlive web site to interview them as to the authenticity of the astonishing personal transformation changes they had reported witnessing in their patients.

As a result of their confirmation, she mentioned that her boss, Dana Brooks, had an interest. I was amazed and delighted. She wondered if I would take the time on a Friday to come to Chicago to do an in-training of eight staff members at Harpo Studios to create custom blends they would all use for a three month trial period. She said to me, "If even a few of our staff that are volunteering for this study experience the types of changes seen on the testimonials on your web site – just from adding floral drops to their drinking water – we will film a similar type trial and present updates of its outcome on segments with Oprah doing a Lifeclass."

Wouldn't it be wonderful for that experiment to take place!

[13] Due to some very clever sleuthing and serendipity, Jamal found her on a Saturday when she was walking her dogs. In his research he had discovered that Lifeclass (which airs on Oprah Winfrey Network) was a special project of Oprah. It is the type of powerful educational forum that she always wanted but didn't really have the freedom to develop previously when she was on network television.)

Appendix 2

Corruption In Scientific Research

One of the starkest examples of corruption in scientific research that is costing many people their health and wasting untold billions of dollars is falsification of drug studies – perversion of scientific research integrity by pharmaceutical giants bent on profit.

Mainstream media is now so tightly controlled by corporate interests that news events with potentially negative implications for major corporate powers rarely, if ever, show up on the evening news. Such is the case for drug companies' falsification and manipulation of "scientific" research data produced for the purpose of drug "safety and efficacy" approval and, of course, for marketing (indoctrination of physicians and the public).

Drug company corruption and the fallout from it has been –and is – massive, and yet the reporting of these events is largely relegated to internet blogs and online news services, the most influential probably being the Huffington Post. Its March 18, 2011 issue[1] reported the enormous scientific fraud of Scott Reuben, M.D. who completely fabricated 21 research papers (or more) supporting the effectiveness of Vioxx , the pain killer (manufactured by Merck) which caused at least 3,400 deaths.

"Merck organized a ghostwriting campaign that involved some 96 scientific articles to support Vioxx. Key ones did not mention the death of some patients during clinical trials. Through a class action lawsuit against Vioxx in Australia, it was discovered that [respected medical publisher] Elsevier had created a fake medical journal for Merck – the Australasian Journal of Joint and Bone Medicine – and perhaps 10 other fake journals for Merck and other Big Pharma companies."[2]

Pharmaceutical fraud law firms have arisen such as Nolan and Auerbach, P.A. who report on their website[3]

> that "500 drugs are now under investigation by the U.S. Department of Justice under the False Claims Act." It describes sub-sections of drug companies' illegal activities as:

[1] Fraudulent Medical Research Could Affect Your Diagnosis http://www.huffingtonpost.com/dr-sherri-tenpenny/fraud-an-examination-of-m_b_835771.html?view=print&comm_ref=false.

[2] Source: Beware the Ghostwriters of Medical Research http://www.cchrint.org/tag/clinical-trials/page/2/.

[3] Pharmaceutical Fraud/Overview http://www.whistleblowerfirm.com/.

- Clinical trial fraud
- Kickbacks (for which it lists seven different types.)
- Off-label marketing
- Good Manufacturing Practices (GMP) Fraud

In 2011 The Hals Report[4] wrote: "In September of 2009 Pfizer settled civil and criminal charges in the amount of 2.3 billion dollars with the federal government for illegally marketing four types of drugs. The Pfizer corporation made over 180 billion dollars selling twelve kinds of drugs and only paid 2.3 billion dollars in fines, talk about a phenomenal business plan!"

There is a another matter that is not immediately as glaring and costly as the pharmaceutical cartel's corruption, but is one that should cause concern due to its insidious nature: censorship of scientists' free access to gather and disseminate information that departs from the status quo.

In his article, "Covert Censorship by the Physics Preprint Archive," Nobel Prize laureate Brian Josephson (Physics, 1973) reports on the manipulative and dubious activities of the physics preprint archive, arXiv.org, administered by Cornell University. Scientists who have unorthodox views or who have chafed the egos of unknown power brokers may suddenly find that they cannot submit their research to this critical forum for sharing information with colleagues. They may be quite literally black-listed.

Seasoned scientist, J. Marvin Herndon (geophysics, Ph.D. in nuclear chemistry, Texas A&M), corroborates Dr. Josephson's findings relating to arXiv.org's preprint archive. Much worse, however, is Dr. Herndon's discussion of how something central to the authentication of valid science – anonymous peer review – originated, and how it "has become a tool of suppression."[5]

Dr. Herndon explained that, "In 1951, the U.S. National Science Foundation (NSF) was established to provide support for post-World War II civilian scientific research... NSF invented the concept of 'peer review', wherein a scientist's competitors would review and evaluate his/her/their proposal for funding, and the reviewers' identities would be concealed. The idea of using anonymous 'peer reviewers' must have seemed like an administrative stroke of genius because the process was adopted by virtually all government science-funding agencies that followed and **almost universally by editors of scientific journals** [emphasis mine.] But no one seems to have considered the

[4] Fraud, Cover-ups and Corruption: Welcome to the Drug Industry!
http://www.thehalsreport.com/2011/01/fraud-cover-ups-and-corruption-welcome-to-the-drug-industry/.

[5] The Corruption of Science in America
http://www.sott.net/articles/show/234225-The-Corruption-of-Science-in-America.

lessons of history with respect to secrecy. Secrecy is certainly necessary in matters of national security and defense. But in civilian science, does secrecy and the concomitant freedom from accountability really encourage truthfulness?"

Dr. Herndon definitively concluded that it does not. Obviously if there is collusion between peer reviewers in supposedly trustworthy scientific journals, such that innovative work is refused publication, or false "science" is allowed publication, the credibility of science is dealt a grievous blow.

For reasons above, generally invoking the "sacred cow" of "science" to substantiate research findings (and conversely that a novel idea seems "unscientific") may be quite meaningless.

What is truly important for meaningful discovery is that the scientist must have an honest love of the subject under investigation (and hence a real appreciation of whatever "truth" or acceptance of whatever invalidation may be revealed relating to it); he should strive to be intellectually honest; and he must be comfortable divulging the sources of his funding with complete transparency.

Appendix 3

Dr. Fritz-Albert Popp Study Comparing ReviveAll™ to Dr. Bach's five-flower rescue formula (created in the early twentieth century.)

Dr. Fritz-Albert Popp achieved pre-eminent status worldwide in the fields of bio-photonics and German biological medicine. His laboratory has been a leader in being able to scientifically measure the amount of "life force" or vital energy in foods and natural medicines. Over many years he developed a highly controlled and reproducible scientific protocol (derived from the field of bio-photonics) to measure how much light is re-emitted from the substance being studied after it has been exposed to a measured amount of light. **The higher the re-emitted light, the greater the vital energy of the substance.**

In a 2005 study privately commissioned by Dr. Brent Davis, Popp reported "significantly higher" vitality (27% greater growth stimulus) in ReviveAll™ when compared to the five flower Bach rescue essence that accounts for more than one half of the world sales of all flower essences.

Since 2005, the FlorAlive® uncut flower extraction method has been significantly enhanced, and appears to be producing flower essences that are significantly more powerful than the samples originally submitted to Dr. Popp for the analysis in this study. In 2012 an effort to contact Dr. Popp was made so that the experiment could be repeated with the new and upgraded essence. At that time this type of analytic service was not available.

The graph below is from Dr. Popp's 2005 report. The y-axis below (vertical) is a measure of re-emitted photons (particles of light) per 50 milliseconds from the sample of flower essences that were placed in the measurement system.

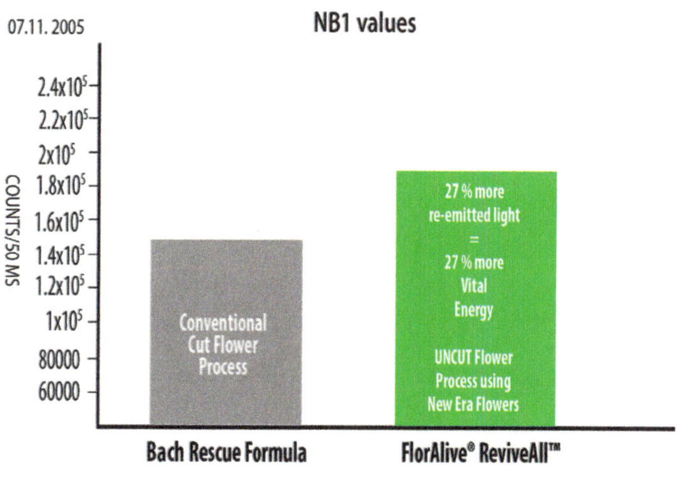

Appendix 4

Dr. Bach's Leading Sales Formula compared to FlorAlive® ReviveAll™ (FERV Sample)- April 2014

Comparison of samples in 100 ml aqueous solution (tap water). Analyzed with the Bioscope bioharmonic spectrum detection system that permits (by direct vortex antenna measurement) the detection and analysis of electrical field interactions in biological systems and bioactive matter.

Samples:

1. Dr. Bach's Emergency Formula in Tap Water (5 sprays)
2. FlorAlive® FERV Sample = ReviveAll™ in Tap Water (5 drops)

Surface Spectrum - Low Frequency Range

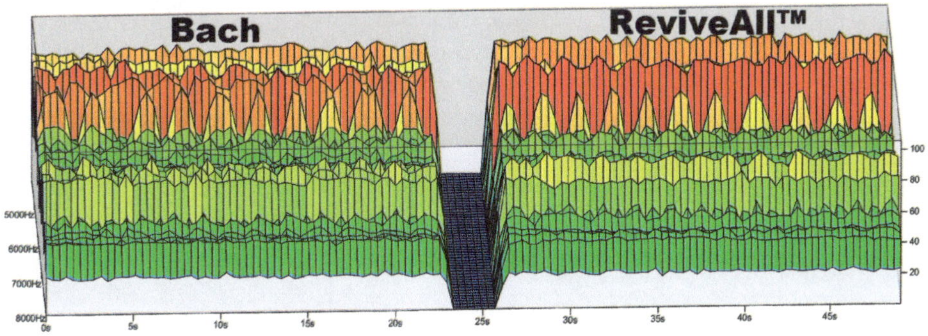

Fig 1. Surface Spectrum. The sample electrical dynamics shown over a time period of 15 seconds (X axis) with Frequency (Y axis) and Amplitude (Z axis) in the lower frequency range.

Interpretation:

The wave structure pulsations of the FlorAlive® sample (on the right) shows a more clear and regular character as compared to the graph on the left (especially the 5500 Hz range.) This is an indicator of greater coherence. That is associated with a greater ability to harmonize our emotional/physical structure.

Average Spectral Amplitude

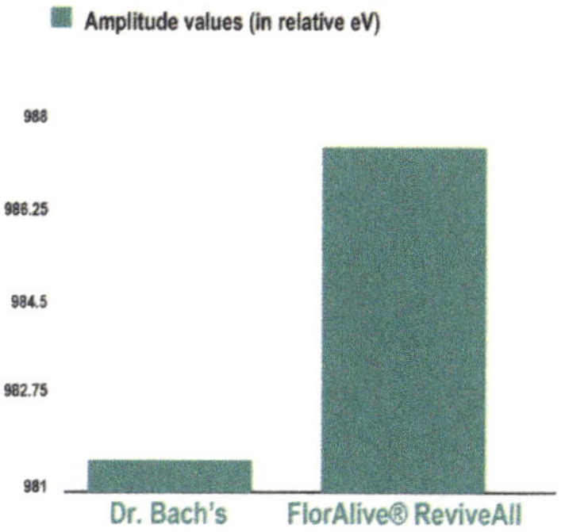

Fig 3. Spectral Amplitude. The sample average electrical charge response indicating electrical absorption (lower values) and reflection (higher values).

Interpretation:

Higher electrical reflection values suggest that ReviveAll™ may repel electrical field energies externally influencing our body in an undesirable way.

Appendix 5

FlorAlive Human Biocompatibility Testing - FEFFB (Combination #4)

Biocompatibility evaluation of the human body's electrical response to FlorAlive samples. Subject is a healthy 40 year old female . FlorAlive Sample FEFFB . The images display three subject states:

1) No sample (this is used as a reference measurement);
2) FlorAlive sample held in the left hand (the sample is in a closed container); and
3) Three drops of FlorAlive sample placed on the tongue.

Field Dynamics - High Frequency

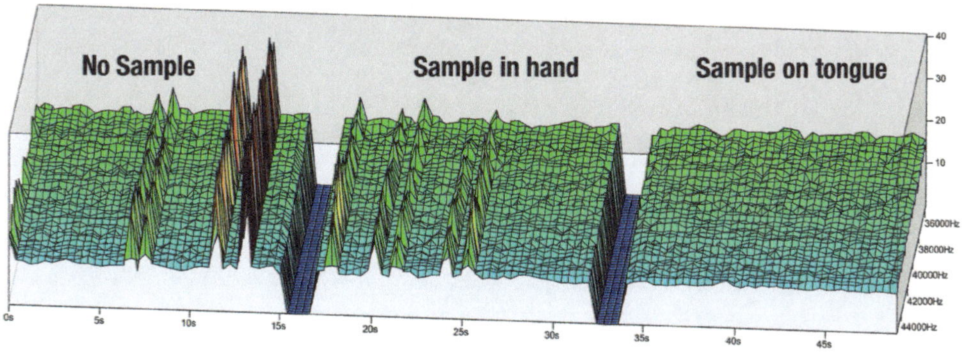

Fig 1. Surface Spectrum. The body's electrical dynamics shown over a time period of 15 seconds (X axis) with Frequency (Y axis) and Amplitude (Z axis) in the higher frequency range related to microscopic biological activity.

Interpretation:
The spikes of electrical discharge show a disharmony in the body at rest, and are diminished somewhat by just holding Combination #4, and are completely eliminated by dropping the essences on the tongue. This represents a significant calming effect. The anti-stress and balancing effect of FEE2P (Combination #3) is even stronger, and is demonstrated below.

Field Dynamics - High Frequency – FEE2P (Combination #3)

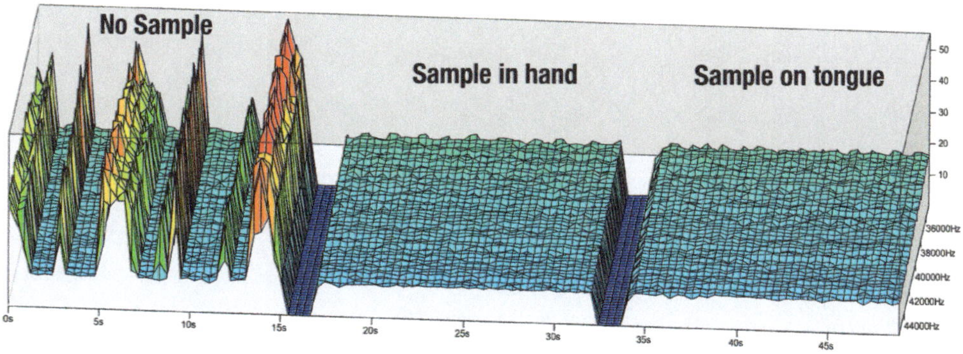

Appendix 6

Clinical Evaluation of FlorAlive® Flower Essences

October 1 to November 1, 2005

Marcelline Burns, Ph.D.
Brent W. Davis, D.C.

Measurement Instrument

With the assistance of cognitive research specialist, Marcelline Burns, Ph.D., Brent Davis, D.C. designed a questionnaire to serve as a test instrument. It presents a respondent with 20 negative statements about emotions, self-esteem, and energy states. (The statements are listed in Table 1 below.) Response is made to each of the 20 items by circling one number in a series 1 to 9 that appear adjacent to the statement. The number 1 signifies that the statement is not true for the respondent. A mid-range number signifies that the statement is moderately true, and the number 9 signifies that the statement is definitely true. Thus, high values reflect currently negative evaluations of the respondent's affect, circumstances, and experiences.

Procedures

Upon arrival at the session, 35 participants signed an Informed Consent document that described the content of the flower essence and each individual's responsibility. They then completed the measurement instrument. These pre-treatment questionnaires were collected onsite without inspection and submitted directly to Marcelline Burns, Ph.D.

Each participant was given sufficient flower essence for a 30-day period. They also were given a copy of the questionnaire with instructions to complete it after finishing the course of treatment. They were given the address of Dr. Burns' office and wereinstructed to mail the post-treatment questionnaires directly to that address. The post-treatment questionnaires were received largely during November of 2005. The rate of return for the post-treatment questionnaire was 66% (23 participants).

Results

Figure 1 graphs the participants' total scores pre- and post-treatment. The difference between the two sets of scores by the paired t-test is statistically significant (t 5.89, 22 df, $p<.001$). As can be seen, the responses of 20 of the 23 participants were more positive (lower scores) after the 30-day regimen of FlorAlive® flower essences. Their scores decreased on the post-treatment questionnaire compared to their scores on the pre-treatment questionnaire, changing on average by 34 points, which is a 41%

improvement.

An analysis of the total response scores reveals a statistically significant relationship between pre- and post-treatment responses (Spearman Rank Correlation $r = 0.61$, $p < .02$).

Scores for each of the 20 items were totaled and ranked across participants (Table 1). Pre-treatment and post-treatment scores are significantly related (Spearman Rank Correlation $r = 0.8$, $p < .01$).

Figure 1

Total Scores Pre & Post
FlorAlive® Flower Essence Treatment
23 Participants

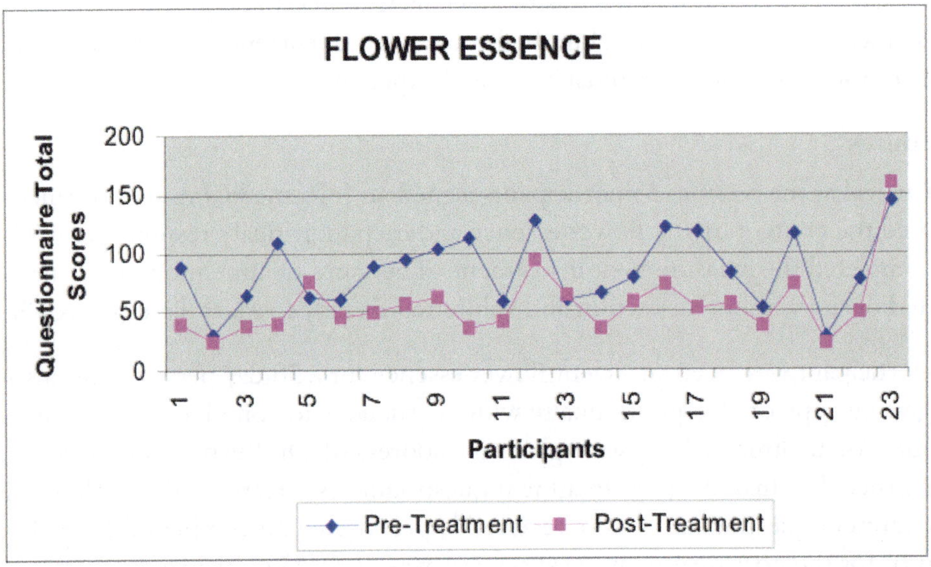

Note: lower score correlates with more positive outlook (post-treatment.)

Table 1

Pre and Post Treatment Responses, Ranked
Rank 1 = most negative response;
Rank 20 = least negative response

Item	Pre-treatment Rank	Item	Post-treatment Rank
1	17.5	Regardless of my efforts, I feel I cannot influence the outcome.	19
2	12	I feel cut off from others.	13.5
3	19	My future does not feel bright.	17.5
4	20	I frequently feel rage.	8
5	3	I feel the resentment of being controlled.	6
6	8	I hardly have any energy.	11
7	10	I feel shut down.	15
8	9	I have low self-esteem.	8
9	13	I am shy and awkward around others.	17.5
10	17.5	I feel worthless.	20
11	6.5	I very often feel discouraged.	10
12	1	I am not attracting the kind of man I desire into my life.	1
13	2	I defend my comfort zone most of the time.	2
14	5	I do not feel comfortable with my appearance.	3
15	15.5	I feel ashamed.	12
16	14	I don't have the resources to deal with undesirable men.	16
17	6.4	I feel alone.	5
18	4	I frequently feel fragmented mentally.	4
19	11	I have low energy most of the time.	8
20	15.5	I feel I cannot change my pattern of poor choices with men.	13.5

Conclusion

Relative to the 9 feeling/affect statements which improved (Table 2), "I feel shut down" (item 7) showed 52% improvement and more positive movement in its ranking than any of the other questionnaire statements (see Table 1).

Emotional and physical abuse are the primary causes of emotional "shut down." Further, they are fundamental components of the deepest cause of stress. The marked pre to post questionnaire improvement in item 7 of Table 2 especially, and in the other eight items as well, corroborates the clinical observation that FlorAlive® UNCUT Flower™ essences can significantly reduce the effects of major stressors, and cause an opening to positive consciousness and to the potential of a more exuberant life.

Table 2
Percentage Improvement of Affect & Consciousness in 20 of 23 FlorAlive Flower Essence Consumers Over 30 Days

Item #	Pre-test Score	Post-test Score	Pre (-) Post	% Improve-ment	Test phrase correlating with belief.
5	107	54	53	50	I feel the resentment of being controlled.
6	92	42	50	54	I hardly have any energy.
11	92	47	45	49	I very often feel discouraged.
7	82	39	43	52	I feel shut down.
2	78	41	37	47	I feel cut off from others.
9	70	36	34	49	I am shy and awkward around others.
1	67	35	32	48	Regardless of my efforts, I feel I cannot influence the outcome.
10	66	35	31	47	I feel worthless.
16	68	43	25	37	I don't have the resources to deal with undesirable men.

Postscript:

The implications of the following study are enormous. It was disseminated only to a small group of health professionals after it was conducted, and I trust that now it will stimulate reflection in a much larger body of people.

Procedures exist, that have been described herein, to measure evolutionary states of consciousness BEFORE and AFTER an individual encounters an experience or receives therapeutic input.

If a book, a seminar, a particular practice, a dietary supplement, or a flower essence purports that it will shift consciousness, properly trained practitioners can evaluate the extent to which that is true.

If, for example, all the attendees of a motivational seminar were pre-screened to measure their existing limiting unconscious beliefs – tested upon entry before the seminar begins – and then were measured upon exiting the seminar and two weeks after the seminar, we could chart the percentage of change and the duration of change experienced by the attendees.

I have essentially been doing that exercise with my patients for my whole professional career and especially in the last decade of developing uncut flower essences. I wanted to expand my test model to a large group of people who were not my patients and who had experienced lots of holistic practices that could have removed their limiting beliefs. Following (in Appendix 7) you will read about the critical limiting beliefs that still were present in the individuals tested and that were removed by my uncut flower essences.

Appendix 7

The L.A. 100 Phenomenon:

Astonishing Consciousness Paradox Revealed

by Brent W. Davis, D.C.

In October of 2007, I issued an invitation to a Los Angeles radio audience of highly informed holistic devotees. I asked for 100 people with special characteristics to show up at an event I envisioned taking place the evening of November 28, 2007. I asked for people to participate in my research study who had spent the majority of their adult life in the pursuit of the evolution of consciousness and holistic healing. When that evening in November came, 170 people from the greater Los Angeles area showed up at an auditorium in the Culver City Senior Citizens Center. The volunteer staff could not adequately handle that many people, so it was challenging. Nevertheless, what an extraordinary experience it turned out to be!

Before explaining the method that I and the doctor assisting me would be using for screening participants to find the extent of their limiting subconscious beliefs, I qualified the audience in the following way. I asked for a showing of raised hands in response to three questions:

Question 1:

Who among you has read books by at least one of the following authors?

a) Deepak Chopra
b) Wayne Dyer
c) Carolyn Myss
d) Don Miguel Ruiz
e) Eckhart Tolle

Question 2:

Who among you has participated in at least one of the following:

a) Holistic health conferences and conventions?
b) Weekend workshops to improve consciousness and health?
c) Viewing the movie, *The Secret*, one or more times?

Question 3:

Who among you has participated in at least one of the following:

a) Body/mind therapies to clear and balance your inner being?
b) Holistic psychotherapy and counseling?
c) Regularly practiced meditation?

Virtually everyone in the audience raised their hand after each question. I then commented, "Good! I know I have the right group of people for this experiment. To the extent that the inspiring wisdom and the state-of-the-art practices that you have embraced produce measurable transformation, then we should not find many core limiting beliefs in your SUBconscious minds." Continuing I said, "Unfortunately over the last several years that I have been doing careful screening of subconscious mind beliefs, that is not what I have found, nor has Dr. Garcia who is assisting me found that either. What has astonished us is to find that the wonderful practices people are doing and the events they attend frequently uplift only the conscious mind. They help us to make conscious choices toward a healthier life. For the most part, however, they do not change the deeply embedded negative subconscious beliefs that largely cause the problems and limitations in our lives.

"What we will be testing tonight in all the participants we screen is the prevalence of six limiting beliefs and noting how often they occur. Then we will test whether the UNCUT flower™ quantum frequencies found in the FlorAlive® combination essence, ReviveAll™ (and two other single essences, Flor de la Luna and Madame Fate), remove the limiting beliefs by overwriting them with higher and clearer frequencies. We will measure this using applied kinesiology evaluation with semantic screening of self-referential statements."

Following are the limiting subconscious beliefs for which we screened:

1. Regardless of my efforts, I cannot influence the outcome.
2. I am disconnected from the source of ALL life.
3. I am free from the effects of emotional abuse.
4. I am free from the influence of negative thoughts and beings.
5. I allow myself to receive.
6. I allow myself to receive love.

As an example, if a person has a strong arm indicator muscle, and upon evaluation, they make the statement, "I allow myself to receive love" and they weaken upon making that statement, it means that at the SUBconscious level, the person is not allowing herself/himself to receive love. (There are video clips on the www.FlorAlive.com site showing this.)

That evening when we screened 100 participants, the implications of what we found were staggering.

Among this very select group of people, individuals who had spent significant resources and a lot of time for the purpose of clearing themselves, we nevertheless found:

- 33% believed at the subconscious level, "Regardless of my efforts I cannot influence the outcome."
- 27% believed at the subconscious level, "I am disconnected from the source of ALL life."
- 33% were NOT "free from the effects of emotional abuse."
- 36% were NOT "free from the influence of negative thoughts and beings."
- 33% did NOT allow themselves "to receive."
- 34% did NOT allow themselves "to receive love."

The FlorAlive® UNCUT flower™ essences, ReviveAll® and the two others, overwrote and removed the frequencies of those limitations in the vast majority of those we tested. Often, consuming the indicated FlorAlive® essences for about three weeks causes a permanent shift. Based on individual needs, most people consume different essences over a period of months as they rapidly shift and remove different limiting beliefs.

Appendix 8

The FlorAlive® Training and Certification Program

(Excerpted from the "Training" tab on the FlorAlive.com home page.)

Would you be happy helping your loved ones – family and friends – noticeably improve their lives? Would you like to be the person who is instrumental in their positive life transformation?

Or, if you are a massage therapist, yoga instructor, Reiki practitioner, nurse, or primary care licensed health professional, would you like to add another income stream while providing your clients and patients major stress relief, valuable personal growth, and better manifestation ability?

You can deliver profound healingWITHOUT the requirement of numerous workshops and EXTENSIVE TIME COMMITMENTS

The possibility of profound transformation with FlorAlive® comes from the life force emitted by UNCUT Flowers™, collected around the world in areas that often have a legendary reputation for healing energy. It is not necessary for the practitioner to be trained to have highly advanced personal skills for healing. It is the flowers that do the work. All that is required of you is benevolent motivation and the acquired ability to match the correct flower frequencies to the individual.

Our purpose is not to place you in a long track of education but to enable you to effectively and easily help accelerate the evolution of consciousness in those that seek your services.

Since the turn of the millennium, Dr. Brent Davis has been developing a streamlined method that allows healthcare practitioners to match the complete energetic profile of the transformational frequencies in FlorAlive® UNCUT Flower™ essences to each individual client or patient. This process makes use, in a simple way, of a sophisticated screening process that derives from the discipline of applied kinesiology muscle testing combined with a pre-screening method he developed and named "holographic scanning."

Holographic scanning is a reflex measurement technique that serves to rapidly pre-screen all the flower frequencies produced by FlorAlive®, in a very short time, to find potential matches for the client/patient before turning to the more lengthy process of muscle testing. When the potential matches are found, then the more accurate method of confirming the selection with muscle testing is employed. You avoid unnecessary, time-consuming muscle testing by this process.

This dual confirmation approach is a hallmark of FlorAlive®, and is a much more precise tool for selecting healing essences than the customary questionnaires and interview sheets that are used by other flower essence companies.

For this reason, when you become a certified FlorAlive® practitioner, you will have a skill that gives your clients the knowledge that the essences you recommend for them to take are actually having an effect. Other systems of flower essence matching rely on whether the client/patient happens to notice benefits. Many times they do not, and it is simply a matter of faith whether the client should continue with the flower essence program.

Equipped with the unique capability you learn during the FlorAlive® certification training, you will be able to confidently and ethically recommend purchase of FlorAlive packages that sell the essences and the follow up assessments which measure if the product has had a beneficial and transformational effect. You will be able to comfortably charge for your time that you spend in assessing the action of the essences, and you will be well compensated for this very valuable service, which will provide an additional income stream for your business.

FlorAlive® provides THREE LEVELS of practitioner training in workshops:

■ Level I – Registered Practitioner

- Acquire the knowledge and beginning skills to select the correct FlorAlive® essences.
- You can start practicing with clients after 14 hours of training with minimal investment.
- We offer a scholarship at $188 U.S. to start implementing the FlorAlive® program.
- Test Kits required for client screening are sold at cost: $69.11 U.S.
- We have 4 attractive, full value FlorAlive® programs you can offer your clients.
- Marketing support including promotional brochures, your own FlorAlive® web page listing, and PowerPoint presentations for the promotion of your practice are available to enhance your visibility with minimum cost.

■ Level II- Certified Practitioner

- In the Level II training, more time will be spent studying the energetic character of the most profoundly transformational FlorAlive® wild flowers. This assists the practitioner in being able to more effectively match which flower frequencies are needed by the client at each session of care.

- Personal attention will be provided to each student to improve proficiency in whatever areas of client examination and delivery of care are deemed necessary.
- After acquiring Level I registration, the FlorAlive® practitioner must complete documentation requirements relating to client/patient management. These will be examined for proficiency before issuing certification.

■ Level III-Certified Instructor

- Application to become a certified instructor requires that you have successfully used FlorAlive® UNCUT Flower™ essences on clients/patients for a period of at least one year. Additionally you will have to fulfill the delivery of care documentation required for Level II certification on a minimum of 36 clients/patients. (Click the Level I seminar link for details under: "Documentation For Level II Certification.)
- The Level III training for certification includes four hours of instruction in the basics of NLP (neuro-linguistic programming) to increase your effectiveness at communication when you present training courses. You will receive additional guidance in marketing strategies to create the number of training venues you desire to teach.
- Personal attention will be provided to each instructor candidate to improve proficiency in whatever areas of client examination and delivery of care are deemed necessary.
- You will receive personal clearing and life enhancement from the most current advanced level essences that Dr. Davis has developed, before they have been released for general use. Dr. Davis will formulate for you a combination essence toward the beginning of the Level III training to take during the seminar.

Notice: FlorAlive® products and FlorAlive® training seminars are not part of any medical model. FlorAlive® training does not constitute medical, psychological, or psychiatric care or treatment. FlorAlive® UNCUT Flower™ essences are not intended to diagnose, treat, cure or prevent any disease.

Appendix 9

Description of Holographic Scanning

Holographic scanning is a rapid screening technique to enable more precise administration of individualized therapies (for example, flower essences, homeopathics, and nutrients) and physiological therapeutics (such as chiropractic and osteopathic procedures, acupuncture treatment protocols, etc.). It was developed by Dr. Brent Davis for health professionals but can be successfully employed by bright and motivated lay people.

It is now a primary tool to assist in the highest level matching of the affinity between various FlorAlive® UNCUT Flower™ essences and the individual that will be consuming them. It vastly speeds and improves the selection process.

It requires the faith that it can work, plus belief and confidence in one's own power to mediate healing. It uses the examiner's mind plus the patient's or client's innate intelligence or super-consciousness as a scanning device, and the patient's body as a readout. It is a skill developed with concentration. It is not a psychic technique.

The mechanical aspect of the scanning is not new. It is a type of leg length check utilized in several chiropractic techniques. What is unique and valuable about holographic scanning is its conceptual framework, which is critical to its success.

Holographic scanning is a four step procedure:

1. It requires the creation of a still space… a sacred place where there is the possibility for truth and knowledge to manifest within a magnetic domain that encompasses the practitioner and client or patient together as one. In this domain the creative super-intelligence residing in the patient can be questioned by the practitioner. If the motive is pure, and if the patient is in a relaxed, trusting state, that intelligence will generally respond accurately with an answer if the question is unambiguous.

   For the answer to be perceived, there must be an instrument independent of the health professional through which the answer can manifest. That instrument is the patient's own body.

   Answers can be received most easily in a yes/no response by using reflexive leg length changes of the patient. Shortening of the patient's right leg in response to an energetic question projected into the super-consciousness of his body is generally a "yes" response; left leg shortening generally a "no".

2. Solid intellectual knowledge at least, and preferably as well as, practical experience on the part of the practitioner in the domain which he is investigating.

3. The practitioner renouncing, temporarily, the satisfaction and pride he takes in his intellectual mastery of health-related subjects so that he can perceive an answer from a Higher Source.

4. Re-entry into the intellectual/clinical framework in which the practitioner operates for rational assessment of the Answer. The practitioner must then determine if it makes sense considering the patient's history, exam, and responses to previous therapy.

Appendix 10

Photos of Facial Transformation
As a Result of Consuming Uncut Flower Essences

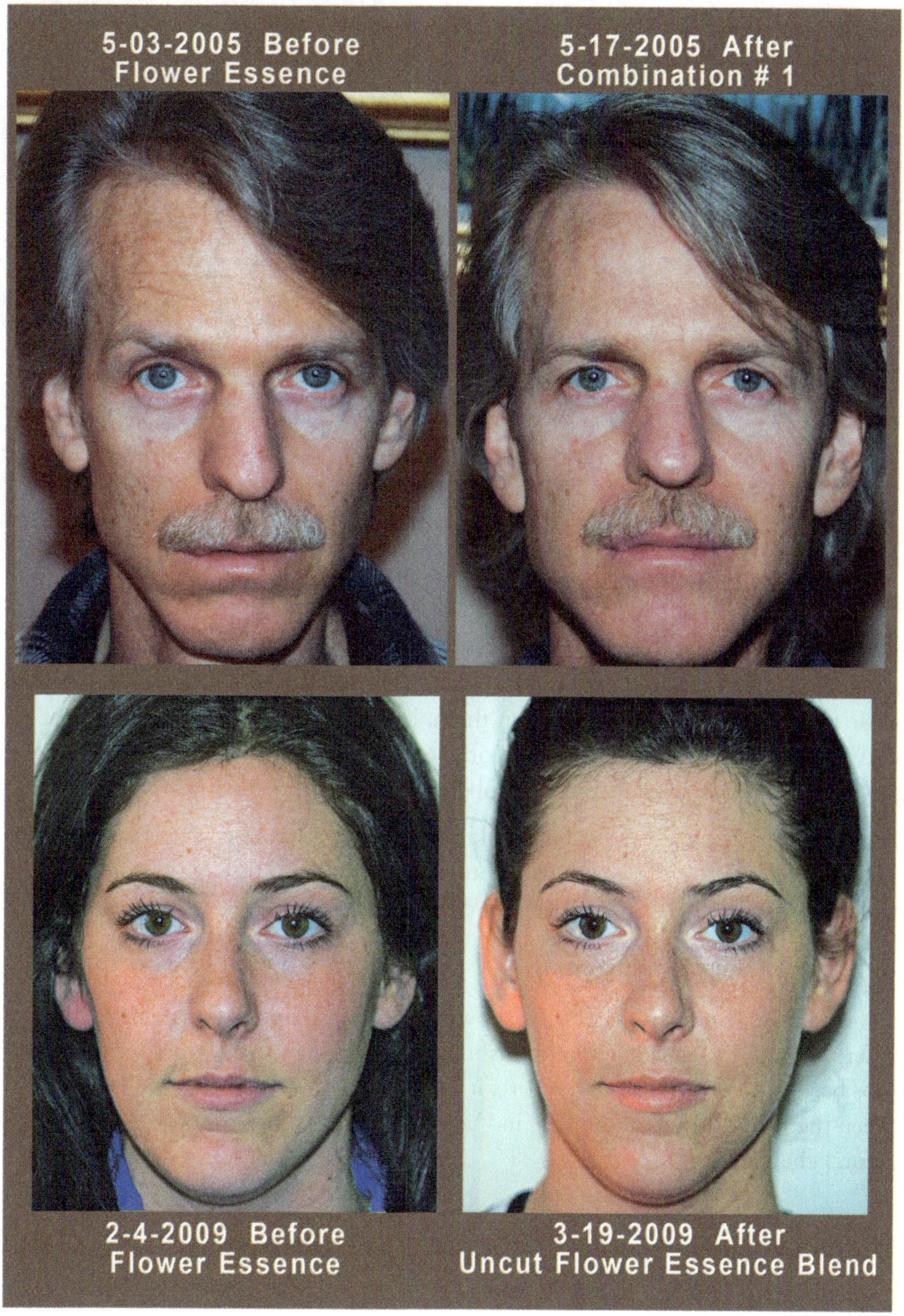

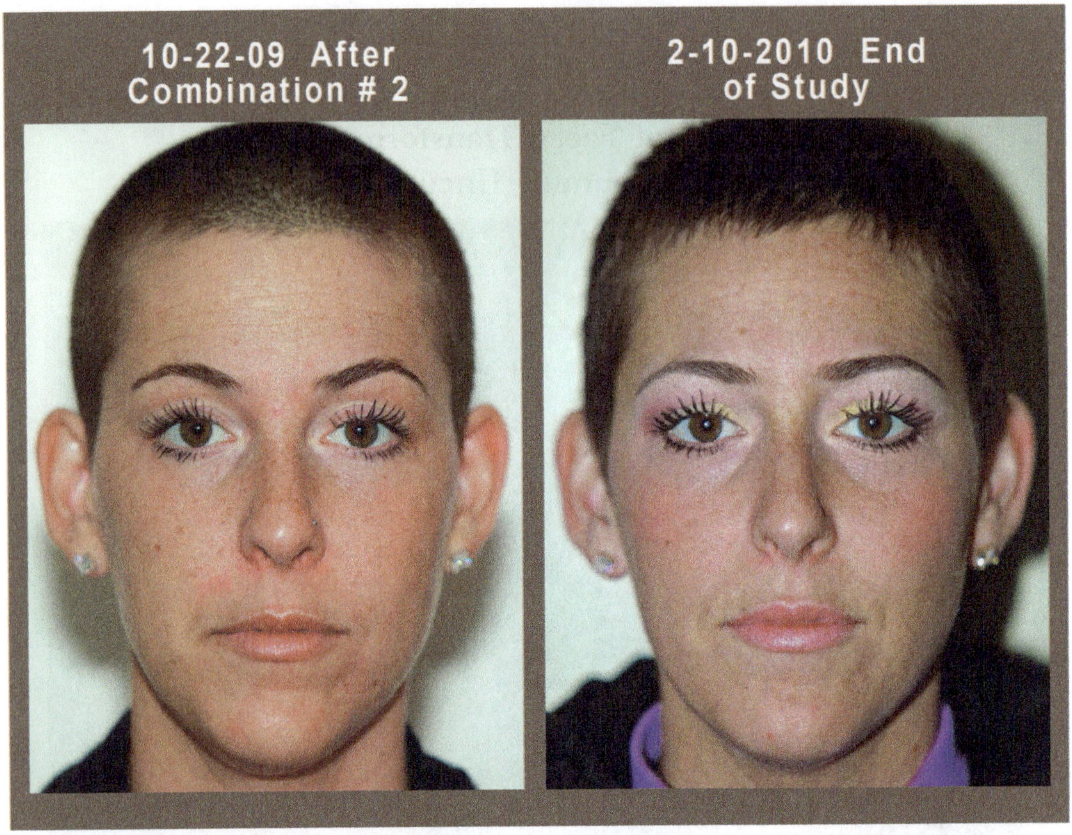

Instructions to Subjects Being Photographed:

Before being photographed, subjects are instructed to look straight ahead and to adopt a resting, non-smiling expression. To achieve a balanced state, they are instructed to close their eyes and then gently open them, looking straight into the camera at eye level. When there is turning of the face off center or tipping of the head one way or the other, it is due to imbalance in the subject at the time of the photo.

Though smiling in itself is healing, all kinds of energies are projected when people smile. In this type of study, this must be avoided because it entirely obscures very complex energies and characteristics that can be seen in the eyes when they are at rest.

Maintaining Exact Aspect Ratio:

In the "before" and "after" photos shown here, when they are superimposed on one another the pupils exactly align, and this indicates that the aspect ratio between both photos has been maintained. Therefore, it is valid to compare them, and differences between the proportions of the face in "before" versus "after" photos represent real structural change.

Interpretation of Facial Changes:

Photos of these two subjects were chosen because they demonstrate two rather fascinating phenomena that are occurring in some individuals that consume the uncut flower essences I have developed.

(1) They both show very clear "energetic" shifts in a rather short time.

(2) They exhibit actual facial bone (cranial bone) movement and reshaping solely as a result of consuming the uncut flower essences. Neither of these subjects had other therapies that might have influenced facial bone molding and reshaping.
These subjects are two of about one dozen patients I have personally examined that

(a) report that they notice their face has changed shape as a result of the flower frequencies, and

(b) demonstrate these changes photographically. The FlorAlive.com website has shown very interesting facial photos of change for years. Any intervention that can change and reshape cranial bones (when no manual procedures have been used) is very powerful.

Male Subject:

The male subject asked for help when he was in a very dejected condition, feeling that he had failed to achieve his professional goals. He was given the six transformational flowers in Combination# 1 to start with, and it was those healing frequencies that produced his dramatic change. In this case, two of the six flowers in that combination that really exerted a strong force for change were: Blue Eyed Grass (to overcome feelings of emotional trauma) and Tulip Poplar (to strengthen self-esteem).

Even though the camera was directly in front of the subject's face and he was directed to look straight into it, he nevertheless had his chin tipped down, resulting in the appearance of a condition in Oriental facial diagnosis called *sanpaku*. It is when the whites of the eyes show on three sides around the pupil, and in Japanese facial diagnosis it is considered a pathological sign indicative of imbalanced mental health.

Within five days of starting the six-flower Combination#1, he reported: "I am totally amazed – everything feels so much brighter." Even though in the "before" picture the subject's face is slightly turned to his left, making it harder to analyze facial structure, my in-office clinical exam two weeks later on 5-17-05 did demonstrate that cranial bone re-modeling had taken place. His mandible was substantially different in shape. The follow-up photo was taken before I treated him. Significantly, he maintained his head position differently, and all signs of *sanpaku* were gone. His resting expression demonstrated a marked increase in self-confidence.

Female Subject:

The female patient first saw me at 25 years of age and mentioned that among other things she wanted to experience a higher quality relationship with a man.

By combining her history with her facial-appearance changes, this is how I would summarize her profound transformation. In the 2/4/2009 photo there is considerable vulnerability and submissiveness evident. This corresponded with the types of relationships that she had encountered involving rather superficial men that took advantage of her. In response to her condition I customized an uncut flower essence blend for her that included Maroon Bethroot. Observe the change in energy emitting from her eyes after six weeks had transpired. She clearly appears to be less vulnerable. Then, over several months, she received the uncut flower essences that now comprise Combination#2 (and the transformational force from its many extraordinary flowers). This patient also received no other therapeutic interventions that would have remodeled her cranial bones, yet this photo shows clear and incontrovertible evidence that change took place. Compression on the right side of her face and distortion of the mandible gradually leaves in the time period between the first and last photo. On her own, the patient commented that she was aware of the bony change in her facial structure.

A movement from initial vulnerability and compliance to "ferocious" resolve in the 10-22-09 photo, finally ending with a softening, is evident to me. You may also perceive a sense of spiritual authority showing in the last photo. Interestingly, when I polled several men asking which photo they liked best, there was a fascinating split between those that liked the "before" photo and those that liked the last photo. The men that preferred the last photo were much closer to what this lady wanted in partnership. (Note: the subject grew her hair to conventional length starting after the last photo.)

Book Introduction

(All following annotations are in Doc's words.)

The rock walls and this canyon at 13,000 feet in the Peruvian Andes are the actual site that I saw in my mind's eye when I was in college in Los Angeles. More than twenty years later I found myself guided to explore this homeland of powerful herbs that yield amazingly transformational flowers.

(Introduction: p.xii)

The needle formation of rock seen below juts into the air more than 150 feet.

FlorAlive Forest – Davis Farm 1

Pictures of my herb farm in the middle of the FlorAlive forest.
Over twenty of the uncut flower essences that I have developed come from this sacred and blessed land.

Teasel (below) grown from wild seed is used to produce a product called SpiroNIL™ – the first herbal product of its type to strongly support Lyme disease recovery.

FlorAlive Forest – Davis Farm 2

I spent a crazy amount of time building this pond/pool, and I am so glad I did. It provides a wonderful energetic balance to the land. Each summer I look forward to pond floating (below.)

It serves as a great recreational area during the summer FlorAlive® health professional training seminars.

Above near Iquitos – My first experience drinking Cat's Claw liquid from the vine. p.16
Below - "Original" scrawny me with the Bosque Gamitana development team as we occupied our newly constructed "village" as part of the FHHC project p.16 footnote.

Jungle 2

My third visit to a remote Peruvian jungle. I was still experiencing health challenges, but nevertheless enjoyed this trip very much. I was fortunate to have the guidance and assistance of the tribal chief, Regner (bottom of photo)(p.44).

My return visit to Regner's tribal land, this time for a week-long flower essence extraction trip. My physical stamina had finally returned. This is where I prepared the "Aseñac" sample that Dr. Tiller analyzed. (p.161)

On the way to El Místico I felt closer to heaven (p.234).

Our group had to pass the "Dragon Mountain" to reach our final destination...

Packing into "El Místico" with my flower essence extraction equipment.

Storming in "El Místico"

Setting up camp for the beginning of flower essence extraction. This site was at the lowest altitude of about 13,000 feet.

The home of Flor del Oso – Flower of the Bear (The King of the High Places.) Read about its characteristics in the Single Essences section. I was overjoyed in this spectacular energy.

That's me hangin' on the mountainside (p.233.)

If you are thinking, "Is someone tilting the camera?" Nope, they weren't!!

Heck of a place to try to extract the head of a living flower inflorescence (of sorts), especially when it is that large.

My friend Serena assisted me on this trip.(p.113)

My great pleasure to commune with Green Hellebore flowers before their extraction (p.40).

My Invitation To You

If some part of *The Floral Hand of God* (FHOG) has touched you deeply, intrigued you, amused you, or most especially, has given you hope, then it has achieved its purpose. That is my wish, and I invite you to visit The Floral Hand of God website to join our community and to be informed of upcoming events, training opportunities, webinars, ecotourism trips to experience flowers in pristine energy centers, and special offers.

If you are or intend to become a health professional, I urge you to investigate the revolutionary training program that can require as little as two seminars to begin flower essence client assessments and creation of custom blended formulas to assist in personal transformation. Please register at : *www.TheFloralHandOfGod.com/training.*

Beyond that, if FHOG inspires in you the desire to personally take hold of and develop one of the many ideas put forward in this book that can speed the awakening of consciousness, please register at the following link: *www.TheFloralHandOfGod.com/awaken* so that you can communicate your particular interest to me. Initially, an outreach coordinator will respond to what you submit.

The new thought movement arising from this book will be profoundly accelerated by a select few people who are strongly aligned in purpose at their core. What a pleasure it will be to create a network consisting of those individuals!

The motive force of human potential presents itself in two poles separated by a time line of experience. On one side rests a particular group of mature individuals who have withstood the opposition of *un*consciousness around them for many years. They have persevered, and, due to exceptional skills in areas such as executive management, writing, finance, marketing, or philanthropy, have, by their intention, cleared a light-filled path for others seeking consciousness to follow more easily.

On the other side is a special breed of youth – a new breath of life – who are free to create, for they carry little within themselves to which the powers of opposition can cling. Rather effortlessly, these individuals may achieve mastery in computer and new era technologies, social media communication, and networking. When young adults in this category apply their own genius to the challenge of how to rapidly shift consciousness toward the light, equilibrium in our world has a much better chance to be restored.

If you fall into either of these categories, I encourage you to apply your skills to strengthen our community.

Dr. Brent W. Davis
CHIROPRACTIC PHYSICIAN
HERBALIST

Dr. Brent Davis is a chiropractic physician whose life's mission is to help people clear their sabotaging subconscious beliefs through advanced healing frequencies extracted from flowers by a method that is now patented internationally.

Since the turn of the millennium, he has witnessed hundreds of people overcome grief, reduce stress, strengthen relationships, and improve their life in many ways by taking the FlorAlive uncut flower essences he has developed.

From the remote mountains and jungles of Peru to the plains of western Australia to the San Juan mountains of Colorado, Dr. Davis is inspired to locate rare flowers worldwide that can act as divine gifts to bring greater ease and joy to life, and assist in the evolution of humanity's consciousness.

Throughout his life, Dr. Davis has had a compelling interest in the world of medicinal plants. He has focused especially on bringing to light both forgotten and new applications of master herbs as they relate to use in general clinical practice.

In addition to being a licensed chiropractor in California and Tennessee, he has advanced post-graduate training in classical homeopathy and applied kinesiology, as well as solid core training in numerous other natural diagnostic and therapeutic techniques. When he is not treating patients or traveling on "floral adventures," he lives on his organic herb farm in the center of the FlorAlive Forest, 75 miles outside of Nashville.

Dr. Davis has collected and prepared herbs in the wild from around the world; clinically validated their usefulness in holistic practice; brought lost herbs to the attention of the academic research community; and co-authored two articles in prominent peer-reviewed scientific journals. He is the author of *Healing Herb Rapid Reference.*

Dr. Davis has developed a streamlined new approach to flower essence administration which he now teaches in workshops. This helps practitioners rapidly achieve transformational responses in patients and clients by identifying the most appropriate uncut flower essences for each individual.

If you have enjoyed this book, I thank you for your interest in my life's work and look forward to connecting with you.

Dr. Brent W. Davis

www.floralive.com
www.facebook.com/floralive

Davis Holistic Chiropractic Center

550 Rosedale Ave

Nashville, TN 37211

(615) 780-5927

CPSIA information can be obtained at www.ICGtesting.com
Printed in the USA
BVOW10s1314041214
377941BV00002B/2/P

9 780996 004343